DATE DUE

ABOUT ISLAND PRESS

Island Press is the only nonprofit organization in the United States whose principal purpose is the publication of books on environmental issues and natural resource management. We provide solutions-oriented information to professionals, public officials, business and community leaders, and concerned citizens who are shaping responses to environmental problems.

In 1994, Island Press celebrates its tenth anniversary as the leading provider of timely and practical books that take a multidisciplinary approach to critical environmental concerns. Our growing list of titles reflects our commitment to bringing the best of an expanding body of literature to the environmental community throughout North America and the world.

Support for Island Press is provided by The Geraldine R. Dodge Foundation, The Energy Foundation, The Ford Foundation, The George Gund Foundation, William and Flora Hewlett Foundation, The James Irvine Foundation, The John D. and Catherine T. MacArthur Foundation, The Andrew W. Mellon Foundation, The Joyce Mertz-Gilmore Foundation, The New-Land Foundation, The Pew Charitable Trusts, The Rockefeller Brothers Fund, The Tides Foundation, Turner Foundation, Inc., The Rockefeller Philanthropic Collaborative, Inc., and individual donors.

ABOUT ISEE

Ecological economics is concerned with integrating the study and management of nature's household (*ecology*) with humanity's household (*economy*). Ecological economics acknowledges that, in the end, a healthy economy can only exist in symbiosis with a healthy ecology. Ecological economics is the name that has been given to the effort to transcend traditional disciplinary boundaries in order to address the interrelationship between ecological and economic systems in a broad and comprehensive way. Ecological economics takes a holistic worldview with human beings representing one component (albeit a very important one) in the overall system. Human beings play a unique role in the overall system because they can consciously understand their role in the larger system and manage it for sustainability. Ecological economics seeks to constitute a true marriage of ecology and economics so as to give meaning and substance to the idea of **sustainable development**.

The International Society for Ecological Economics (ISEE) is a not-for-profit organization with more than 1600 members in over 60 countries. Regional chapters have been established in Russia and Canada, with plans being made for chapters in China, Africa, and Southeast Asia. ISEE promotes the integration of ecology and economics by providing information through its membership journal, *Ecological Economics,* and the Quarterly Newsletter, and encourages the exchange of ideas by supporting major international conferences and smaller regional meetings on topics of interest to members, as well as research and training programs in ecological economics.

Investing in Natural Capital, a video providing an overview of ecological economics, and membership information can be obtained by contacting the ISEE Secretariat, P.O. Box 1589, Solomons, MD 20688 USA.

Toward Sustainable
Development

Titles published by Island Press in the
INTERNATIONAL SOCIETY FOR ECOLOGICAL
ECONOMICS SERIES include:

R. Costanza, B.G. Norton, B.D. Haskell
(Editors), *Ecosystem Health,* 1992

A.M. Jansson, M. Hammer, C. Folke, R.
Costanza (Editors), *Investing in Natural
Capital,* 1994

Toward Sustainable Development

*Concepts, Methods,
and Policy*

Edited by
Jeroen C.J.M. van den Bergh
Jan van der Straaten

Technical Editor, Sandra Koskoff

INTERNATIONAL SOCIETY
FOR ECOLOGICAL ECONOMICS

ISLAND PRESS

Washington, D.C. ❑ Covelo, California

Copyright © 1994 by Island Press

All rights reserved under International and Pan-American Copyright
Conventions. No part of this book may be reproduced in any form or by
any means without permission in writing from the publisher: Island Press,
1718 Connecticut Avenue, N.W., Suite 300, Washington, DC 20009.

ISLAND PRESS is a trademark of The Center for Resource Economics.

Library of Congress Cataloging-in-Publication Data

Toward sustainable development : concepts, methods, and policy /
    edited by Jeroen C.J.M. van den Bergh, Jan van der Straaten.
        p. cm.
        "International Society for Ecological Economics."
        Includes bibliographical references and index.
        ISBN 1-55963-349-2 (paper)
        1. Sustainable development--Congresses. 2. Economic development-
    -Environmental aspects--Congresses. 3. Environmental policy-
    -Congresses. I. Bergh, Jeroen C. J. M. van den, 1965- .
    II. Straaten, Jan van der.
    HD75.6.T69 1994
    333.7--dc20   94-36174
                                                             CIP

Printed on recycled, acid-free paper

Manufactured in the United States of America

10 9 8 7 6 5 4 3 2 1

Toward Sustainable Development

Concepts, Methods, and Policy

Edited by
Jeroen C.J.M. van den Bergh
Jan van der Straaten

Technical Editor, Sandra Koskoff

INTERNATIONAL SOCIETY
FOR ECOLOGICAL ECONOMICS

ISLAND PRESS
Washington, D.C. ❑ Covelo, California

Copyright © 1994 by Island Press

All rights reserved under International and Pan-American Copyright
Conventions. No part of this book may be reproduced in any form or by
any means without permission in writing from the publisher: Island Press,
1718 Connecticut Avenue, N.W., Suite 300, Washington, DC 20009.

ISLAND PRESS is a trademark of The Center for Resource Economics.

Library of Congress Cataloging-in-Publication Data

Toward sustainable development : concepts, methods, and policy /
    edited by Jeroen C.J.M. van den Bergh, Jan van der Straaten.
        p. cm.
    "International Society for Ecological Economics."
    Includes bibliographical references and index.
    ISBN 1-55963-349-2 (paper)
    1. Sustainable development—Congresses. 2. Economic development-
-Environmental aspects--Congresses. 3. Environmental policy-
-Congresses. I. Bergh, Jeroen C. J. M. van den, 1965- .
II. Straaten, Jan van der.
HD75.6.T69 1994
333.7—dc20   94-36174
                                                CIP

Printed on recycled, acid-free paper

Manufactured in the United States of America

10 9 8 7 6 5 4 3 2 1

CONTENTS

PART THREE: IMPLEMENTATION AND POLICY

CONTRIBUTORS

R.K. Blamey	Centre for Resource and Environmental Studies, Australian National University, Canberra, Australia
M. Common	Centre for Resource and Environmental Studies, Australian National University, Canberra, Australia
Robert Costanza	MD International Institute for Ecological Economics, University of MD, Solomons, MD
Paul P. Craig	Dept. of Applied Science and Graduate Group in Ecology, University of CA, Davis, CA
John H. Cumberland	MD International Institute for Ecological Economics, University of MD, Solomons, MD
Paul Ekins	Dept. of Economics, Birkbeck College, University of London, U.K.
Harold Glasser	Dept. of Civil and Environmental Engineering, University of CA, Davis, CA
Friedrich Hinterberger	Wuppertal Institute for Climate, Environment, and Energy, Germany
Willett Kempton	Center for Energy and Environmental Policy, University of DE, Newark, DE
Jane King	Centre for Human Ecology, University of Edinburgh, Scotland
Juan Martinez-Alier	Dept. d'Economia i d'Historia Econmica, Universitat Autònoma, Spain
Thomas Maxwell	MD International Institute for Ecological Economics, University of MD, Solomons, MD
Malcolm Slesser	Centre for Human Ecology, University of Edinburgh, Scotland
Jeroen C.J.M. van den Bergh	Dept. of Spatial Economics, Free University, The Netherlands
Jan van der Straaten	European Centre for Nature Conservation, Tilburg University, The Netherlands

PREFACE

The fields of *Environmental* and *Ecological Economics* are attracting wide attention. Witness the number of publications in books and journals on issues such as instruments for environmental policy, economic valuation of environmental damage and environmental policy benefits, economic and ecological indicators for sustainable development, institutional and distributional elements in environmental policy, environmental ethics and philosophy, and integrated modelling and analysis. In addition, the growing interest in these issues is reflected in international meetings of economists, ecologists, and scientists from related disciplines, e.g., social and economic geography, human ecology, sociology, and political science.

All the chapters in this book were presented at the second meeting of the *International Society for Ecological Economics* (ISEE), titled "Investing in Natural Capital: A Prerequisite for Sustainability," held from August 3 to 6 in 1992, at Stockholm University in Sweden. This meeting attracted much attention from all over the world. One of the very important subjects considered in Ecological Economics, *Sustainable Development*, received ample attention at the conference, and was consequently chosen by the editors as the central subject of this book. Since the term is often being used as a catchword, detailed attention is devoted to it in the various chapters, at the conceptual, methodological, and implementational levels. Several basic questions in the context of sustainable development motivate the topics dealt with in this book: How can sustainable development be analyzed, defined, modeled, and evaluated? What is the role of ethics and human tastes with regard to the human relationship with the natural environment? What distributional and institutional obstacles are encountered in the implementation of sustainable development policies and strategies? The editors have carefully selected papers of high quality and standards for inclusion in this volume, which represent significant original contributions to the young field of Ecological Economics.

The chapters following may be characterized by an attempt either to provide a well-argued critique on existing, traditional methods and ideas, or to present a novel framework for analysis of issues related to environmentally sustainable economy, development, or policy. The order of the papers is such that the reader is first confronted with conceptual and theoretical considerations in Part I of the book, then with discussions of methods and techniques in Part II, and finally with

xi

examinations of policy and implementation issues in Part III. It is our hope that readers will find a good introduction to recent developments and material for establishing their own ideas about an Ecological Economics for Sustainable Development.

Finally, we would like to thank Robert Costanza for his suggestion to compose a book from papers of the ISEE conference, and Sandra Koskoff, ISEE Publications Coordinator, for final editorial support and preparation of camera-ready copy.

1 THE SIGNIFICANCE OF SUSTAINABLE DEVELOPMENT FOR IDEAS, TOOLS, AND POLICY

Jeroen C. J. M. van den Bergh
Department of Spatial Economics
Faculty of Economics
Free University
De Boelelaan 1105
1081 HV, Amsterdam
The Netherlands

Jan van der Straaten
European Centre for Nature Conservation
Tilburg University
P.O. Box 1352
5004 BJ, Tilburg
The Netherlands

INTRODUCTION

At the end of the eighties the concern for environmental issues became widespread. An increased concentration by scientists, environmentalists, and policymakers on global and long-term problems accompanied this concern, which reflected a renewed interest in long-term environmental issues that takes serious account of the interdependence of various political, social, distributional, economic, industrial, and environmental problems and processes. As part of this trend, the phrase "sustainable development" was introduced and became more well-known after the publication of the report *Our Common Future* (WCED 1987). Since then, a mass of literature has been generated in various fields of science, most of which does not go far beyond the descriptive stage. In addition to the more or less traditional fields applying their knowledge and techniques to environmental issues, both mainstream science and alternative approaches are more intensively exploited in what is commonly regarded as a new and fruitful field of application. This growing interest is indicated clearly by many international meetings and publications of new books and journals in the field. Interestingly, and surprisingly to some, the catch-word "sustainable development" still remains present in both professional and other literature.

The use of the concept of sustainable development is a starting point for broader examinations of economics, environment, and development, and is even becoming more accepted now in specialized sub-disciplines, giving rise to notions of sustainable agriculture, sustainable energy patterns, sustainable transport, sustainable land use, and sustainable industry. Sadly enough, much work emanating from sustainable development does not seem to be able to go beyond abstract or descriptive studies, and sometimes even results in a repetition of arguments and definitions. One consequence of this is that many scientists are becoming somewhat cautious in using the term. The purpose of this book is to open up the discussion related to sustainable development on multiple levels. Thus different theoretical perspectives are seriously considered, with the aim being to extend the traditional, dominant monodisciplinary views and to provide alternative views and methods for dealing with a multitude of sustainable development-related problems. For this reason, as the title of the book already suggests, some critical view on traditional theory and tools may be useful.

A HISTORY OF THE CONCEPT OF SUSTAINABLE DEVELOPMENT

Although sustainable development as a policy objective was stimulated by the mentioned WCED report, it could be argued that it implicitly was included already in some classical economic theories. For instance, notions of limits to growth and development towards a steady state can be found in the works of Ricardo, Malthus, and Mill. From the perspective of natural resources providing inputs for production processes, a steady state may be considered as a specific type of sustainable development, in which the availability of natural resources determines the physical scale of the economy.

Several economic issues are related to the idea of a steady state. Ricardo addressed questions related to the distribution of economic produce and the consequences of it for development. Malthus considered the objective of a stable and sustainable population level, given the fertility of mankind and minimum welfare conditions. Mill investigated the economic contents of a steady state.

With the introduction of neoclassical economic theory at the end of the nineteenth century, classical theory lost its influence. The formal and rigid analysis, which is so characteristic of the neoclassical approach, was a main reason for not incorporating the dependence of economic production, consumption, and welfare on natural resources and ecosystems. The role of the market is stressed in these theories, so that account was taken of natural resources only as far as they were being traded on a market. The implication is that non-renewable resources, such as fossil fuels and ores, are easily dealt with, but clean air and water, as well as functions of ecosystems, are labeled as free goods. The main result of this theory is that such goods require governmental intervention that corrects the functioning of the market process. Otherwise, a disoptimal level of such goods will result. Generally, one can say that the market can only deal with the optimal allocation of private goods. The optimal scale of production of goods and the optimal level of natural resource stocks is something that requires additional considerations, since the optimal scale of production and consumption is not related to market processes (Daly 1989). This requires that one has to take account of the physical and biological base of economies. Optimality is not an unprejudiced goal in this case. One has to realize that this concept is dependent on welfare aspects and ethical issues related to the existence of future generations, living nature, and abiotic elements of the natural environment.

The mainstream reaction to environmental disruption as a result of economic activities has been in terms of (1) the formulation of so-called negative externalities, and associated with these, (2) price corrections (Pigouvian taxes) to restore economic efficiency. The proposed procedure is that the national state calculates the social costs of environmental disruption and assigns them to the associated sources as to attain an optimal economic allocation of "functions of nature." One should not overlook, however, the societal reality during the period of Pigou early this century that was partly responsible for such a view. The most important element may well have been the fact that environmental issues played only a small role in the public debate. When one adopts a more extensive—and hopefully appropriate—view of a complex natural system subject to a complex interaction of negative influences, it seems that sustainable development cannot simply and straightforwardly be founded on the notion of an externality in the sense of Pigou. In addition, the structural character of environmental effects asks for a more integrated and dynamic analytical approach. The externality concept assumes too much static and partial character of cause-effect relationships that go through both economic and environmental systems. Between the economic activity, the physical-material output, the environmental consequence, and the welfare impact is a whole system of complex dynamic processes that should receive more careful and explicit attention. One can seriously doubt whether the neoclassical method can absorb so much reality. It would, in any case, be interesting to apply this method to the above issue. It seems very likely, for instance, that one should leave the analytical world of neoclassical economics and move to more experimental—and less general—methods of numerical simulation, based on artificial and empirical data (Braat and Van Lierop 1987; Faber and Proops 1990; Van den Bergh 1991, 1993).

A second element that is typical of the mainstream economic approach can be phrased as the "substitution principle." It is based on the argument that market processes will bring forward a substitution of less for more scarce inputs, whether into production, consumption, or welfare. What is generally assumed, in theory, is that the main input relationship between various production factors leaves much scope for various types of substitution. However, from a materials balance perspective (Ayres and Kneese 1989), it is readily clear that there is much to say against this, and in favor of complementariness of, for instance, labor and capital on the one hand, and natural resource inputs and conditions on the other hand. Although this debatable assumption is not necessarily linked to the formal neoclassical approach, it is a common one that is not often enlightened.

Until the sixties, environmental problems were largely disregarded in social decision making as well as in economic theory. From the sixties on, it was increasingly recognized that environmental problems have a structural character and may not be approached simply from an market-allocation perspective using externality and substitution concepts (Boulding 1966; Daly 1969; Ayres and Kneese 1969). In spite of increased "environmental awareness," the seventies did not show sufficient implementation of environmental policies for dealing with resource use, waste emission, or ecosystem destruction. In particular, international trade and economic growth caused an increase in environmental stress that often more than compensated efforts to cut it back. In this context the recognition of the structural and wide-reaching character of environmental problems by the WCED (1987) can be regarded as a logical next phase in dealing with environmental issues.

LITERATURE ON SUSTAINABLE DEVELOPMENT

Some important previous events and political actions that have paved the way for the emergence of the concept of sustainable development are:

- the Stockholm Conference on the Human Environment and the establishment of the UNEP in 1972;

- the *Limits to Growth* report (Meadows et al. 1972);

- the *U.S. Global 2000 Report to the President* (Barney 1980) and its response *The Resourceful Earth* (Simon and Kahn 1984);

- the *World Conservation Strategy* (WCN/IUCN 1980);

- the IIASA report *Sustainable Development of the Biosphere* (Clark and Munn 1986); and, of course,

- the previously mentioned U.N. report *Our Common Future* (WCED 1987).

In general, the reactions to the latter report have been very positive, mainly because of its political effect and stimulus for scientific research. As a critique, the possibility of inconsistency between its growth objective and regard for ecological limits has been noted (Daly 1990; Hueting 1990).

Finally, as a meeting that may have reinforced the work on sustainable development, one may also note the UNCED meeting on Environment and Development in Rio de Janeiro in 1992 (see Chapter 4).

Much of the literature related to sustainable development has a strong bias towards developing countries (Bartelmus 1986; Redclift 1987; Repetto 1986; Tolba 1987; Schramm and Warford 1989; Pearce et al. 1990; Simonis 1990; Pearce and Warford 1993; Van Pelt 1993). Some authors prefer a historical or theoretical economic argument that ends with proposals for sustainable development (Barbier 1989; Pezzey 1989; Young 1992). Various papers show the variety of opinions and approaches that are possible (Collard et al. 1988; Turner 1988; Pearce and Redclift 1988; Archibugi and Nijkamp 1989; NAVF 1990; Costanza et al. 1991; Gilbert and Braat 1991; Breheny et al. 1992; Dietz et al. 1992; Opschoor 1992; IIASA 1992; Bannister and Button 1993). Studies focused on models usually deal with dynamic theoretical and systems-dynamic models (De Vries 1989; Van den Bergh 1991). Kuik and Verbruggen (1991) present a range of attempts to monitor and evaluate the unsustainability of actual patterns and levels of economic activity.

Various older and recent studies of interest for sustainable development stay close to the realm of the growth debate, relating environmental problems to economic (GDP) growth (Mishan 1967, 1977; Daly, 1977, 1991; Hueting 1980). On a more theoretical level one can distinguish between a rather pure neoclassical perspective (Solow 1974, 1986; Hartwick 1977; Dasgupta and Heal 1979), and alternative approaches (Siebert 1982; Barbier 1990; Van den Bergh 1991). Finally, there is also a related literature dealing with the fundamental question of whether to base ecological sustainability on anthropocentric, (i.e., intergenerational) or non-anthropocentric, (i.e., "ecocentric," "holistic," or "bio-egalitarianism") arguments. A whole literature is now concerned with this debate (Maclean and Brown 1983; Kneese and Schulze 1985; and a new journal, *Environmental Values*).

Definitions of sustainable development abound. Some attempts show a systematic approach to construct a definition (Brown et al. 1987) or to provide a collection of different viewpoints (see the Appendix in Pezzey 1989). It is generally agreed upon that "ecological sustainability" is a more clear concept than "sustainable development." The confusion usually arises, of course, from what is meant by "development," and how broadly or specifically the term is defined. "Sustainable growth" is also a frequently used term, although many authors believe that it is a contradiction of terms.

In addition to the above books and articles, there is by now a mass of publications in scientific journals devoted to sustainable development. To review the variety of approaches, one may consult Goodland and Ledec (1987), Van Pelt et al. (1990), Klaassen and Opschoor (1991), Van den Bergh and Nijkamp (1991a, b), Dietz and Van der Straaten (1992), Common and Perrings (1993), Pezzey (1993), and Opschoor and Van der Straaten (1993). Although it is impossible here to be complete in the overview of literature on "sustainable development," the above references provide a broad introduction to the various issues, opinions, methods, and applications. In the next section these aspects are briefly discussed.

SOME VIEWS ON SUSTAINABLE DEVELOPMENT

As it is generally agreed upon that *sustainable development* refers to both system-wide and very long-term processes and conditions, it may be interesting to start the discussion here with a broad and historical view on the relationship between man and nature. Man depends on nature in multiple ways, most clearly by depending on the existence of a foodweb from which to extract his necessary inputs. In a way even, man has placed himself at the top of the foodchain at various levels, from local to global. But this perspective is, of course, only a partial one. To obtain a more complete picture, one should add to the ecological and ecosystems approach the dependence of man on non-renewable energy and mineral resources, as well as the fact that natural systems are sensitive to human sources of pollution, noise, and other disturbance. A recent trend in the man-nature relationship is that nature nowadays is increasingly dependent on mankind. Since happiness of people seems to be determined to a large extent by the direct and indirect presence of nature, in all its variety and quality, the dependence exceeds a merely physical level. The history of the relationship between mankind and natural environments shows quite some turbulence, even before the present age of culmination of environmental problems. This relationship has now begun to be documented and analyzed more purposefully (Wilkinson 1973; Common 1988; Simmons 1989; Ponting 1991; Pezzey 1993).

The new perspectives of sustainable development are quite multidimensional, as is clearly demonstrated by Pezzey (1993), who discusses physical, ecological, economic, psychological, sociological, and especially, historical elements of sustainable development. The interaction of economic and ecological knowledge is already often referred to in interdisciplinary research, although we are still in the process of early learning (Costanza 1991).

The approaches in this book focus on the following aspects of sustainable development:

- a broad interpretation of economic costs (Ekins, Chapter 2);
- evolutionary processes related to physical and cultural economic-environmental interactions (Hinterberger, Chapter 3);

- normative backgrounds in policy making (Glasser, Craig, and Kempton, Chapter 4);

- spatial dimension in economic-environmental systems (Maxwell and Costanza, Chapter 5);

- energy as a common denominator for economic and environmental processes (King and Slessor, Chapter 6);

- psychological issues in economic valuation studies (Blamey and Common, Chapter 7);

- historical development and policy aspects in a systems setting (Van den Bergh and Van der Straaten, Chapter 8);

- distributional conflicts in shaping international and global environmental policy (Martinez-Alier, Chapter 9); and

- integration of ecological knowledge, standards, and economic incentives in environmental policy (Cumberland, Chapter 10).

New ideas and concepts in themselves are attractive, but especially in the context of sustainable development, one is inclined to look ahead at the practical implications of proposals for changing perspectives. Of course, one may argue that this is legitimate in view of the pressing need for quick actions in the related field of policy. On the other hand, it is also true that one must be careful in hastily diving into new enterprises of quick implementation of untested ideas and tools, especially since in the context of sustainable development the focus lies, by definition, on long-term processes. This two-sidedness, of large scale and long-term issues on the one hand and the need for policies on the other hand, explains why one may observe two streams of thought. On the one hand, a search exists for new frameworks, models, and theory with regard to sustainable development problems. And on the other hand, quite specific and seemingly operational plans for policies and instruments are proposed, including very creative ones like bonds for natural areas and the proposals in Chapters 9 and 10.

Given the multiple approaches to analysis for sustainable development, one may wonder how to proceed. Some researchers agree that a total systems view may serve a good purpose (see Chapters 2, 3, 5, 6, and 8). In a systems view one can put together parts that are usually separately dealt with in different disciplines. At this point it is not too important to spend much time on different possible choices one can make, such as whether or not to take a division into sub-systems as a reference point.

New dialogue is especially interested in phenomena that extend over long periods of time and large areas in space. Thus one may conclude, for instance, that it is relevant to focus on interactions between changing subsystems (in space) that are continuously changing themselves (over time). This then provides one with good reasons to use extensive computerized models based on, for example, an evolutionary framework (see Chapter 3), a geographic analysis approach (see Chapter 5), or a dynamic systems approach (see Chapters 5, 6, and 8). Of course, many considerations necessarily fall outside the central scope of formal analysis tools, such as political, institutional, and social details. For this reason, one must also rely on qualitative analyses, the value of which is convincingly illustrated in Chapters 4 and 9.

The next important activity that both policy-advising and scientific research organizations should be engaged in is conducting international and interdisciplinary case studies. These will help us to see where our new ideas add to our understanding. In addition, it would be interesting to have studies that allow us to implement theory in an experimental way. This may necessitate more formal studies that allow us to experiment with artificial systems that are projections of reality. Thus one can learn more in terms of relevance and applicability of new tools. Sadly enough, such research is still rare, and, of course, requires more serious attention from all participating disciplines—social, natural, and political. Although methodological differences do not necessarily hinder such efforts, it does seem that some structural improvements of education, research, meetings, and financing can still be realized.

Case studies have to be performed at all levels, including the project, regional, national, fluvial, continental, and global levels. Since most of these levels have been discussed extensively (Costanza1991), the important thing left to do is actual applications. Various publications are under way, which gives one hope. Of course, much attention has been put on global studies with regard to the Greenhouse Effect. It is as yet quite uncertain what to expect from these. On the one hand, it seems favorable that attention is addressed to both physical and social aspects. However, these studies are performed quite separately from each other, and feedback, (e.g., from human reactions to predicted climate change on climatic and global processes), is hardly dealt with (Cline 1992). Furthermore, such a task may be too demanding on present science and perhaps coordination of dispersed knowledge will prove too difficult at the moment. It is also not entirely clear whether one should put more emphasis on linkages between different environmental, including poverty and distributional, issues. Such ideas are not easily translated to analytical studies, especially to those that use formal or quantitative approaches. Hopefully, however, some progress in this direction can be made.

What we are ultimately aiming at when investigating sustainable development is, of course, some implementable plans based on a rather mixed qualitative/quantitative analysis. Such analyses mean in the first place, that we must again take a long-term perspective with regard to policies and institutions. In order to make statements about long-term phenomena in an environmental-economic-social context, it may turn out to be extremely relevant that more attention than at present is devoted to a description and analysis of past interrelationships between socio-economic and environmental processes. These may extend to millennia rather than decennia (Simmons 1989; Ponting 1991). Such considerations are certainly very uncommon in long-term economic analysis, particularly in the field of formal economic growth theory, upon which much of the environmental economics literature on this topic is based. The formal environmental science literature has taken a systems view, relating economic and environmental processes in a rather mechanistic way (Meadows et al. 1973; Odum 1986). Both approaches are rather ahistorical in scope, and it seems that historical and evolutionary understanding may have to be included to obtain more realism and relevance in long-term inquiry. It is furthermore important that we learn from past mistakes. Reviewing concrete policy failures can be very insightful (see Chapter 9). Finally then, one can come to suggestions about new or mixed types of instruments, as in Chapter 10. It will be clear, however, that no simple list of instruments can indicate the extent of possible influences that may be exerted to change trends in favor of sustainable levels. It will be clear that ultimately, for instance, land policy and public decisions with respect to transport and infrastructure are also very important. For that reason, the contribution of specific fields of application to the discussion of sustainable development remains necessary.

STRUCTURE OF THE BOOK

The book is subdivided into three parts. The first one deals with some theoretical and conceptual underpinnings of sustainability analyses. The second one is devoted to the application of methods and techniques in sustainable development studies. The third one deals with aspects and implementation of policies for sustainable development.

Part I opens with *Chapter 2*, which addresses an analytical framework for estimating the costs of tackling the problems of environmental unsustainability of economic processes. The costs of unsustainability are generally impossible to compute with any accuracy, since they are usually characterized by chronic uncertainty, irreversibility, and wide and indirect socio-economic impacts on a global and intergenerational scale. Therefore, it is more attractive to focus on the costs of achieving environmental sustainability. A requirement for this is that conditions for sustainability are agreed upon. Briefly, the procedure comes down to estimating the costs of adequate use of instruments to meet the conditions. It is clear then that the following steps have to be taken: deciding to achieve sustainability; establishing conditions; mapping causes and effects of unsustainable processes, as well as spatial or geographical demarcation of effects and policies; identifying instruments; and calculating costs of using instruments. The costs can be used to assess the macroeconomic effects as well as economic implications for specific industrial sectors. Also, one may work towards calculating a figure for sustainable national income. The various steps mentioned receive ample attention in this chapter. The discussion includes the conceptual, schematic presentation of causes and effects giving rise to unsustainability, as well as useful general classifications of costs, and policy instruments. Therefore, Chapter 2 may be regarded as a good introduction to many of the issues appearing in successive chapters.

A more specific issue is covered in *Chapter 3*. There, a formal framework of the economy-ecology relationship from an evolutionary perspective is introduced. Analogies are drawn from biological Darwinian evolution to economics. It is argued that evolutionary phenomena may be found in both nature and the economy, and that, accordingly, the proposed framework can serve an especially useful purpose for the study of interactions between the two. For this reason, an extended interpretation of evolution is considered, consisting of biological, cultural, and economic levels. The usefulness of the approach is argued on the basis of three essential characteristics underlying the evolutionary concept, which not only apply to natural systems but which are also critical to economic systems. First, the driving force behind evolution in nature is relative scarcity. Second, evolution takes place in historical time, (i.e., it is path dependent and non-predictable). And third, nature is a complex system in which non-linear feedbacks are important. *Replication* and *interaction* are key notions in representing evolution, usually associated with genes and organisms respectively. In the economic sphere, innovative ideas or information ("memes") can be regarded as replicators of cultural evolution, while individual humans act as interactors. One element of correspondence of biological and cultural evolution follows from the fact that the interactors—humans—are identical in terms of playing the important role of interactors on the level of biological and cultural evolution. A distinction from other species derives from the fact that humans are the only organisms that can effectively pass on knowledge non-genetically. Matters become more complex when one includes institutions and organizations, communication within larger groups, interaction between individual decisions and group phenomena, and purposeful action. For instance, in addition to individuals, various types of groups may act as interactors as well. An important conclusion is that, because cultural processes influence and constrain individual actions, their single effects remain modest. Therefore, evolutionary socio-economic processes may be self-organizing, but can hardly be regarded in terms of human design. As a second approach followed to deal with economic evolution, the author suggests regarding commodities as interactors, and preferences and technologies as replicators. The advantage is that this remains closer to standard microeconomic traditions in economics, and therefore, permits use of neoclassical concepts (e.g., relating stability to change). Communication occurs on markets that serve as a selection mechanism. For instance, technologies survive only if related products survive. The environment can be included in the evolutionary economic framework by feedback loops. On the one hand, these link environmental processes to economic ones, and on the other hand, they allow for an endogenously modeled environment. In view of the evolutionary traits, the latter can be seen as a dynamic interpretation of ecological sustainability. A special element introduced is that the evolutionary processes are enforced by interactive economic-ecological processes. Then the question is raised how important it is to take notice of differences in the velocity of evolutionary phenomena in economies and natural systems. Finally, institutions, as representing normative aspects and environmental policy, are placed within the economic-ecological evolutionary framework. This immediately gives rise to a problem of how to correctly separate facts and norms. A subsequent study may implement the framework via a computer simulation approach.

In *Chapter 4* the role of environmental (non-use, non-instrumental and/or intrinsic) values within governments is investigated. Many experts and influential policy documents, (i.e., the *World Conservation Strategy* [IUCN 1980] and *Our Common Future* [WCED 1987]) do not refer much to non-use values, as opposed to the general public who often use more subjective arguments and notions of intrinsic values. As a consequence, such non-use values are rarely mentioned in policy debates, even by pressure groups. In order to see whether this separation is extended to individuals in the policy institutions, interviews were held with senior policy advisors to four European governments that are active in global climate change negotiations and the U.N. Conference on Environment and Development. Questions were asked with respect to environmental values and descriptions of these values. It became clear that many advisors felt a friction between personal and professional opinions and responsibilities. Investigations made clear what the advisors thought about the role of economic analysis in the context of environmental policy preparation, including the problems of multi-dimensionality, aggregation, discounting, and inclusion of environmental values. Responses showed that most advisors hold deeply personal environmental values, which they keep separate from their professional environmental policy activities. The findings are interpreted in the context of recent literature on environmental ethics and values. The conclusion is drawn that environmental policy could be improved if widely held environmental values were articulated, validated, and admitted into the process of policy analysis and deliberation.

Part II opens with *Chapter 5* on spatial analysis of natural systems. The starting point for the ideas conveyed here is that computer simulations are becoming important tools for the investigation of protection and preservation of ecosystems that are being threatened. Especially in view of a combination of direct and indirect, as well as delayed, effects caused by human activities, it is necessary to deal with rather complex model systems. Many case studies will subsequently have to be performed on a detailed spatial level. Spatial ecosystem modeling is aimed at providing for more realistic representations of natural processes, and allows for interesting and new applications such as landscape modeling. A wider field of application of spatial analysis and modeling is opened up by current developments in Geographic Information Systems (GIS), for collection, storage, and manipulation of spatially referenced data. Applied modeling of economic-environmental processes may, in light of these developments, increasingly occur along temporal and spatial axes simultaneously. Together with the wide spectrum of aspects aimed to be covered by sustainable development analysis, it appears that complicated models may result, which can cause computation problems. Until recently the development of such models has, in fact, been severely limited by data requirements, conceptual and computational complexity issues, and insufficient computational resources. In the chapter these various problems receive attention, and discussion of the technical support offered by computer devices and packages is included. The architecture of an intelligent, user-friendly location for ecological-economic model development in a parallel, distributed computational environment is presented, along with examples of actual applications to spatial ecosystems. The resulting spatial modeling working station is based on development and testing of a basic model on Macintosh computers, and the use of, among other tools, a dynamic simulation development package and an interface package for guiding users through the model development process. The system allows for generating model versions for other parallel or serial computers. The approach presented combines user-friendliness, efficiency in design and programming, powerful computability, and flexibility in terms of translation to other computer systems.

Chapter 6 describes an application of the ECCO methodology, aimed at investigating the problem of natural capital depletion. Natural capital is defined as being composed of depletable recyclable and renewable forms. Development is related to a human-made physical capital stock. In the model the latter is focused on the production of technology for capturing solar energy. In order to have sufficient trade-offs, the study allows for the substitution of depletable energy sources by solar energy, nuclear fission, and fusion energy. To deal with investment in solar energy, capturing capital, land, and human capital is important, in addition to sectoral information on capital formation and energy requirements. The ECCO methodology being used is a dynamic natural capital accounting procedure, which allows for tracing dynamic substitution processes. The chapter specifically addresses whether it is possible for the world's economy to build—in time—the systems to capture solar energy on a scale sufficient to replace non-renewable natural capital sources, before these become seriously depleted. The world is expressed as a two-regional system, comprising the developed and less developed countries. Various scenarios are investigated, based on the speed of penetration of solar electricity, nuclear energy production, consumption patterns, fuel conservation, and population policies. A provisional conclusion is that the transition from a world economy based on the depletion of natural capital to one that is truly sustainable is only possible if both coal and nuclear energy continue to be used as energy sources for at least the next fifty years.

In *Chapter 7* a very central issue in ecological economics is addressed, namely that of the foundations of economic valuation of environmental damage and policy benefits. The important and previously little researched assumption investigated is whether individuals have utility functions defined over arguments that comprise both ordinary commodities and evironmental commodities. In order to provide a critical review and a discussion of alternatives to the standard mainstream approach of valuation of natural assets, a division of perspectives into four schools of thought is proposed and indicated by the keywords: *efficiency, equity, ecological,* and *philosophical*. The mainstream *efficiency* school is especially compared to the *philosophical* school, which stresses differences between subjective and ethical preferences, as well as between people in their roles as "citizens" and "consumers." Furthermore, it questions the validity of the principle of consumer sovereignty, and addresses issues such as preference shaping and intrinsic values of biological entities. In order to come up with an alternative basis for valuation, the Sagoff hypothesis is proposed, which is stated as: individuals respond to questions with regard to their non-use relationships with the natural environment as a citizen rather than a consumer. The implications of this and a variant hypothesis—based on whether they think they *should* act as citizens—for interpreting results of studies based on contingent valuation methods are discussed. For instance, the difference between Willingness-To-Pay and Willingness-To-Accept measures is clarified on the basis of it. The authors conclude that the extant approach to pseudo market valuation and their use is likely based on weak foundations, and that there is a case for new directions of research in regard to environmental valuation and its use in social decision making.

In *Part III*, *Chapter 8* opens with an examination of several issues related to the environmental sustainability of long-term development. Both conceptual economy-environment relationships and environmental policy issues are considered. Attention is devoted to the use of systematic and formal approaches for dealing with the topic of integrating knowledge and analysis in economics and ecology. For this reason several types of formal integration are discussed: calculating environmentally admissible economic activity levels; including also costs of adjustment actions into the analysis; adding economic-monetary valuation of environmental goods and services; and describing phenomena on a physical-material level of economic-environmental interactions. It is argued that frameworks used to elucidate the potential development interactions with the natural environment must be capable of recognizing and characterizing unsustainable—in addition to sustainable—patterns within economic/environmental systems. For policymaking, one must go beyond merely offering pictures of a system reflecting static, unstable, unlikely, or very sensitive time patterns. One approach may be to build systems that include at least the fourth type of integration concept mentioned. A second possible route is examination of the total past, in the sense of devoting attention to phenomena that extend beyond periods of decades and even centuries. In the context of long-term development and natural environment, attention is devoted to some frameworks of relationships between economy, society, institutions, and environment at different important phases in the history of mankind. These represent periods of a traditional hunting and fishing society, an agricultural society, a mineral economy, and a modern economy that includes the use of both minerals and fossil fuel resources for energy conversion and material production activities. Two elements are distinguished, namely sketching economic-environmental interactions in various periods of historical time, and indicating processes relevant to long-term change affecting such interaction schemes. The final part of the chapter is devoted to particular inconsistencies in the steps to be taken when the implementation of sustainable development is attempted. These are partitioned into valuation and analysis, evaluation and social decision making, and instruments and institutions. It is argued that there are fundamental problems associated with partial valuation of environmental systems and elements, and that this implies a shift to using methods stressing interrelationships between elements in environmental systems, consistent with the discussion in the first part of Chapter 8. One other issue dealt with here is whether and how institutional arrangements and economic instruments should be combined to realize an effective and efficient policy toolbox.

Chapter 9 is concerned with the relationship between distributional elements and environmental policy, with particular reference to the global international level. Much attention has been devoted to the intra- and intergenerational distributional impacts of the regulation of external effects, since these are associated with expropriation of environmental property rights. However, the relationship in the other direction, namely the influence of inequalities in income distribution on social values placed on environmental resources, as well as on environmental policies, has received much less attention. The discussion in the chapter provides for an interesting combination of theoretical, historical, environmental, political, institutional, and international issues with a focus on the latter relationship. Two cases where it did become a problematic one receive more detailed attention. They are related to the global emissions of CO_2, and the erosion of the global diversity of agricultural genetic resources. The relevance of the first example is based on the proposals for owner- ship rights to the CO_2 sink function. Questions derived from this are whether quota availability changes if countries become richer, and what price would be charged for them. Genetic resources for agriculture have been developed in many different places around the world over the last few thousand years by traditional methods of plant breeding, mostly out- side the market. The ownership rights to and the values placed on such environmental resources are now a subject of political contest. It is, therefore, first necessary to create a social perception that environmental resources have values, including option and use values. Subsequently, one can think about these resources as marketable commodities, acquir- ing suitable chrematistic values so that ecologically extended markets become instruments of environmental policies. The important argument in this chapter is then that market valuations depend partly on the distri- bution of income at present, and therefore, environmental policies based on markets will not be the same if the distribution of income changes. Diverse examples are investigated more accurately, such as a European ecotax, free trade agreements in North America, fuelwood versus fossil fuels for domestic cooking in poor countries, and the choice of potato varieties. The main conclusion drawn is that distributional obstacles to environmental policy should be removed by redistribution rather than growth. This opposes the common mainstream opinion, also expressed in the WCED report, that growth may solve both poverty and environmental problems. In the chapter this view is regarded as a rather easy way out.

The final contribution in *Chapter 10* is devoted to the choice of environmental policy from the perspective of combining the positive elements of different pure instruments. This is, in fact, a powerful idea that combines many nice characteristics of separate instruments. Three instruments are usually distinguished, namely property rights, economic incentive-based, and regulatory instruments. Failures in environmental policy might be attributed to deficiencies of single separate instruments. It is not surprising that, in response, an instrument of a quite mixed character, such as a tradable permit system, has received much attention the last few years. Objections to the adoption of purely economic incentives have been based upon such issues as concerns among scientists about information availability and environmental standards, concerns among regulators about loss of command and control authority, and concerns among emitters about increased costs. A tripartite approach is proposed to meet these concerns. Within an initial property range, over which no damage occurs, emitters would be allowed to emit. Beyond this, within an economic incentive range, further emissions would be taxed. In a third regulatory range any further emissions would be prohibited. The latter would be determined by pace of accumulation and irreversibility of damages occurring as a result of emissions. In this way goals of economic efficiency and environmental effectiveness may be served simultaneously, thereby taking notice of cost and ecological sustainability and human health considerations.

A NEED FOR CRITIQUE AND NEW APPROACHES

Although at the end of the eighties some scientists were of the opinion that "sustainability" and "sustainable development" would soon disappear, being no more than fashionable terms, it seems that the interest in these concepts is still very much alive. Furthermore, attention comes from both more or less traditional fields—notably neoclassical economics, welfare economics, public finance, and growth theory—and more pluriform and practical fields, (i.e., ecological economics, institutional economics, regional science, agricultural science, development fields, human ecology, and social/economic geography). Thus the concepts seem to offer opportunities for monodisciplinarists, multidisciplinarists, theorists, empiricists, optimists and pessimists alike. Which of the approaches is more needed and relevant is, to some extent, a matter of personal taste. Although one can never be certain that new approaches will be successful, it is clear that some of the old ones are, in any case, not always providing required solutions or even useful insights. The chapters in this book offer critical observations on old approaches, as well as guidelines for and applications of recent innovative developments in the field of "ecological economics." We feel that they are a necessary element of scientific research that aims to contribute to a realization of environmentally sustainable development.

REFERENCES

Archibugi, F., and P. Nijkamp, eds. 1989. Economy & Ecology: Towards Sustainable Development. Dordrecht: Kluwer.

Ayres, R. U., and A. V. Kneese. 1969. Production, consumption and externalities. *American Economic Review* 59: 282–97.

———. 1989. Externalities, economics and thermodynamics. In Economy and Ecology: Towards Sustainable Development, eds. F. Archibugi and P. Nijkamp. Dordrecht: Kluwer.

Bannister, D., and K. Button, eds. 1993. Transport, the Environment and Sustainable Development. London: E&FN Spon.

Barbier, E. B. 1989. Economics, Natural Resource Scarcity and Development: Conventional and Alternative Views. London: Earthscan.

———. 1990. Alternative approaches to economic-environmental interactions. *Ecological Economics* 2: 7–26.

Barbier, E. B., A. Markandya, and D. W. Pearce. 1990. Environmental sustainability and cost-benefit analysis. *Environment and Planning A*, 22: 1259–66.

Barney, G. O., ed. 1980. The Global 2000 Report to the President of the U.S.: Entering the Twenty-First Century, 2 Volumes. Harmondsworth: Penguin Books.

Bartelmus, P. 1986. Environment and Development. Boston: Allen and Unwin.

Bergh, J. C. J. M. van den. 1991. Dynamic Models for Sustainable Development. Ph.D. dissertation. Amsterdam: Thesis Publishers for Tinbergen Institute.

———. 1993. A framework for modelling economy-environment-development relationships based on dynamic carrying capacity and sustainable development feedback. *Environmental and Resource Economics* 3: 395–412.

Bergh, J. C. J. M. van den, and P. Nijkamp. 1991a. Operationalizing sustainable development: dynamic ecological economic models. *Ecological Economics* 4: 11–33.

———. 1991b. Aggregate dynamic economic-ecological models for sustainable development. *Environment and Planning A*, 23: 1409–28.

Boulding, K. E. 1966. The economics of the coming spaceship earth. In Environmental Quality in a Growing Economy, ed. H. Jarret. Baltimore: Johns Hopkins Univ. Press.

Breheny, M. J., ed. 1992. Sustainable Development in Urban Form. European Research in Regional Science Series, Vol. 2. London: Pion

Brown, B. J., M. E. Hanson, D. M. Liverman, and R. W. Meredith Jr. 1988. Global sustainability, towards a definition. *Environmental Management* 11: 713–19.

Clark, W. C., and R. E. Munn, eds. 1986. Sustainable Development of the Biosphere. Cambridge: Cambridge Univ. Press.

Cline, W. R. 1992. The Economics of Global Warming. Washington, DC: Institute for International Economics.

Collard, D., D. W. Pearce, and D. Ulph, eds. 1988. Economics, Growth and Sustainable Environments. New York: St. Martin's Press.

Common, M. 1988. Poverty and Progress Revisited. In Economics, Growth and Sustainable Environments, eds. D. Collard, D.W. Pearce, and D. Ulph. New York: St. Martin's Press.

Costanza, R., ed. 1991. Ecological Economics: The Science and Management of Sustainability. New York: Columbia Univ. Press.

Daly, H. E. 1991. Steady-State Economics, 2nd ed. San Francisco: Freeman.

———. 1990. Toward some operational principles of sustainable development. *Ecological Economics* 2: 1–6.

Dasgupta, P. S., and G. M. Heal. 1979. Economic Theory and Exhaustible Resources. Cambridge: Cambridge Univ. Press.

Despotakis, V. K. 1991. Sustainable Development Planning Using Geographical Information Systems. Ph.D. dissertation. Amsterdam: Free University.

Devall, B., and G. Sessions. 1984. Deep Ecology. Layton, UT: Peregrine Smith.

Dietz, F. J., and J. van der Straaten. 1992. Rethinking environmental economics: missing links between economic theory and environmental policy. *Journal of Economic Issues* 26: 27–51.

Dietz, F. J., U. E. Simonis, and J. van der Straaten, eds. 1992. Sustainability and Environmental Policy—Restraints and Advances. Berlin: Sigma Verlag.

Faber, M., and J. L. R. Proops. 1990. Evolution, Time, Production and the Environment. Heidelberg: Springer Verlag,

Gilbert, A. J., and L. C. Braat, eds. 1991. Modelling for Population and Sustainable Development. London: Routledge.

Goodland, R., and G. Ledec. 1987. Neoclassical economics and principles of sustainable development. *Ecological Modelling* 38: 19–46.

Hartwick, J. M. 1977. Intergenerational equity and the investing of rents from exhaustible resources. *American Economic Review* 67: 972–4.

Hueting, R. 1980. New Scarcity and Economic Growth: More Welfare Through Less Production? Amsterdam: North-Holland.

———. 1990. The Brundtland report: a matter of conflicting goals. *Ecological Economics* 2: 109–17.

IIASA. 1992. Science and sustainability. Selected papers on IIASA's 20th Anniversary. Laxenburg, Austria: International Institute for Applied Systems Analysis.

Klaassen, G. A. J., and J. B. Opschoor. 1991. The economics of sustainability and the sustainability of economics. *Ecological Economics* 4: 93–117.

Kneese, A. V., and W. D. Schulze. 1985. Ethics and environmental economics. In Handbook of Natural Resource and Energy Economics, Vol. 1., eds. A. V. Kneese and J. L. Sweeney. North-Holland: Amsterdam.

Kuik, O., and H. Verbruggen, eds. 1991. In Search of Indicators of Sustainable Development. Dordrecht: Kluwer.

Maclean, D., and P. G. Brown, eds. 1983. Energy and the Future. Totowa, NJ: Rowman and Littlefield.

Meadows, D. H., D. L. Meadows, J. Randers, and W. W. Behrens III. 1972. The Limits to Growth. New York: Universe Books.

Mishan, E. J. 1967. The Cost of Economic Growth. London: Staples Press.

———. 1977. The Economic Growth Debate: An Assessment. London: George Allen and Unwin.

NAVF. 1990. Sustainable Development, Science and Policy. Conference report of the Norwegian Research Council for Science and the Humanities. Oslo: NAVF.

Odum, H. T. 1987. Models for national, international, and global systems policy. In Economic-Ecological Modelling, eds. L. C. Braat and W. F. J. van Lierop. Amsterdam: North-Holland.

Opschoor, J. B., ed. 1992. Environment, Economy and Sustainable Development. Groningen, The Netherlands: Wolters-Noordhoff.

Opschoor, J. B., and J. van der Straaten. 1993. Sustainable development: an institutional approach. *Ecological Economics* 3: 203–22.

Pearce, D. W., and M. Redclift, eds. 1988. Sustainable development. *Futures* 20: special issue.

Pearce, D. W., E. B. Barbier, and A. Markandya. 1990. Sustainable Development: Economics and Environment in the Third World. Aldershot: Edward Elgar.

Pearce, D. W., and R. K. Turner. 1990. Economics of Natural Resources and the Environment. New York: Harvester Wheatsheaf.

Pearce, D. W., and J. J. Warford. 1993. World Without End—Economics, Environment, and Sustainable Development. Published for the World Bank. Oxford: Oxford Univ. Press

Pelt, M. J. F. van. 1993. Sustainability-Oriented Project Appraisal for Developing Countries. Ph.D. dissertation. Wageningen, The Netherlands: Agricultural University.

Pelt, M. J. F. van, A. Kuyvenhoven, and P. Nijkamp. 1990. Project Appraisal and Sustainability: Methodological Challenges. *Project Appraisal* 5: 139–58.

Pezzey, J. 1989. Economic Analysis of Sustainable Growth and Sustainable Development. Environmental Department working paper no.15. Washington, DC: The World Bank.

———. 1992. Sustainability: an interdisciplinary guide. *Environmental Values* 1: 321–62.

Ponting, C. 1991. A Green History of the World. London: Sinclair-Stevenson.

Redclift, M. 1987. Sustainable Development: Exploring the Contradictions. London: Methuen.

Repetto, R. 1986. World Enough and Time—Successful Strategies for Resource Management. New Haven: Yale Univ. Press.

Schramm, G., and J. J. Warford, eds. 1989. Environmental Management and Economic Development. Washington, DC; Baltimore: World Bank; Johns Hopkins Univ. Press.

Siebert, H. 1982. Nature as a life support system: renewable resources and environmental disruption. *Journal of Economics* 42: 133–42.

Simmons, I. G. 1989. Changing the Face of the Earth: Culture, Environment, History. Oxford: Basil Blackwell.

Simon, J. L., and H. Kahn. 1984. The Resourceful Earth. Oxford: Basil Blackwell.

Simonis, U. E. 1990. Beyond Growth: Elements of Sustainable Development. Berlin: Sigma Verlag.

Solow, R. M. 1974. Intergenerational equity and exhaustible resources. *Review of Economic Studies* 41: 29–45.

———. 1986. On the intergenerational allocation of natural resources. *Scandinavian Journal of Economics* 88: 141–49.

Tolba, M. K. 1987. Sustainable Development: Constraints and Opportunities. London: Butterworths.

Turner, R. K. 1988, ed. Sustainable Environmental Management: Principles and Practice. London: Belhaven.

Vries, H. J. M. de. 1989. Sustainable Resource Use: An Enquiry into Modelling and Planning. Groningen: University Press.

WCED. 1987. Our Common Future. World Commission on Environment and Development. Oxford; New York: Oxford Univ. Press.

WCN/IUCN. 1980. World Conservation Strategy: Living Resource Conservation for Sustainable Development. Gland, Switzerland: World Conservation Strategy/International Union for the Conservation of Nature.

Wilkinson, R. 1973. Poverty and Progress—An Ecological Model of Economic Development. London: Methuen and Co.

Young, M. D. 1992. Sustainable Investment and Resource use—Equity, Environmental Integrity and Economic Efficiency. Man and the Biosphere Series, Vol. 9. Published for UNESCO. Carnforth, U.K.: Parthenon.

PART I

THEORY AND CONCEPTS

2 THE ENVIRONMENTAL SUSTAINABILITY OF ECONOMIC PROCESSES: A FRAMEWORK FOR ANALYSIS

Paul Ekins
Department of Economics
Birkbeck College
University of London
7-15 Gresse Street
London, W1P 1PA U.K.

INTRODUCTION

During the last twenty years, an increasingly pronounced scientific consensus on the environmental unsustainability of current human ways of
life has emerged. This chapter provides a simple classification of the
main symptoms of that unsustainability.

Policy to address unsustainability often involves a stated commitment
to "sustainable development," a term which has acquired many different
meanings and interpretations, but which is comprised of two distinct
components—"development" and "sustainability." The chapter notes the
multi-dimensional nature of sustainability before focusing on environmental sustainability.

Environmental sustainability is related subsequently to the environmental functions that sustain human ways of life. The loss or impairment
of these functions entails costs that are often very difficult or impossible
to measure using normal methods of economic valuation. For many of
these costs, the only method that arrives at reliable computations is the
calculation of the costs entailed in reaching agreed-upon standards of
environmental quality. This is accordingly the method of cost-calculation
incorporated in the chapter's subsequent framework for the analysis of
the environmental sustainability of economic processes.

This framework first entails the mapping of the processes contributing to environmental sustainability. The boundaries of the processes and their environmental impacts need to be considered. Instruments to act on the processes to promote sustainability need to be devised. Standards of sustainability need to be set, and the costs of the instruments required to meet these standards must be calculated.

One use of these cost calculations is to enable instruments to be chosen that meet the standards at least cost. Another is to permit the macroeconomic implications of shifts towards sustainability to be assessed, using an appropriate macroeconomic model. A third is to permit calculations of adjustments to national GDP figures in order to arrive at a figure closer to sustainable national income. Each of these uses is important for the formulation of policies to move towards environmental sustainability.

THE ENVIRONMENTAL PROBLEM

Unsustainability: A Consensus

In the 20 years (1972–92) between the U.N. Conference on the Environment in Stockholm and the one on Environment and Development (UNCED) in Rio de Janeiro, a scientific consensus has gradually been established that the damage being inflicted by human activities on the natural environment render those activities unsustainable. It has become clear that the activities cannot be projected to continue into the future, either because they will have destroyed the environmental conditions necessary for that continuation, or because their environmental effects will cause massive, unacceptable damage to human health and disruption of human ways of life.

This is not the place to review the evidence that has led to the scientific consensus, but the now perceived seriousness of the problem can be illustrated by a number of quotations from the conclusions of reputable bodies that have conducted such a review. Thus the Business Council for Sustainable Development stated bluntly in its report to UNCED: "We cannot continue in our present methods of using energy, managing forests, farming, protecting plant and animal species, managing urban growth and producing industrial goods" (Schmidheiny 1992, 5). The Brundtland report, which initiated the process that led to UNCED, had formulated its perception of unsustainability in terms of a threat to survival: "There are thresholds which cannot be crossed without endangering the basic integrity of the system. Today we are close to many of these thresholds; we must be ever mindful of the risk of endangering the survival of life on earth" (WCED 1987, 32–3).

The World Resources Institute (WRI), in collaboration with both the Development and Environment programs of the U.N., concludes on the basis of one of the world's most extensive environmental databases that "The world is not now headed toward a sustainable future, but rather toward a variety of potential human and environmental disasters" (WRI 1992, 2). The World Bank, envisaging a 3.5 times increase in world economic output by 2030, acknowledged that "If environmental pollution and degradation were to rise in step with such a rise in output, the result would be appalling environmental pollution and damage." (World Bank 1992, 9). The Fifth Action Program of the European Community acknowledges that "many current forms of activity and development are not environmentally sustainable" (CEC 1992a, 4), as indicated by "a slow but relentless deterioration of the environment of the Community, notwithstanding the measures taken over the last two decades" (CEC 1992b, 3).

In its annual *State of the World* reports, the Worldwatch Institute has documented current environmental damage, concluding in 1993: "The environmentally destructive activities of recent decades are now showing up in reduced productivity of croplands, forests, grasslands and fisheries; in the mounting cleanup costs of toxic waste sites; in rising health care costs for cancer, birth defects, allergies, emphysema, asthma and other respiratory diseases; and in the spread of hunger." These trends mean "If we fail to convert our self-destructing economy into one that is environmentally sustainable, future generations will be overwhelmed by environmental degradation and social disintegration" (Brown et al. 1993, 4–5, 21).

Little wonder, therefore, that in 1992 two of the world's most prestigious scientific institutions saw fit to issue a joint statement of warning: "Unrestrained resource consumption for energy production and other uses...could lead to catastrophic outcomes for the global environment. Some of the environmental changes may produce irreversible damage to the earth's capacity to sustain life....The future of our planet is in the balance" (RS and NAS 1992, 2, 4)

Unsustainability: The Symptoms

An environmentally unsustainable activity is one that cannot be projected to continue into the future because of its negative effect either on the environment or on the human condition of which it is a part. The main symptoms of unsustainability, with their principal causative agents and the geographical level to which they mainly apply, can be simply grouped as in Table 2.1.

Table 2.1. Symptoms of Environmental Unsustainability

PROBLEM	PRINCIPAL AGENTS
Pollution	
Greenhouse effect/climate change (global)	Emissions of CO_2, N_2O, CH_4, CFCs (and HFCs), O_3 (low level)
	Deforestation
Ozone depletion (global)	Emissions of CFCs
Acidification (continental)	Emissions of SO_2, NO_x, NH_3, O_3 (low level)
Toxic pollution (continental)	Heavy metals, hydrocarbons, agrochemicals, eutrophiers radiation, carbon monoxide, organo-chlorides, noise
Renewable Resource Depletion	
Species extinction (global)	Land-use changes (e.g., development, deforestation), population pressure, unsustainable harvest (e.g., overgrazing, overfishing, poaching), climate change (possible), ozone depletion (in future)
Deforestation (global, regional)	Land-use changes, population pressure, unsustainable harvest (e.g., hardwoods), climate change (possible in future)
Land degradation/loss of soil fertility ([bio] regional, national)	Population pressure, unsustainable agriculture, urbanization, "development," climate change, (possible in future)
Water depletion ([bio] regional, national)	Unsustainable use, climate change (possible in future)
Non-renewable Resource Depletion	
Depletion of various resources (global, national)	Fossil fuels, minerals
Other Environmental Problems	
Congestion (national)	Waste-disposal, traffic

Two immediate observations can be made about the symptoms of un-sustainability. The first is the extent to which the problems are inter-linked. The second is the fact that the most important problems are those of pollution and depletion of renewable resources. It is somewhat para-doxical that the depletion of non-renewable resources (e.g., minerals, fossil fuels), which caused much of the anxiety about unsustainability in the 1970s (Meadows et al. 1972), and which appears to be an unsustain-able activity by definition, has declined dramatically in perceived impor-tance. New discoveries, and more efficient use of and substitution away from non-renewable resources have tended to keep constant, or even lengthen, their life-expectancies (defined as the known reserves/annual production, or R/P ratio). As an example, the R/P ratio of oil and natural gas increased from 31 and 38 to 41 and 68 years respectively from 1970 to 1989 (Meadows et al. 1992, 68). In one sense, any level of use of these resources is unsustainable, but the timescales involved now seem much less pressing than for pollution and the depletion of renewable resources.

Sustainability: The Solution

The increasingly conclusive evidence of environmental unsustainability has led to a rise in prominence of the concept of *sustainable develop-ment*. While some have claimed that the term was first used in the mid-1970s "to make the point that environmental protection and development are linked" (Holmberg and Sandbrook 1992, 19), it first became widely accepted when it was used as the flagship concept of the Brundtland re-port (WCED 1987). Since then, it has come to mean many different things to different people. Pearce et al. (1989, 173–85) were able to cite a "gallery of definitions," which by 1993 could have been much extended. To Lele, "Sustainable development is a 'meta-fix' that will unite every-body" (1991, 613). To Beckerman, "It is far from clear what concept of 'sustainable development' can be both morally acceptable and opera-tionally meaningful" (1992, 491).

Part of the definitional problem clearly arises from the composite na-ture of the concept of sustainable development, involving both *develop-ment* and *sustainability*. Now the debate about what constitutes develop-ment has a considerable history that has spawned an enormous literature. For present purposes, development may be crudely considered as a pro-cess that results in the increased welfare of the group under considera-tion, both on average and with regard only to the least well-off members of the group. This is consistent, for example, with UNDP's recent attempts to indicate levels of development by combining average per capita income figures with statistics on infant mortality and literacy to formulate a Human Development Index (UNDP 1990, 1991, 1992).

Barbier (1987) has suggested that sustainable development should be viewed as an interaction between three systems—biological, economic, and social. "The general objective of sustainable economic development, then, is to maximize the goals across all these systems through an adaptive process of trade-offs" (Barbier 1987, 104), although the difficulty of expressing these trade-offs in the same units suggests that the process is likely to be at best one of attempted optimization through the political process rather than strict maximization. The same multi-dimensionality is present in the concept of "primary environmental care" (PEC), which is clearly related to sustainable development and has become widely accepted among development organizations in their attempts to put sustainable development into practice. PEC is defined as "the umbrella term for development approaches in the interactive and zone between economic, environmental and social systems" (Holmberg and Sandbrook 1992, 31–32). Its "integral elements" are:

- meeting and satisfying of basic needs—the economic goal;

- protection and optimal utilization of the environment—the environmental goal; and,

- empowering of groups and communities—the social goal.

Turning specifically to sustainability, the basic meaning of the word is the capacity for continuance indefinitely into the future. While current concern about unsustainability largely has an ecological basis, it is clear that human situations or ways of life can be unsustainable for social and economic reasons as well. Provided that the inter-relatedness of these dimensions is kept in mind, it can be useful to distinguish between the implications for sustainability of human mores, relationships, and institutions (the social dimension); of the allocation and distribution of scarce resources (the economic dimension); and of the contribution to both of these from, and their effects on, the environment and its resources (the ecological dimension). Clearly human relationships may be socially unsustainable (for example, those leading to civil war) independently of economic or ecological factors; and a particular allocation of resources may be economically unsustainable (leading, for example, to growing budget deficits) independently of social or ecological factors. Similarly, a given level of economic growth may be unsustainable for purely economic reasons, insofar as it is leading to increased inflation or balance of payments deficits; on the other hand, it may be socially unsustainable insofar as it is increasing income inequalities or undermining structures of social cohesion such as the family or community; or it may be environmentally unsustainable insofar as it is depleting resources on which the economic growth itself depends.

One way of illustrating the complexities involved is through the matrix shown in Table 2.2, where the rows show the types of sustainability, and the columns the influences on those types across the same dimensions. In the example above, the sustainability of economic growth would be considered across the second row, with environmental influences (e.g., resource depletion) in box A, economic influences (e.g., inflation, balance of payments) in box B, and social influences (e.g., social cohesion) in box C.

Table 2.2. Types of Sustainability and Their Interactions

Type of Sustainability	Influences		
	Environmental	Economic	Social
Environmental		D	
Economic	A	B	C
Social			

Environmental sustainability may always be considered a desirable characteristic of a human situation, though some states of such sustainability may be better than others. In contrast, economic and social sustainability have no such happy connotation. As Hardoy et al. stress, "When judged by the length of time for which they (were) sustained, some of the most successful societies were also among the most exploitative, where the abuse of human rights was greatest" (1993, 180–1). Also, poverty and the evils that go with it may be all too sustainable. Similarly, in many countries structural unemployment is showing worrying signs of long-term sustainability.

The principal focus of this chapter is environmental unsustainability of many current human ways of life, with special reference to the economic influences involved (i.e., box D in Table 2.2). But a "way of life" is a complex bundle of activities, institutions, values, and objectives with all the above dimensions, and which can relate to and involve individuals and communities at different levels, from the village to the "global community." Changing the economic conditions leading to environmental unsustainability is likely to have implications for economic sustainability (e.g., international competitiveness) as well. These interlinkages must be constantly kept in mind in any policy analysis based on the considerations of environmental sustainability which are to follow. In a situation of any complexity, the dimensions of sustainability will generally interact in a multiplicity of ways. Any attempt to proceed from the symptoms of unsustainability to their practical remediation, which fails to take these interactions into account, will be in grave danger of ineffective, and perhaps counterproductive, intervention.

CONSIDERATIONS OF ENVIRONMENTAL SUSTAINABILITY

Environmental Functions

Following Hueting (1980), the contribution of the environment to human life is perceived to be through the operation of a wide range of "environmental functions." This concept has been extensively developed by de Groot, who defines environmental functions as "the capacity of natural processes and components to provide goods and services that satisfy human needs" (1992, 7). These "natural processes and components" can in turn be identified as "natural capital" (though de Groot does not use the term), which features in various definitions of sustainability and sustainable development (Pearce et al. 1989, 34ff.). De Groot (1992) identifies thirty-seven environmental functions, which he classifies under four headings: regulation, carrier, production, and information.

Pearce and Turner (1990) and Ekins (1992a), for example, have used another method of grouping these functions, under three headings:

- Provision of resources for human activity,
- Absorption of wastes from human activity, and
- Provision of environmental services independently of or interdependently with human activity.

These two classifications are not contradictory. The resource functions in the second typology correspond broadly to the production functions of the first, but also include some carrier functions. The waste absorption functions are included among the regulation functions, and the provision of services includes the information functions and some regulation and carrier functions.

With the increase of the human population and the scale of its activities, the environmental functions are increasingly in competition with each other. Choices have to made between them, and some functions are lost. Lost functions represent costs to be ascribed to the chosen functions. It is in this sense that the environment has become an increasingly scarce economic factor. The uses to which it is put are increasingly competing, and it is an important ingredient of human welfare. The choices between environmental functions are therefore precisely analogous to other economic choices.

Environmental Sustainability

As already defined, sustainability means the ability to be continued indefinitely in time. The environmental sustainability of human ways of life refers to the ability of the environment to sustain those ways of life. This, in turn, depends on the maintenance of the environmental functions that provide this sustenance, according to the classification described above. Which functions are important for which ways of life, and the level at which they should be sustained, will vary to some extent by culture and society, although there are obviously basic biophysical criteria for human existence. Such considerations provide the context for the setting of standards of sustainability, to be discussed later.

In part, the concern over the environmental unsustainability of current ways of life has an ethical basis: some consider it wrong to diminish the environmental options of future generations below those available today; others consider wrong the impacts on other life forms that unsustainability implies. The concern derives also in part from perceived self-interest. Unsustainability threatens costs and disruption to ways of life in the future that are or may be greater than those incurred by moving voluntarily towards sustainability now. The self-interested concern about unsustainability will obviously become stronger as the time-scale within which the costs and disruption will be experienced is perceived to shorten. This is probably the reason for the current strengthening of public anxiety about the environment.

While some would view environmental sustainability as an ethical imperative—one that is becoming an increasingly important, though not yet dominant, objective of public policy—it is not usually viewed as an end in itself. It is, rather, a present desirability with regard to future human development, yet the conditions for sustainability can act as a constraint on present development. Sustainability guarantees certain life opportunities in the future at the cost of the modification or sacrifice of life opportunities in the present. The political argument, and the tension in the concept of sustainable development, is over the acceptability of and uncertainties involved in the trade-offs. The task for science is to clarify the uncertainties as far as possible. The task for economic analysis is to elaborate the economic implications of moving towards sustainability, and show how the costs can be minimized, once the definition of and need for sustainability have been accepted.

Costs of Unsustainability

To apply the standard economic approach to problems of unsustainability, one should seek to equate the marginal benefit produced by the activity causing the unsustainability with the marginal cost of that unsustainability. Where both costs and benefits are expressed in well-functioning markets with socially just property rights, this job can be left to those markets. Unfortunately, as a cursory examination of the symptoms of unsustainability shows, these problems are not usually mediated by such markets. Most of the effects escape the market mechanism (i.e., they are externalities), and there can be insuperable problems, with regard to basic feasibility and the level of transaction costs, and with applying the Coasian remedy of defining property rights in order to create those markets (Pearce and Turner 1990).

Where costs or benefits escape markets and markets cannot be created to capture them, the economic approach is to apply some valuation technique in order to express the cost or benefit in monetary terms and so bring it into the calculus. Environmental systems have many different kinds of values relating to their different functions. Pearce (1993) considers that the total economic value (TEV) of these systems can be expressed as:

TEV = Direct use value + Indirect use value + Option value + Existence value,

where the direct use value relates broadly to the production of at least potentially measurable, marketable outputs; the indirect use value relates to other uses of production functions and of the regulation, carrier, and information functions; the option value relates to peoples' desire to sustain these functions for possible future use, even if they are not being used currently; and existence value relates to peoples' desire to sustain these functions regardless of their use. Pearce considers existence value to capture at least part (the humanly defined part) of "intrinsic" value (Pearce 1993).

Within this basic formulation of value, there are several possible ways of trying to calculate the value of environmental functions, and thus the economic implications of their loss:

    a. *Costs in surrogate markets*: peoples' valuation of environmental functions may be deducible from the costs they are prepared to incur to make use of them (e.g., by paying more for well-situated houses or paying to travel to parks).

    b. *Damage costs*: the impairment or loss of a function may damage economic productivity or human welfare. Such damage may or may not be remedied and may or may not give rise to compensation, which might include actual payments, the provision of substitutes or hypothetical willingness to accept valuations. Any of the costs of the damage, its remedy or compensation for it may be used as a valuation of the environmental function.

    c. *Maintenance and protection costs*: the costs of maintaining and protecting environmental functions can be regarded as expressions of their worth to human society. These costs may be actual payments made or hypothetical costs, as in willingness-to-pay evaluations; or they may be opportunity costs, that is, the costs of foregoing otherwise beneficial activities that would unacceptably impair or destroy an environmental function.

    d. *Restoration costs*: the costs associated with the impairment or loss of a function may, under some circumstances, be equated to the cost of restoring that function to some agreed level.

Figure 2.1 illustrates the economic problem and the necessity for cost-evaluation in order to arrive at a solution. In Figure 2.1a the horizontal axis has two variables on different scales: the output of a good, and the environmental damage associated with its production, which rises in proportion to output. S_P is the (private) supply curve of the good. S_E is the marginal external environmental cost curve, and can be thought of as the "supply curve" of the environmental damage, which is an unintended output of production. The total social supply curve of the good is therefore represented by S_T, where $S_T = S_P + S_E$. The good's demand curve is D. The optimal economic solution to the problem is to levy a tax, t, equal to the difference between the private and total cost curves at the optimal output level Q^*. t is also equal to the external social cost at that output.

Figure 2.1b reverses the horizontal axis for the environmental damage, so that S_E can now be viewed as the demand curve for the environmental function(s) affected by the good's production. S_F is the marginal cost curve for preventing or remedying the environmental damage and can be regarded as the supply curve of the relevant environmental function(s) for this use. Expenditures on preventing environmental damage will change the relationship between output and environmental damage, and thus may enable damage to be reduced without reducing output. In this formulation, the economic problem becomes the location of E^*, the optimal level of the environmental function, where the current level of the function might be given by E.

The various techniques for measuring the kinds of costs described under a, b, and c above represent attempts to determine the S_E curves in Figure 2.1, the "total economic value" (as earlier defined) of the environmental sacrifice. Both de Groot and Pearce acknowledge the controversial nature of some of these techniques, especially contingent valuation (willingness-to-pay/accept, WTP/WTA), for arriving at a credible valuation of environmental functions. Option and existence value are particularly difficult to measure. As Pearce says, only contingent valuation can be used in these cases (1993). De Groot believes that "accurate economic quantification of existence values attached to ecosystems is quite impossible" (1992, 134) and that "it is quite difficult if not impossible to assign a monetary value to the option value of natural ecosystems" (1992, 136). It must also be kept in mind that the environmental costs (or benefits) may be incurred in the future, in which case the calculation of their present value involves the use of a discount rate, the appropriate value of which for distant, large environmental effects is a further matter of great controversy.[1]

---

1. In addition to de Groot and Pearce, see Cline (1993) and Birdsall and Steer (1993) for a discussion of this issue with regard to global warming.

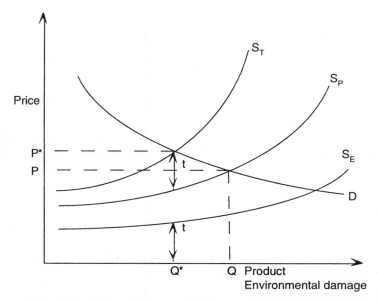

a. Supply and demand of a good with an environmental externality

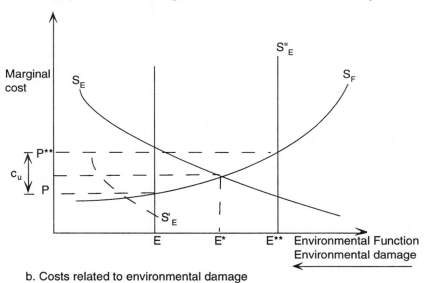

b. Costs related to environmental damage

Figure 2.1. Environmental costs and their internalization.

The values of environmental functions produced by these techniques can vary enormously. Pearce (1993) reports implicit willingness-to-pay valuations for tropical forests that vary by a factor of 400 without any evidence that this difference relates to difference in forest quality. Again, different methods of valuing the potential benefits in OECD countries of medicinal forest plants under threat of extinction produced results that varied between $17.2 billion and $720 billion. Another example that enters into some environmental valuations is the value of a human "statistical life," taken in one study to be $1 million, and in another $4 million. Such variations, of course, undermine the credibility and usefulness of the evaluating techniques (Pearce 1993).

These differences in valuation are not surprising given the common characteristics of the symptoms of unsustainability listed earlier, which make them most intractable for economic analysis and which include chronic uncertainty often verging on the indeterminate; irreversibility; profound social and cultural implications; actual or potential grave damage to human health, including threats to life; global scope; and a long-term, intergenerational time-scale.

There is rarely any generally acceptable way of putting a monetary value on costs with these characteristics, especially when the characteristics are combined. Microeconomic techniques of hedonic pricing, contingent valuation, and cost-benefit analysis are not able to realistically assess the economic costs of displacing millions of people from low-lying coastal areas (global warming); of hundreds of thousands of extra eye-cataracts and skin cancers (ozone depletion); of other processes of large-scale environmental degradation, such as current rates of deforestation, desertification, and water depletion, which entail considerable national or international threats to life and livelihood; of the possible unraveling of ecosystems (species extinction); of the persistent release of serious toxins (radiation); or the effects of major disasters (Chernobyl, Bhopal).

A danger of seeking to arrive at a monetary valuation of effects such as these is that they will be underestimated and decisions will be made in favor of the far more certain, near-term benefits that accrue from environmental destruction. In pictorial terms this amounts to the derivation of only a partial demand curve such as S_E' in Figure 2.1b, which leads to an excessive level of environmental damage. It is here that the concept of sustainability can be useful.

The rhetoric in favor of environmental sustainability at gatherings such as UNCED suggest that it is an increasingly important human priority. Insofar as it is taken to be an over-riding priority, the implicit costs of unsustainability can be thought of as approaching infinity. In Figure 2.1b, if E^{**} is taken to be the minimum sustainable level of the environmental function(s), then accepting the priority of environmental sustainability amounts to deriving a demand curve for the function(s) of S_E". E^{**} will not necessarily be the same as the efficient level of the environmental function (E^*), for, as Pearce (1993, 47) says: "An efficient use of resources need not be a sustainable one." S_F has already been identified as the marginal restoration or abatement cost associated with supplying the environmental function(s) and corresponding to costs type D in the earlier discussion. These costs normally are determinable to acceptable levels of accuracy. The point of intersection of the S_F curve with the S_E" curve gives the shadow price of environmental sustainability (P^{**}), which, in turn, puts a value on the extent to which current economic activity is unsustainable, c_u (= $P^{**}-P$). The E^{**} levels of environmental quality are derived from sustainability standards (see later section). The first step in deriving the S_F curve is to trace the causes of unsustainability.

Mapping Unsustainable Processes

Unsustainability arises from activities of production and consumption. At a certain level these cause competition between environmental functions. Following Hueting (1980), again, this competition can be quantitative, qualitative, or spatial. Quantitative competition results from the extraction and depletion of resources. Qualitative competition results from the emission of substances (or noise) at or resulting in disruptive levels or concentrations. Spatial competition arises from occupation of space resulting in congestion. Unsustainability arises from some of the effects of the depletion, concentration, and congestion on living things, including people (biotic effects), or on the human way of life.

All competition between environmental functions entails costs and is appropriate for economic analysis. However, not all such competition results in problems of unsustainability. Noise is an example of qualitative competition, which can be disruptive but is not necessarily a problem of unsustainability. It is an economic problem but need not be a sustainability problem. The boundary between the two is defined by the sustainability conditions and standards.

It is, however, important to attempt the economic evaluation of even non-sustainability problems, because, in the event that they are resolved as a by-product of measures directed at sustainability problems, the net cost of these measures is reduced by the now foregone cost of the resolved (non-sustainability) problem. Such examples might include a transport policy aimed at reducing emissions that also reduces noise because of a diminution of road traffic (cost foregone), or an agricultural policy aimed at reducing pesticide concentrations that results in a landscape of greater aesthetic or amenity value (benefit gained). While the cost and benefit may be incidental to the achievement of sustainability, they should still be accounted for when computing the cost of the sustainability measure itself.

In mapping processes of unsustainability, the following steps are required, with reference to Figure 2.2:

1. The effects on the biota or human way of life (V) must be identified and, if possible, quantified.

2. The causes of these effects must be determined scientifically, whether they are due to concentration, depletion or congestion (IV).

3. These causes must in turn be related to the emissions, extraction, or occupation patterns of particular human activities (II). The boundaries and levels of these activity patterns and their effects must be established (see following section). Thus far the task is one of scientific analysis and the production of appropriate environmental statistics.

4. Standards must be set for the effects on biota and the human way of life that are compatible with sustainability. These standards must then be traced back through the lines of cause and effect established in 2 and 3 to arrive at sustainability standards for emission, depletion, and occupation (see the following section).

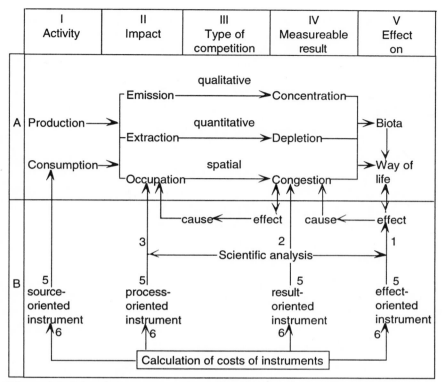

Figure 2.2. Mapping processes of unsustainability.
A=causal sequences; B=analytic sequences
Numbers 1–6 refer to the numbered paragraphs

5. Instruments, which might be market-based, regulatory, or technical, must be devised to meet these standards.[2] These instruments can either be effect-oriented (applied to the effects), result-oriented (applied to the concentrations, depletion, or congestion), process-oriented (applied to the emissions, extraction, or occupation) or source-oriented (applied to the activity, either reducing its volume or changing its nature). The instruments themselves might have environmental implications (e.g., the quarrying and transporting of lime for use in counteracting the acidification of lakes), which should themselves be subject to the mapping process of Figure 2.2. Suppose, for example, that the unsustainability effect was health problems caused by water-pollution (an example of qualitative competition). An effect-oriented instrument would be the

---

2. See Opschoor and Vos (1989) for a discussion of economic instruments in general.

administration of a drug to affected persons; a result-oriented instrument would be water purification; a process-oriented instrument would be emission controls; and a source-oriented instrument would be the restriction of production or the replacement or reduction of the pollutant's use. Not all the types of instrument will be feasible for all problems. Alternatively, the use of instruments in all categories may be required to effectively tackle a problem.

6. The costs of the instruments need to be calculated (1) for comparisons between them so as to be able to choose the most cost-effective option; (2) to estimate, through the use of an appropriate economic model, their sectoral and macroeconomic implications; and (3) to permit the computation of an adjustment to the GNP in order for it to better approximate sustainable income (Hueting et al. 1991). The first objective is obvious. The other two are briefly discussed in a later section.

Boundaries of Sustainability

Environmental impacts can be felt at global, continental, (bio)regional, national, and local levels. To be effective, public policy will have to be formulated at a level appropriate to the impact concerned. Because of the primacy of national governments in political decision making, it makes sense to think of boundaries of sustainability, initially at least, in terms of the nation-state.

Figure 2.3 is a schematic representation of the domestic production and consumption of a country, N, and the environmental impacts caused by these, together with imported pollution. Of course, the environmental effects will not generally be measurable in the same units, so that the additions are descriptive rather than computable. Most of the environmental effects identified are obvious and need no exemplification here. EIP, EIC, PEX, CEX, the imports and exports of environmental effects, are likely to be in the form of air- or water-born pollutants. CIE might be exemplified by the destruction of tropical forests due to hardwood imports, CXE by damage to human health or the environment by the export of pesticides or other dangerous chemicals.

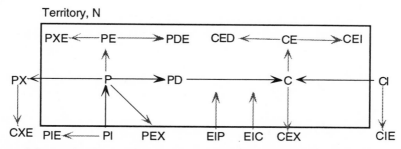

Figure 2.3. Production, consumption, and environmental impacts of and in
Country N.

Key to Figure 2.3:

- Solid lines are processes of production or consumption. Dotted lines are associated environmental impacts.
- E terms: E appearing in any sequence of letters signifies an environmental impact, i.e., emission, extraction, or occupation. All impacts are in N unless stated to the contrary.
- Activity: Production, P; Consumption, C

N	=	Territorial boundary of nation-state
P	=	Production within N
PE	=	Environmental impacts due to production in N
PI	=	Imports for production (capital goods)
PIE	=	Environmental impacts outside N due to PI
PD	=	Domestic product for home consumption
PX	=	Domestic product for export
CXE	=	Environmental effects outside N due to consumption of exports
PDE	=	Environmental impacts due to production of home-consumed domestic product
PXE	=	Environmental impacts due to production of exports

Production equation: P = PD + PX

C	=	Consumption within N
CE	=	Environmental impacts due to consumption in N
CED	=	Environmental impacts due to consumption of domestic product in N
CI	=	Imports consumed in N
CEI	=	Environmental impacts due to consumption of imports in N
CIE	=	Environmental effects outside N due to production of imports of consumer goods

Consumption equation: C = PD + CI

EIP, EIC   = Import of environmental effects due to production and consumption abroad

PEX, CEX   = Export of environmental effects due to domestic production and consumption

Environmental effects equations:

PE   = PDE + PXE

TPE   = Total environmental impacts (in and outside N) due to production in N
       = PE + PEX + PIE + CXE

CE   = CED + CEI

TCE   = Total environmental effects (in and outside N) due to consumption in N
       = CE + CEX + CIE

It is possible to identify three meaningful sets of boundaries:

1. The total environmental impacts in N due to domestic production and consumption are:

    PE + CE = PDE + PXE + CED + CEI

2. The total environmental impacts in N are:

    PE + CE + EIP + EIC

3. The total environmental effects emanating from domestic production and consumption are:

    TPE + TCE = PE + CE + PEX + CEX + PIE + CIE + CXE

Which of these boundaries is relevant and can be made operational will depend on the issue in question and on possibilities of measurement. The measurement of impacts in N is likely to include the contribution of imported impacts (EIP and EIC, as in 2). The measurement of domestic emissions will probably include those that are subsequently exported (PEX and CEX). PIE, CIE, and CXE are likely to be impossible to measure without the co-operation of the exporting/importing country, but may be among the principal contributors to unsustainability. The boundaries must also be kept in mind in the choice of instruments. Tackling domestic emissions may not improve the domestic concentration of pollutants if the pollutants are mainly imported (EIP, EIC), in which case the cheapest way to improve environmental quality may be to subsidize emission-reduction in the neighboring polluting countries (though this has obvious implications for the observation of the Polluter Pays Principle). Similarly, purifying domestic soil or water will not decrease the emissions that are exported to neighbors.

In accounting terms involving more than one country, only case 2 allocates all effects to one country and one only. In case 1, no country is considering the impacts of pollution imports and exports (PEX, CEX, EIP, EIC). In case 3, more than one country (N, and the countries importing from or exporting to N) will be considering, and perhaps taking responsibility for, CIE, CEI, PIE, CXE, PXE. (CXE for one country is equivalent to CEI for the other; PXE is similarly equivalent to the sum of PIE and CIE). While untidy in accounting terms, acceptance of shared responsibility for these effects is likely to produce the best environmental outcome.

Sustainability Conditions and Standards

Unsustainability has been defined earlier as an effect on biota or the human way of life that prevents the way of life from continuing, or incurs an unacceptable risk of preventing it from continuing in the future. Given the uncertainties involved in matters of sustainability, the question of risk is crucial, not least because risk, through insurance premiums, for example, incurs present real (rather than hypothetical future) costs.

The problems of unsustainability arise, as has been seen, from chronic competition between environmental functions:

Qualitative = excessive emissions lead to excessive concentrations, which lead to unsustainable effects

Quantitative = excessive extraction leads to excessive depletion, which leads to unsustainable effects.

Spatial = excessive occupation (of space) leads to excessive congestion, which leads to unsustainable effects.

What counts as an "unsustainable effect" rather than a sustainable economic cost is a matter of judgment that can only partially be resolved by science. Ethics and the attitude toward risk also play a significant role here. It is important that the basis of judgment is articulated clearly, especially as to who is responsible for the effects and who is bearing their costs, and how the contributions played by science, ethics, and risk acceptance or aversion are distinguished:

The following are put forward as a preliminary set of sustainability conditions:

- Destabilization of global environmental features, such as climate patterns or the ozone layer, must be prevented.

- Important ecosystems and ecological features must be absolutely protected to maintain biological diversity.

- Renewable resources must be renewed through the maintenance of soil fertility, hydrobiological cycles, and necessary vegetative cover, and sustainable harvesting must be rigorously enforced.

- Depletion of non-renewable resources should seek to balance the maintenance of a minimum life-expectancy of the resource with the development of substitutes for it. Once the minimum life-expectancy was reached, consumption of the resource would have to be matched by new discoveries of it. To help finance research for alternatives and the eventual transition to renewal substitutes, all depletion of non-renewable resources should entail a contribution to a capital fund. The need to minimize the depletion of all but the most abundant non-renewable resources implies that these resources should be used as intensively as possible by designing for resource-efficiency, durability, and the maximum feasible practice of repair, reconditioning, re-use, and recycling (the four Rs).

- Emissions into air, soil, and water must not exceed their critical load, (i.e., the capability of the receiving media to disperse, absorb, neutralize, and recycle them), nor may they lead to life-damaging concentrations of toxins.

- Risks of life-damaging events from human activity must be kept at very low levels. Technologies, such as nuclear power, which threaten long-lasting ecosystem damage at whatever level of risk, should be foregone.

Ideally, the actual standards following from these conditions should be set and enforced by institutions operating at the level at which the problem is manifest, (i.e., a global problem should be handled globally). However, where the institution at the appropriate level is either absent or ineffective, the standard-setting may need to be undertaken at other levels. Thus, with regard to the depletion of important non-renewable resources, it is desirable that a global view be taken in the allocation of depletion quotas.[3] The extreme unlikelihood of this being politically feasible in the near future argues for individual countries with the institutional capability taking measures to bring depletion of their own resources within sustainability standards. In doing so, they will clearly be constrained by other domestic priorities and the need to remain economically competitive as a nation, but appropriate national action on global problems is likely to produce a better environmental outcome than waiting perhaps indefinitely for global agreement.

The different forms of competition (qualitative, quantitative, spatial) will need to be addressed by different kinds of standards:

- *Qualitative*. A standard can be set at each of the stages of the unsustainable process:
    1. effect, (e.g., a tolerated level of sickness from pollution or disruption from noise);

---

3. Daly (1977, 61ff.) describes proposals for a "depletion quota auction."

2.   concentration, (e.g., maximum levels of pollution in soil, water, air, and organisms); and

3.   emissions, (e.g., maximum emissions levels).

- *Quantitative*. It is more difficult here to relate the standards to the stages in the unsustainability process. For renewable resources the standard is clear—the definition of a minimum acceptable stock and then the definition and enforcement of a strictly sustainable harvest. For non-renewable resources, the situation is more complex, and three overall concepts seem helpful:

1.   minimum reserve—a certain quantity of the resource should be re-garded as untouchable in normal circumstances to insure against uncertainty or emergencies;

2.   minimum life expectancy—for the remainder of the resource, the depletion rate should be balanced by new discoveries to guarantee a minimum life expectancy of the resource. Operating at minimum life expectancy, the relevant formula (derived in Appendix A) is:

$$d_2 = d_1 [1 + (D_1 - d_1)/R_1]$$

where d_2 = period 2 rate of depletion, and

d_1 = period 1 rate of depletion

D_1 = discoveries in period 1

R_1 = stock of resources in period 1

3.   capital fund—from the financial flows arising from depletion of the resource, a proportion should be set aside, either to fund re-search into substitutes for it or to generate a permanent income stream in the future equal to that consumed as income in the pre-sent. El Serafy (1989) has calculated a formula by which this pro-portion can be computed (derived in Appendix B), relating it to the discount rate and the life expectancy of the resource. The formula is:

$$I/R = 1/(1 + r)^{n+1}$$

where I =   that part of receipts to be considered as capital

R =   receipts

r =   discount rate

n =   life expectancy of the resource

Ekins (1992b) applies this formula to the depletion of the U.K.'s North Sea oil, calculating that the royalty receipts of the U.K. government should by now have resulted in a capital fund of £43 or £25 billion, depending on whether a 5% or 10% discount rate is used.

The minimum life expectancy and capital fund approaches could be applied as alternatives or together. Their implications are rather different. Maintaining a minimum life expectancy would guarantee to future generations a continuing flow of the resource in question but, depending on new discoveries, it could be a diminishing one. Creating a capital fund could result in total exhaustion of the resource but should have ensured the development of a substitute or an equivalent income stream from another source. This would only be compatible with sustainability where the asset producing the income stream was a perfect substitute for the depleted resource. Given that the whole notion of sustainable use of a finite resource is somewhat contradictory, a case can be made for applying both approaches, and therefore reaping their different sustainability benefits together.

- *Spatial.* The principal unsustainability effect from spatial competition is species extinction. Because of its irreversibility and the uncertainties involved, an appropriate standard would appear to be that no species be knowingly extinguished. This standard is rendered more imperative by the fact that many extinctions are currently occurring, and many more undoubtedly will occur as a result of processes already under way that cannot be immediately halted (though for sustainability, they must be over time). Other potentially unsustainable examples of spatial competition are waste-dumping, and traffic congestion. Both of these are likely to be much ameliorated by sustainability measures to reduce emissions and depletion, so it may not be necessary to formulate sustainability standards in these areas (although as noted earlier, the cost savings associated with dealing with these problems must be computed and subtracted from the costs of the measures of the sustainability measures in the other areas).

SUSTAINABILITY: MACROECONOMIC IMPLICATIONS

The preceding sections discuss a methodology for tracing the causes of environmental sustainability and analyzing instruments to bring economic activity within defined standards of sustainability. It is clear that the determined application of these instruments across the whole range of activities implicated in unsustainability will have profound effects on the macroeconomy. Of major importance are the implications of a shift towards environmental sustainability for economic growth. Ekins (1993) reviews the debate on this issue since the 1970s, from which it is clear that no consensus on the growth sustainability relationship has yet emerged. Though substantive differences of opinion exist, at least some of the disagreement is due to differing meanings attached to the word "growth" in the context of sustainable development.

Following Daly (1990), one can start by drawing a distinction between development, as qualitative change, and growth, as quantitative increase. Growth then may or may not be a necessary condition for development (there is now wide agreement that it is not a sufficient condition), but this, in turn, depends on what is considered to be growing. At least four different kinds of growth related to the economy can be identified:

1. Growth in the economy's physical throughput of matter and energy and therefore in its generation of wastes,

2. Growth in Gross National (or Domestic) Product, as conventionally measured,

3. Growth in the production of biomass, which one could label Gross Nature Product, and

4. Growth in economic welfare or utility.

In a physically finite world governed by the laws of thermodynamics, indefinite, let alone exponentially indefinite, Type 1 growth is not possible. It is, in fact, quite clear that it is this kind of growth that is responsible for current environmental problems.

Type 2 growth can differ from Type 1 growth through three effects identified by Lecomber (1975): (1) changes in composition of output, (2) substitution between factor inputs, and (3) more efficient use, through technical progress, of the same input. If these three effects add up to a shift away from the limiting resource or pollutant at a rate equal to or greater than the rate of GNP growth, then the physical limits to growth are put back indefinitely, and GNP can go on growing. But Lecomber warns that, "...(This) establishes the logical conceivability, not the certainty, probability, or even possibility in practice, of (GNP) growth continuing indefinitely...." (1975, 42).

Type 3 growth, including many different kinds of biomass, animal and vegetable, clearly cannot be meaningfully expressed in aggregate form. But, for three reasons, it is probably the most important kind of growth considered here. First, the conversion by plants of solar energy from outside the biosphere to biomass within it is the only means by which living systems, including humans, can circumvent the Second Law of Thermodynamics and decrease biospheric entropy. Second, the quantity and quality of biomass is crucial to the stability of important natural processes, such as climate regulation or the carbon and water cycles. Third, and most obviously, biomass includes food. The ability of the earth to support the likely doubling of the present human population depends on great increases in food production.

The production of biomass is currently experiencing two powerful conflicting trends. Positively, genetic manipulation and chemical inputs have greatly increased outputs of foodstuffs in some areas, though not without fears for the future due to soil erosion and the negative effects associated with chemically intensive agriculture and biotechnology. Negatively, environmental degradation (deforestation, desertification) and harvesting beyond sustainable yields (e.g., overfishing) have greatly reduced biomass production. While the future net outcome of these trends is uncertain, reversal of the processes of degradation are likely to be essential to the attainment of "sustainable livelihoods" in many less industrial countries (Chambers 1992).

Type 4 growth is obviously related to Type 2 growth and may be assumed to be positively related ceteris paribus. However, the existence of possibly negative external effects from production on, inter alia, the environment, health, working conditions, income distribution, and leisure (all of which are components of economic welfare) means that the relationship is not necessarily positive overall. Mishan (1967, 1977), Leipert (1989), Daly and Cobb (1989), and Douthwaite (1992) all question the extent to which GNP growth now contributes to net human welfare.

Development is most closely related to Type 4 growth and therefore also has a complex relationship to Type 2 growth. Environmental sustainability is most closely related to Types 1 (probably negatively) and 3. The relationship between sustainable development, which clearly seeks to combine both sustainability and development, and GNP growth therefore has several levels of complexity.

Standards of sustainability derived from the conditions set out in an earlier section will set clear directions and targets for changes in the economy's biophysical throughputs and in the production of biomass. The costs of the instruments necessary to achieve these targets can serve as inputs into an appropriate macroeconomic model to estimate the instruments' impacts on GNP growth and other macroeconomic variables. One such model is the Cambridge MDM (Barker and Peterson 1987), which has been used extensively to model the macroeconomic implications of a carbon tax (Barker and Lewney 1991). Given a model with a sufficiently high level of disaggregation (MDM is disaggregated into 40 industries), the macroeconomic implications of the costs associated with a wide range of sector-specific instruments can be estimated. Obviously the accuracy of these estimates will depend on the degree to which the structural relationships underlying the model persist, but provided these remain essentially valid, the estimates will provide at least a guide to the basic magnitudes and directions of macroeconomic change.

Another use of the cost figures associated with different instruments of environmental policy is to compute adjustments to GNP figures to take account of environmental damage (Ahmad et al. 1989), but there is as yet no consensus as to how the adjustments should be made, in part because of the difficulties of evaluating environmental effects, as discussed above. Provided that the sustainability standards approach to environmental evaluation is accepted, then the use of the costs required to meet those standards as the necessary adjustments to GNP, as described in Hueting et al. (1991), is both theoretically sound and operationally possible.

CONCLUSION

The hardening consensus about the dangers and unacceptability of current trends of environmental unsustainability is increasing the pressure to turn into effective practice the many rhetorical commitments to sustainable development. While the concept of sustainable development can be expected to generate controversial discussion for some time to come, one of its component parts, environmental sustainability, is much easier both to define and to measure.

However, great problems remain in measuring the direct costs of environmental unsustainability, so that the applicability of the traditional economic approach to project and policy analysis (cost-benefit analysis) is much reduced for issues in this area, especially for the more important issues. This could seriously retard progress towards environmental sustainability.

This chapter has developed a methodology in response to this situation, which entails:

1. Mapping the economic processes and activities that cause environmental unsustainability,

2. Considering the boundaries that are relevant to a particular problem or policy approach,

3. Developing appropriate instruments to address the problems,

4. Setting standards of sustainability for different environmental functions, and

5. Calculating the costs of the instruments required to reach these standards.

These cost figures can then be used to compare the relative cost-effectiveness of different instruments. They can be used as inputs into an appropriate macroeconomic model in order to establish the macroeconomic implications of the instruments. And they can be used to adjust figures of GNP in order to arrive more nearly at a figure for "sustainable income."

Together these uses render the methodology of considerable potential importance in putting sustainability thinking into practice.

ACKNOWLEDGMENTS

I am grateful to Roefie Hueting for our many discussions of the issues covered in this chapter. Anyone who knows his work will recognize how much I have been influenced by it.

APPENDIX A: DERIVING THE FORMULA FOR THE DEPLETION RATE AT MINIMUM LIFE EXPECTANCY

Let:

R	$=$	Reserves
d	$=$	Depletion rate, then
L	$=$	Life expectancy $= R/d$
L_{min}	$=$	Agreed minimum life expectancy
D	$=$	Discoveries

Subscripts "1, 2" refer to time-periods, then

$$R_2 = (R_1 - d_1) + D_1$$

At L_{min}:

$$L_{min} = R_1/d_1 = R_2/d_2$$

$$
\begin{aligned}
&= && [(R_1 - d_1) + D_1]/d_2 \\
\Rightarrow \quad d_2 \quad &= && d_1[(R_1 - d_1) + D_1]/R_1 \\
&= && d_1[1 + (D_1 - d_1)/R_1]
\end{aligned}
$$

APPENDIX B: DERIVATION OF CAPITAL/INCOME SHARES OF RECEIPTS FROM DEPLETION OF A NON-RENEWABLE RESOURCE

Let: R   =   Constant stream of receipts from total depletion of a resource over n periods

X   =   Constant income derived from R in each year of depletion, and indefinitely thereafter from capital fund, S

I   =   Constant capital component of R, which contributes to S in each year of depletion

$\Rightarrow$ R   =   X + I in each period

r   =   Interest rate

subscript i refers to time period

Then:

$$
\sum_0^\infty X_i = X/[1 - 1/(1 + r)]
$$

$$
\sum_0^\infty R_i = R/[1 - 1/(1 + r)]
$$

$$
\sum_{n+1}^\infty R_i = R/[1 - 1/(1 + r)]\,(1 + r)^{n+1}
$$

$$
\Rightarrow \quad \sum_0^n R_i = R[1 - 1/(1 + r)^{n+1}]/[1 - 1/(1 + r)]
$$

Set: $\sum_0^\infty X_i$ = $\sum_0^n R_i$

$\Rightarrow$ $X/[1 - 1/(1+r)] =$ $R[1 - 1/(1 + r)^{n+1}]/[1 - 1/(1 + r)]$

$\Rightarrow$ X/R   = $[1 - 1/(1 + r)^{n+1}]$

$\Rightarrow$ I/R   = $1/(1 + r)^{n+1}$

REFERENCES

Ahmad, Y., S. El Serafy, and E. Lutz. 1989. Environmental Accounting for Sustainable Development. Washington DC: The World Bank.

Barbier, E. B. 1987. The concept of sustainable economic development. *Environmental Conservation* 14 (2): 101–10.

Barker, T., and A. Peterson, eds. 1987. The Cambridge Multisectoral Dynamic Model of the British Economy. Cambridge: Cambridge Univ. Press.

Barker, T., and R. Lewney. 1991. A Green scenario for the U.K. economy. In Green Futures for Economic Growth., ed. T. Barker. Cambridge: Cambridge Econometrics.

Beckerman, W. 1992. Economic Growth and the Environment: Whose Growth? Whose Environment? *World Development* 20 (4): 481–96.

Birdsall, N., and A. Steer. 1993. Act now on global warming—but don't cook the books. *Finance & Development* March: 6-8.

Brown, L. R. et al. 1993. State of the World 1993. London: Earthscan.

CEC (Commission of the European Communities). 1992a. Towards Sustainability: a European Community Programme of Policy and Action in Relation to the Environment and Sustainable Development, Volume 1. Proposal for a Resolution of the Council of the European Communities. Brussels: Commission of the European Communities.

———. 1992b. Towards Sustainability: a European Community Programme of Policy and Action in Relation to the Environment and Sustainable Development, Volume 2. Executive Summary. Brussels: Commission of the European Communities.

Chambers, R. 1992. Sustainable livelihoods: the poors' reconciliation of environment and development. In Real-Life Economics: Understanding Wealth Creation, eds. P. Ekins and M. Max-Neef. London: Routledge.

Cline, W. R. 1993. Give greenhouse abatement a fair chance. *Finance & Development* March: 3–5.

Daly, H. E. 1977. Steady-State Economics. San Francisco: W. H. Freeman.

———. 1990. Toward some operational principles of sustainable development. *Ecological Economics* 2: 1–6.

Daly, H. E., and J. Cobb. 1989. For the Common Good. Boston: Beacon Press.

de Groot, R. S. 1992. Functions of Nature. Groningen, Netherlands: Wolters-Noordhoff.

Douthwaite, R. 1992. The Growth Illusion. Devon, U.K.: Green Books.

Ekins, P. 1992a. A four-capital model of wealth creation. In Real-Life Economics: Understanding Wealth Creation, eds. P. Ekins and M. Max-Neef. London: Routledge.

——— 1992b. Sustainability first. In Real-Life Economics: Understanding Wealth Creation, eds. P. Ekins and M. Max-Neef. London: Routledge.

———. 1993. "Limits to growth" and "sustainable development": grappling with ecological realities. *Ecological Economics* 8: 269–88.

El Serafy, S. 1989. The proper calculation of income from a depletable natural resource. In Environmental Accounting for Sustainable Development, eds. Y. Ahmad, S. El Serafy and E. Lutz. Washington, DC: World Bank.

Hardoy, J., D. Mitlin, and D. Satterthwaite. 1993. Environmental Problems in Third World Cities. London: Earthscan.

Holmberg, J., and R. Sandbrook. 1992. Sustainable development: what is to be done? In Policies for a Small Planet, ed. J. Holmberg. London: Earthscan.

Hueting, R. 1980. New Scarcity and Economic Growth. Amsterdam: North Holland.

Hueting, R., P. Bosch, and B. de Boer. 1991. Methodology for Calculating Sustainable National Income. Voorburg: Netherlands Central Bureau of Statistics.

Lecomber, R. 1975. Economic Growth versus the Environment. London: Macmillan.

Leipert, C. 1989. Social costs of the economic process and national accounts: the example of defensive expenditures. *The Journal of Interdisciplinary Economics* 3(1): 27–46.

Lele, S. 1991. Sustainable development: a critical review. *World Development* 19(6): 607–21.

Meadows, D. H., D. L. Meadows, J. Randers, and W. Behrens. 1972. The Limits to Growth. New York: Universe Books.

Meadows, D. H., D. L. Meadows, and J. Randers. 1992. Beyond the Limits. London: Earthscan.

Mishan, E. J. 1967. The Costs of Economic Growth. London: Staples Press.

———. 1977. The Economic Growth Debate: an Assessment. London: George Allen and Unwin.

Opschoor, J. B., and H. B. Vos. 1989. Economic Instruments for Environmental Protection. Paris: Organisation for Economic Cooperation and Development.

Pearce, D. W. 1993. Economic Values and the Natural World. London: Earthscan.

Pearce, D. W., A. Markandya, and E. B. Barbier. 1989. Blueprint for a Green Economy. London: Earthscan.

Pearce, D. W., and R. K. Turner. 1990. The Economics of Natural Resources and the Environment. Hemel Hempstead: Harvester Wheatsheaf.

RS and NAS (Royal Society and National Academy of Sciences). 1992. Population Growth, Resource Consumption and a Sustainable World. London; New York: RS; NAS.

Schmidheiny, S. (with the Business Council for Sustainable Development). 1992. Changing Course: a Global Business Perspective on Development and the Environment. Cambridge, MA: MIT Press.

UNDP (United Nations Development Programme). 1990. Human Development Report 1990. Oxford; New York: Oxford Univ. Press.

———. 1991. Human Development Report 1991. Oxford; New York: Oxford Univ. Press.

———. 1992. Human Development Report 1992. Oxford; New York: Oxford Univ. Press.

WCED (World Commission on Environment and Development). 1987. Our Common Future. New York: Oxford Univ. Press.

World Bank. 1992. World Development Report 1992. Oxford; New York: Oxford Univ. Press.

WRI (World Resources Institute). 1992. World Resources, 1992–93. Oxford; New York: Oxford Univ. Press.

3 BIOLOGICAL, CULTURAL, AND ECONOMIC EVOLUTION AND THE ECONOMY/ECOLOGY RELATIONSHIP

Friedrich Hinterberger
Wuppertal Institute for Climate, Environment,
  and Energy
Division for Material Flows and Structural Change
Döppersberg 19
D-42103 Wuppertal
Germany

INTRODUCTION

This chapter attempts to develop a formal conceptual economic model analogous to biological evolution, which serves to discuss the relationship between economic and ecological processes. Without denying that there are substantial differences between natural and socio-economic processes and without claiming that *every* socio-economic phenomenon can be properly described in evolutionary terms, my claim is that certain similarities of biological, cultural, and economic processes justify an analogous representation, especially when the relationship between these processes is taken into consideration. As we observe similar phenomena (such as selection and adaptation) in nature and in the economy, it is reasonable to look for theoretically analogous descriptions.

The second section will present the theoretical background. We assume a general principle of evolution as acting on three different levels: biological, cultural, and economic. The latter two are described as analogous to the contemporary version of Darwinian evolution. Cultural evolution is responsible for the formation of institutions—such as ethical values, law, and language—and is described as based on ideas as replicators, while human individuals and organizations function as interactors of the evolutionary process. Economic evolution will be described as a replication and selection process using commodities as interactors and ideas (preferences and technologies) as replicators. This model will be described in the third section. Such a view is at least partially compatible with concepts developed by economists such as Marshall, Schumpeter, Hayek, or Boulding. It offers an interpretation of the connections between ecological systems (based on the principles of biological evolution) and the economy (based on the principle of economic evolution to be described in this chapter). These connections will be clarified in the fourth section. Subsequently, in the fifth section the concept is applied to discussions of biodiversity and economic diversity, as well as sustainable economic and ecological development. As cultural evolution can be (theoretically and practically) seen as an intermediation of both (partly showing features of both), it may help when thinking about possible solutions of certain environmental problems as presented in the sixth section. Some thoughts on limits and possibilities for further research will conclude the chapter.

CULTURAL AND NATURAL CHANGE AS CO-EVOLUTION

It is well known that most theoretical approaches to contemporary economics are in their methodology closely related to classical mechanics in physics (Mirowski 1984).[1] Throughout the twentieth century natural scientists have explored the limitations of Newtonian mechanics by developing further, for example, thermodynamics, systems theory, and evolutionary theory. Most economists stuck to the mechanistic paradigm (on important exceptions, see Clark and Juma 1988). Apart from that, biologists developed so-called sociobiological models, which can be applied to certain economic problems. This branch of sociobiology directly explains human behavior on the basis of genetic advantages (Wilson 1975).[2] It provides an application, and thereby generalization of the theory of biological evolution, which was introduced by Charles Darwin and is now interpreted as a clearly non-mechanistic approach (Prigogine and Stengers 1984; Brooks and Wiley 1986).

---

1. This holds not only for neoclassical mainstream economics, but also, for example, for many Keynesian approaches or for the Neo-Ricardian theory following the fundamental work of Piero Sraffa (1960).
2. Tietzel (1983) and Witt (1985) discuss these theories from an economic point of view.

In this chapter, another approach will be presented. We draw *analogies* between biological evolution and economics. This attempt is not at all new. Nelson and Winter (1982), Witt (1987), and Faber and Proops (1990) are only three of a growing number of important contributions to this emerging branch of economics. Such an approach can be interrelated with other approaches to partial economic analysis in order to gain a broader view of how an economy works. Especially if we are interested in the relationship between natural and economic structures and the relationship between ecology and an economy, we can gain additional insights from evolutionary thinking. Although the model is formally presented along the relatively strict lines of Darwinian evolution, it is suggested as a heuristic device. It does not attempt to be an alternative to the traditional way of looking at the issue but presents some long-discussed concepts, such as endogenous preferences and economic selection, in a way that adds insights to the traditional view of the environmental economic issue.

Three basic incentives may take processes of biological evolution as a theoretical basis for economic considerations:

1. The driving force behind evolution is relative scarcity. Natural selection takes place because the number of organisms created by nature is greater than the number that can survive.

2. Evolution takes place in historical time; it is path-dependent and non-predictable.

3. The evolutionary concept views nature as a complex system in which non-linear feedbacks are important.

All three features are crucial features of economic systems, too. Obviously, all three features are tackled insufficiently in predominant economic theories, although it is the declared aim of most economic textbooks to deal exactly with these basic facts of economic systems. Evolution can be examined on a micro level if we look at certain species (markets) and/or on a macro level of a complex evolving system. All three kinds of evolutionary processes—economic, cultural, and natural— are connected to what we call co-evolution (see Norgaard, 1984 for different approaches).[3]

---

3. With such an approach we could also discuss how homo economicus evolved and gained his success over other psychological "traits" (Binmore 1990). We will briefly return to this point later.

Richard Dawkins' (1986, 1989) suggestion to regard so-called "memes" as fundamental units of cultural evolution serves as a starting point for a formal description of an evolutionary economic process. Dawkins' view of biological evolution has been criticized as being reductionistic and mechanistic (Depew and Weber 1985). But it appears that the concept of memes is not necessarily restricted to his concept of biological evolution. The concept presented here can also be related to Konrad Lorenz's (1973) view of a co-evolution of cultural and natural traits. Hinterberger (1993) deals in more detail with the possibilities to develop such a model along the lines of some recent discussions on evolutionary theory in order to gain some further applications for economic problems. The claim will be that Dawkins' version allows us to gain some basic insights, while most of what will be developed is not restricted to Dawkins' version of biological evolution. The advantage of the strictness of this model is that it can serve as a basis for mathematical treatment and, hence, computer simulation models.

Dawkins has based his approach on the concept of replicators, which are defined units (biological or social) that are able to create copies of themselves. The process of replication is seen as *the* necessary element of every evolutionary process (Dawkins 1989). In biological evolution, genes are replicators using the DNA reproduction process; as the replicators are not directly exposed to the process of natural selection, Hull (1981) introduced the concept of interactors. Biological interactors are organisms, which—according to their fitness in the environment—reproduce the replicators by means of interacting with their environments. This differentiation reflects the distinction between genotypes and phenotypes, which represents the contemporary textbook version of evolutionary thinking (Mayr 1978). If a gene creates an interactor (organism) that fits better into the environment than others, the replicator (gene) will have a greater chance to survive.

Dawkins (1989) proposes a generalization of his version of Darwinism by stating that genes are not the only replicators of evolutionary processes. He recommends taking innovative ideas—like tunes, ideas, catch-phrases, clothes fashions, ways of making pots or of building arches—as replicators of social evolution. Dawkins introduces the artificial word "meme" to name these ideas, which are created by certain individuals and copied by others; they serve as replicators of social evolution via direct communication, imitation, and learning, just like genes are the replicators of biological evolution.[4] To turn the theory toward more straightforward reasoning, we should again differentiate between replicators and interactors. But what are the interactors of cultural or economic evolution? For Dawkins, individual humans are interactors, which leads us in the direction of a Boyd and Richerson-type (1985) of cultural evolution.[5] Biological inheritance is accompanied by culturally passing on traits from parents to children and from individuals to other individuals.[6] This approach provides a way to describe the emergence and change of institutions, like language, law, or ethical values. A new word, for instance, has to be passed on by communication and accepted (used) by a sufficient number of individuals in order to become a new item of the common language.[7] Cultural evolution is most closely connected to biological evolution, because the interactors are identical: human individuals pass on information of both types ("memes" and genes). Such a process may be portrayed as in Figure 3.1, which is inspired by Witt's (1985) representation of biological evolution: H_n is a given distribution of individual organisms (i.e., phenotypic traits), among them, humans. These individuals incorporate a certain gene pool, G_n, (passed on to them biologically via natural inheritance) and a meme pool, M_n, (i.e., a set of "ideas" in the sense of Dawkins, passed on culturally from individual to individual by communication and learning). Both memes and genes influence the "fitness" of the individuals and, hence, the distribution of individuals after various selection and adaptation processes take place. Let this new distribution be denoted by H_n'.

---

4. Despite all the critique on the concept of memetic evolution, I believe that it does make sense to use it, although we cannot identify memes physically as we can identify genes. Charles Darwin developed his theory long before the concept of genes was introduced and DNA was discovered. Hence, we can say something about the underlying processes, even if we have only a rough understanding of how to identify the memes.

5. The idea to build a model along these lines goes back at least to Veblen (Hodgson 1992a).

6. Therefore, the approach is analagous to Darwinian, not Lamarckian, evolution and because we are not talking about biological inheritance of the acquired. We refer to communication and learning as means of transmission. The up-to-date view of biological evolution includes concepts of kin selection, punctuated equilibria, saltational evolution, etc.; these can be applied to our analogies, too, but this will not be a subject of this particular chapter.

7. This can be formalized by the concepts of synergetics, as developed by Haken (1977).

There is, of course, a huge difference in velocities of both feedback mechanisms. For certain research programs, it will be appropriate to consider gene pools and phenotypic traits as fixed. Nevertheless, they have to be seen as strongly interrelated. Regarding the economy-ecology relationship, these interrelations play a crucial role. Figure 3.1 can therefore also be understood as a simple formal representation of what Lorenz (1973) describes. A similar view, although much more comprehensive, has been developed by Durham (1991).

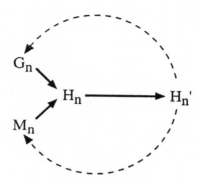

Figure 3.1. Biological and cultural evolution.

Although humans are not the only species with the ability to pass on knowledge non-genetically, we can regard this aspect as relatively negligible for other species compared with human abilities. We then have to discuss what cultural selection and adaptation means. It is obvious that mankind's cultural development led to an enormous "success" of the human species compared to other species. This success is due to technical knowledge as well as to the development of institutions and organizations. Without discussing the extent to which traits are passed on genetically or culturally, we simply postulate here that there is some interaction between both, which has led to the observed development. The development of technical and institutional knowledge also influences the relative success of human individuals among themselves, although this success can usually not be measured in terms of physical survival of the more fit, but rather in economic terms of living standards and political terms of power—human societies are structured according to the cultural knowledge the individuals have access to. As an effect, the new distribution of individuals (between humans and other species, as well as between different cultural groups within human societies) bears a new distribution of genes and memes G_{n+1} and M_{n+1}, which will generally differ from the original one. In Figure 3.1 this is shown by the broken arrows pointing back to G_n and M_n.

To what extent is such a description based on methodological individualism? Thoughts, ideas, and behavior as such can only be individual phenomena. The meme pool is the totality of individual ideas, but not in the sense of aggregation. This chapter deliberately avoids a mathematical representation. Those who prefer to think in mathematical terms may understand a meme pool as a vector. The number of its elements corresponds to the number of individuals times the number of relevant ideas to be examined in a certain research. Respectively, cultural traits consist of nothing other than the sum of individual behavior (the elements of the vector of cultural traits represent the behavior of the individuals with respect to the question examined). Culture is not simply a statistical aggregation of individual behavior. It is crucial how individuals influence each other. Talking about adaptation and selection of cultural traits can improve our understanding of the concept as individualistic without neglecting the importance of collectively acquired knowledge.

Biological inheritance is the crucial mechanism to preserve stability in biological evolutionary processes: "What is required is a degree of inertia in such structures and routines to restrict change so that selection can operate effectively" (Hodgson 1992b). In an analogy with inheritance, "memes" are remembered by individuals and communicated to others. The greater the group of individuals who adopt a cultural trait, the greater is its chance to survive. Technically speaking, cultural traits can be seen as attractors for the individuals' behavior. Cultural traits constrain behavior—though not rigidly. For example, rising consciousness about environmental issues may be heavily influenced by external effects (from certain events, like the Chernobyl accident, and information campaigns via mass media). But individuals also influence each other. Such influences stabilize the effects of external shocks. This may be seen as an element contradicting strict methodological individualism. But both directions of influences cannot be separated from each other. Individuals make up collectives, but collective (maybe unintended) effects constrain individual behavior.[8] This, in turn, serves as a necessary device for individual decisions, without which individuals would be unable to decide consistently. To ask whether individual decisions influence group phenomena or vice versa is like discussing the famous hen-and-egg problem. Both directions of influence are necessary to understand the whole process.

Groups and organizations are interactors as well: mass media, political parties, pressure groups, universities, scientific organizations, and religious groups all pass on information. They seek to establish certain memes in accordance with their specific aims.[9] On the other hand, the emergence of these organizations is based on processes of cultural evolution. In this context, it is a crucial point of evolutionary economics to understand how individual aims (and, hence, individual purposeful actions) influence the evolutionary socio-economic process and its outcomes. As evolutionary self-organization processes have their own laws, the outcomes are based on human action but not on human design (Haye 1967). This is not to say that individual decisions have no influence on cultural developments at all, rather that there is, in turn, some non-negligible influence of cultural processes on individual actions.

A "MEMETIC" MODEL OF ECONOMIC DEVELOPMENT

This section presents, as a third category of evolution, a concept of economic evolution based on a sub-set of memes closely connected to economic decision making. In Hinterberger (1993) I suggest drawing an analogy between biological evolution and economic processes by taking *commodities* as interactors. Economic theories describe transactions as based on ideas, which we usually term "preferences" on the demand side and "technologies" on the supply side. I suggest considering preferences and technologies as "memes" of economic processes. This goes along with the standard notion of microeconomic theory that sees technologies (production functions) and preferences (utility functions) as analogous concepts that mirror each other. Economic agents found their individual plans on these ideas. Supply and demand behavior of economic agents is

---

8. Collectives are, of course, structured entities. Individuals may join different collectives under different circumstances. In certain instances, class will matter; in others, nationality will.

9. Of course, individuals and individuals within pressure groups also try to do so. We have to consider the power relationships between and within groups to understand the relative possibilities of individuals and groups to establish their ideas.

based on these ideas, and the market serves as a selection mechanism for economic memes. Preferences and technologies "communicate" on the market. As a result, only a part of the individuals' ideas ("wants") can be realized. Although this type of evolution will be analyzed separately, it is closely related to both biological and cultural evolution: ideas are replicators of economic and of cultural evolution. The latter is, in turn, connected with biological evolution via interactors, which are individuals in both cases. Now the interactors are different: economically speaking, individuals and organizations (like firms) do not interact directly. They interact by selling and purchasing commodities; this is why I take commodities as interactors of economic evolution.[10] (We will see that direct interaction of individuals influences, of course, their behavior on markets.)

Because this chapter is concerned mainly with the *connections* between various evolutionary processes, it provides merely an overview of the memetic economic process.[11] The relevant memes on the supply side of a specific market refer to the technologies of production and of the product itself. Technologies will only "survive" if the product "survives" on the market. The market provides the selective environment for the products, functioning as interactors of the economic evolution. In the short term, the usual mechanisms of neoclassical economics apply. Prices deliver the necessary information, according to which entrepreneurs may make rational decisions. If they fail to do so, the product may be selected out of the market. It is an open discussion, to the extent it is true that rationality, in the sense of neoclassical axioms, is really the outcome of this process. Selten (1991), for example, states that selective forces are quite weak near an evolutionary equilibrium .

Economic selection is triggered because entrepreneurs want to produce and sell more than they are able to sell due to scarce resources and due to the conditions on the demand side. The products remaining in the market will be more adaptive to the current conditions than the products that lost the struggle for economic survival. One problem is that such a process is by no means future-oriented. Traits may be selected out that could be advantageous in the future. But in addition to the passive selec-

---

10. Hodgson (1992b) hints at a similar procedure used by Winter (1964): "The genotype-phenotype distinction in biology suggests to Winter an analogous distinction in the socio-economic sphere: between rules of action and action itself."

11. Hinterberger (1994) gives a full formulation of the memetic economic process.

tion that works analogous to biological processes, intelligent, conscious entrepreneurs have a possibility to *perceive* the selective process and to make decisions, and thus go beyond passive adaptation.

Similar processes can be discussed on the demand side, although in this case, the analogy is less strict and less developed in the literature. Consumer behavior depends on what the consumers experience in the market. They may change their demand when new products enter the market. We may say that preferences will not "survive," if they are not satisfied. Gowdy (1993) shows this for the case of environmental issues. For example, the willingness-to-accept environmental damage is much higher than the willingness-to-pay for environmental benefits: "Once it is gone, it is much harder to elicit public support (in terms of collecting money to pay for it) for bringing back an environmental amenity than to prevent the loss. Once something has disappeared people adjust to the new situation and have a different view of what is theirs "by right" (Gowdy 1993, 237). This contradicts the standard notion of microeconomic theory, because it takes preferences as endogenous. Nevertheless, it seems reasonable to use the concept of exogenous preferences for short-term descriptions of the demand side. Again, in addition to simply reacting to given market conditions, conscious beings have the possibility to perceive the evolutionary process and make active decisions. Of course, supply and demand are closely interrelated. This can be described as depicted in Figure 3.2.

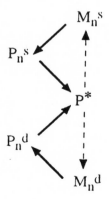

Figure 3.2. Memetic feedback loops in an evolutionary economic model.

M_n^s and M_n^d refer to technologies and preferences, while P_n^s and P_n^d denote the ex ante supply and demand, respectively. Hence, the arrow between M_n^s and P_n^s represents a general description of a production function, whereas the arrow from M_n^d to P_n^d can be seen as a general preference function. Economic selection leads to the *ex post* supply, which necessarily equals *ex post* demand, depicted by P^*. If the market is not in equilibrium, P^* will select for certain technologies and preferences, which are passively changed by direct selection and actively changed according to the participants' perception of the situation. This is represented by the broken arrows. If the market is in equilibrium M_n^d and M_n^s will remain unchanged. [12]

Although cultural and economic evolutionary processes are seen as similar, the latter works much faster. Most short-term changes in markets within an economy can be regarded as working within a given institutional setting. But the model also indicates how, in the long run, economic results may influence institutions. For example, the introduction of new household applicants may (help to) change family structures (by enabling both parents to work outside the household, which, in turn, increases the demand for these commodities), and this may lead to new political challenges (e.g., the introduction of a nursing insurance). The model could be developed further and made more explicit to gain empirically testable results. To keep the model simple, the argument will not be developed further here. These rough statements and few examples should merely indicate the research program to which the model presented above could be applied.

A major feature of the memetic view analogous to biological evolution is that it stresses the importance of an interrelation between stability, arranged by the working of negative feedbacks, and change, caused by dynamic factors of a system that is not in equilibrium. From this follows that the role of ceteris paribus conditions appears in a different light. In order to describe an evolutionary process, it is crucial to incorporate at least the "local" environment into the observation. Evolution is only

---

12. This view is similar to the approaches of Boulding (1981), Nelson and Winter (1982), and Mohr (1990). It may also be seen as an interpretation and further development of Marshall's partial equilibrium approach (see the interpretations of Dardi 1991, and Foster 1991). A general equilibrium would require that the evolutionary process has come to an end.

possible, if individual—social as well as biological organisms—react with each other.

MEMES AND THE ENVIRONMENT

How can we incorporate the natural environment into our model? Although an economy, as well as the environment, are immensely complex structures, it may serve as a first step to represent "the environment" by a single feedback loop, as depicted on the right side of Figure 3.3, and "the economy" as one consolidated market on the left of this figure. Here, "the environment" is defined as living nature. It is the totality of living organisms, including humans.[13] The biological concept of evolution serves on a macro-level as a general description of ecological processes. It refers to the dynamic aspect of environmental sustainability (as discussed later). The advantage of such an approach is that it identifies nature as endogenous. Nature supplies resources and consumption goods, and it absorbs waste (Siebert 1987). For various reasons, markets fail to provide the competition necessary to coordinate competing uses with respect to limited capacity of nature to provide these services. Due to the co-evolutionary view, economic and ecological processes are formally similar. Despite all differences in qualitative and quantitative respects, this makes it easier to deal with the interrelatedness between them. Figure 3.3 is based on this insight.

Nature "produces" commodities that can be used by human households and firms, and it provides possibilities to get rid of human waste. But it also competes with humans for certain "inputs"; we can say that nature "consumes" naturally produced "commodities" that could otherwise be used by human households and firms for consumption or production. But something more important might be the absorption of waste that is competitive with other species' own use of natural resources. Moreover, humans heavily influence natural selection processes by agri-

---

13. Inanimate nature provides an additional set of goods that are not really produced (at least not in our time) and can be seen as a direct (potential) import into the economic-ecological system. There are, of course, indirect effects on animate nature as, for example, the earth's atmosphere. Another problem in this context is that the economic system does not pay attention to the basic fact of increasing entropy by use of fossil fuels in order to raise its level of production and, hence, socio-economic self-organization. This is the main topic of Georgescu-Roegen's "bioeconomic program" (Georgescu-Roegen 1976), which will not be developed in this chapter.

cultural (and, nowadays, genetic) techniques. Figure 3.3 gives a simple representation of all this. We have competition on the demand side for products of both the natural and the commercial "sectors." Nature is depicted as analogous to the biological evolutionary process in Figure 3.1, while the left side represents "the market" as derived in Figure 3.2. We have genes as natural replicators, which ensure the reproduction of plants and animals (including humans). H represents the phenotypic traits (i.e., the interactors of our ecological system).

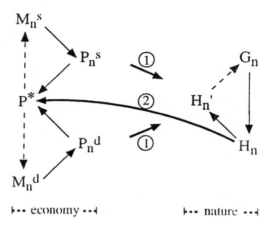

⊢·· economy ··⊣   ⊢·· nature ··⊣

Figure 3.3. Memetic and genetic feedback loops in an economic-ecological model.

Ecologists will have a lot to say about the circular flows representing the ecological system on the right side of Figure 3.3, while the economic relations depicted on the left side will draw comment from economists (Hinterberger 1993). According to the main theme of this chapter, the connections between both sides will be the primary focus here. The bold arrows represent aspects of biological and economic adaptation and selection between the two systems. To make this plausible, we may start with a simple example: if a firm lays out a plantation, it intervenes in the ecological cycles. By fertilization and the use of herbicides, it promotes certain plants against other living beings. This is represented by arrow 1. The plants and animals produced enter the market of consumer goods and raw materials (arrow 2).

A plantation is, of course, a rather specific example of human impairments of natural processes. Here, the effect on the environment is identical with the human purpose. Most ecological problems come from "side-effects" of human activity rather than deliberate steering. Human activities impose "external effects" on nature. The formation of human cultures, however, can be seen as an analogous process on a long-term, global scale. It influences the global gene pool, predominantly by the extermination of many species. A large number of species disappears every day (and with them a certain fraction of the global distribution of genes), while a very restricted number of species is promoted (Norgaard 1992).[14] It is reasonable to neglect the factor of newly emerging traits via combination and mutation if developments that take place within years or decades are considered; the direct impact of human activities on the distribution of traits, however, is clearly non-negligible. The distribution of species changes by what we may term *passive* adaptation. Complex ecological processes are triggered. The main problem is that, as soon as we give up the simple representation of Figure 3.3, the main factors appear as highly intertwined on a much more disaggregated level, so that predictability of processes is very low.

ON THE CONTRIBUTION OF THE EVOLUTIONARY IDEA TO THE STUDY OF ECOLOGY-ECONOMY PROBLEMS: SUSTAINABILITY AND DIVERSITY IN ECONOMICS AND ECOLOGY

Sustainability means the capacity to be continued in time more or less indefinitely.[15] Mature ecosystems are in continuous equilibrium and do not produce waste (Costanza 1991). In that sense they are perfectly sustainable, because the possibilities for future generations to flourish are not being diminished. This is a theoretical statement, describing a hypothetical reference state of the ecological system. Real-world ecosystems are evolving and, hence, necessarily *not* in equilibrium. If we broaden our view and incorporate cultural and economic developments, the same

14. Besides the deliberate promotion of cultivated plants and animals, we indirectly promote cultural parasites, such as rats and roaches.

15 . "Sustainability is a relationship between dynamic human economic systems, in which (1) human life can continue indefinitely, (2) human individuals can flourish, and (3) human cultures can develop; but in which effects of human activities remain within bounds, so as not to destroy the diversity, complexity, and function of the ecological life support system" (Costanza, Daly, and Bartolomew 1991, 8–9).

must be true: our point of reference would be a hypothetical socio-economic equilibrium. With this view, the economy can analytically
be separated from nature, and human activity is not problematic for nature. Because a real-world socio-environmental system is never totally in
equilibrium, the economy-ecology relation becomes important.

In technical terms, sustainability means to economize on natural capital. The traditional, non-evolutionary economic view seems to be sufficient as long as natural capital incorporates inanimate material only.
Including living nature in the concept of natural capital makes things
more complex. One of the nature's most important achievements is biodiversity (Wilson 1992), which is crucially connected with the workability of the evolutionary processes. Its destruction would also endanger the
survival of our species (Ehrlich 1992).

For humans, at least for most of those living in developed countries,
the socio-economic selection process is not yet a struggle for physical
life; it is a struggle for certain living conditions within the household
sector and for the economic survival of firms, rather than the physical
survival of the entrepreneurs. But for most species in nature, mankind's
economic development *is* a struggle for life, and many of them lose this
fight. One may say that there is nothing special in this process if we look
at it as an evolutionary process, because quite a huge percentage of
species lost the natural struggle throughout natural history and disappeared irrevocably; mankind simply *is* the "fittest" species on earth. But
there are two aspects that we should not overlook (Verbeek 1990).

One is that man's "success" in this struggle is only partially due to biological facts, such as the development of the brain.[16] The velocity of
cultural and economic processes exceeds most natural processes. Hence,
cultural and technical developments of modern societies enable mankind
to be, to a certain degree, independent from biological restrictions. Most
species do not "have enough time" to adjust genetically; this fact may
have created the most decisive advantage of human societies over the rest

---

16. In order to keep the argument relatively simple, we abstract from the fact that
    biological and cultural developments are closely interrelated in the sense that, for
    example, the use of tools induced a further development of the brain and vice versa.
    As we discuss historical developments rather than human biological evolution, the
    genetic developments other than those directly created through extermination of
    species can be left out of consideration.

of nature. As long as we do not have any ethical incentives to think in a different way, this may still be seen as an advantage.

The second difficulty is that, generally speaking, nature reacts so slowly that the effects of certain activities react too late on the actors, while they are quite immediately "hit" by the economic reactions of other firms and/or consumers and maybe also by social sanctions within the cultural community (at least within sufficiently small societies). Only in the last decades, the dimension of the ecological problems became evident, so that they are perceived not only as unpleasant, but also as dangerous. The danger became a biological one—it damages health and threatens lives. This means, that the feedback mechanisms of the evolutionary process, which worked so "well" for a long time and insured the—from a biological, cultural, and economic point of view—incredible rise of the human species, now fail to solve the vital ecological problems (Kafka 1991). In other words, humans created themselves a world into which they no longer fit biologically. Only in the short term have technical achievements reduced the problem significantly. Humans did not *need* to adapt biologically because they created technical substitutes (Selten 1991). Today, ecological damages became so severe that sustainability of the human species and its social, cultural and economic artifacts is not guaranteed.[17] Kafka (1991, 1) puts the fundamental problem concerning the velocity of evolutionary processes as follows:

> At the front of evolution in the space of possibilities, the speed of innovation has itself a selective advantage. The faster conquers the slower and is conquered by something still faster—until the front loses the context with its roots and destroys more complexity than it can build.

Will this lead necessarily to an end of our cultural and economic achievements? Boulding (1991) puts it in the following way:

> The sustainability of biological evolution on this planet, punctuated as it seems to have been by catastrophes from which it recovered, is a fascinating story of which we have very imperfect knowledge. There seems little doubt, however, that the human race is an ecological catastrophe, simply because its intelligence has enabled it to spread over the whole planet and to produce very large numbers of artifacts which have an im-

---

17. We may add that cultural (and political) development might also fail to follow economic evolution: the basic political institutions on which our policy is built (parties, organizations) were founded in the 19th century and were adjusted less rapidly than economic and even institutional change took place.

pact on biological populations. Most evolutionary catastrophes seem to have been followed by an increase in complexity of organisms, perhaps because of the empty niches created by the catastrophe itself, and one wonders whether this is a possible guide for the future.

Is there an escape? I see another difference between human abilities and, more or less, the abilities of all other species, which may help to overcome this dilemma: mankind's ability to *understand* evolutionary processes and to evaluate, to some extent, the future. We do have at least the possibility to revise preferences and plans, if certain negative effects are to be expected. Today, we are able to predict probable global consequences of certain emissions, which provides, at least theoretically, the possibility to intervene. "The evolution of ideas must come to front again..." (Kafka 1991, 2). At first sight, this seems to contradict the former statement that human actions are not restricted by possible negative impacts on themselves. The problem is that individuals do not have very strong *incentives*, except from strong ethical arguments, to do something in favor of society if it leads to substantial individual disadvantages. As a result, they are forced to act contra-productively with respect to society or environment in the sense that every individual would desire another state of the world, achievable only if a substantial group within the society acted appropriately. This is due to an individual's almost infinitesimal impact on the aggregate behavior, so that one is hardly forced to act in favor of society, which would reflect their interests only if a substantial proportion of the society does the same. This well-known argument is based on the game theoretic prisoners' dilemma. The next section will discuss whether the society as a whole has possibilities to do so.

NORMATIVE ASPECTS AND ENVIRONMENTAL POLICY IN AN EVOLUTIONARY CONTEXT

For the longest time in history, man lived in ecological "harmony" with nature—at least to a large extent (Norgaard 1984). This harmony was due to a low population and fewer technical opportunities for substantially destroying nature, as well as to a set of norms within societies that protected the natural basis of human life. Such a behavior may be explained by an extension of the idea that altruism can lead to genetic—and certainly also memetic—advantages in fitness in the case of reciprocity, and thus to a kind of symbiotic relationship between humans and other natural beings. With industrial development this relationship changed substantially, perhaps due to the mechanistic world view that dominated Western societies (including those of Eastern Europe) for more than three centuries. Mechanistic economic theories, from neoclassical to Keynesian, are only one expression of such a point of view. Today, substantial changes might be expected, if government activities—legislative and executive—based on democratic decision making could force a sufficiently great number of individuals within the society to act according to the rules. Hence, there is no conceptual difference, regarding the possibility of collective actions, between the quest for non-egoistic actions emerging from ethical reasons or from the necessity to avoid dangerous environmental damages.

One sub-set of "non-economic" memes are individual preferences regarding certain states of the society, the environment, etc. These memes may be termed "norms" or value judgments; they influence political processes.[18] Individuals will change their political decisions due to certain experiences they have. They will influence other individuals, and politicians have to take these processes into account. Given the general coverage of this chapter, concrete political measures cannot be included (see Dietz and Van der Straaten 1992). So this chapter can only give some preliminary hints about which direction the discussion on environmental policy should take once the evolutionary view of both the economic and the natural world is accepted.

The theory of public finance describes a need for environmental policy measures when certain environmental *values* and the observed outcomes of socio-natural processes do not match. A deviation between normative "wants" and economic outcomes may justify state interventions, if and only if the problems of such an intervention (policy failure) are not regarded as being worse. Traditional welfare-economic norms are fulfilled by the economy if it behaves as neoclassical theory predicts—at least in a situation of perfect competition and in the absence of so-called market failure such as external effects, natural monopolies, and preferences for public goods. But as soon as we change the norms and add environmental sustainability, such an economy would, in general, not fulfill these goals (Dietz and Van der Straaten 1992). And if the economic pro-

---

18. Political processes are not necessarily restricted to existing organizational settings (elections, legislative and executive bureaucracies, political measures designed by elected representatives to reach certain aims, etc.). Generally speaking, policy is based on collective actions, which can be described as societal feedback mechanisms.

cess is described differently from the neoclassical predictions, the norms of Pareto efficiency will, in general, not be seen as fulfilled (Hinterberger 1992).

The latter is the case with our evolutionary description of the economy as part of a complex evolving socio-economic system. This may include natural, psychological, social, political, and economic subsystems, as have been described in the previous sections. If our meme pool contains preferences for certain supra-individual (societal, environmental, etc.) situations, which are partially influenced by economic and other social processes but also by the ecological interrelatedness, it is necessary to understand under what circumstances and to what extent certain changes are accepted by voters and politicians. This means to give up the strict separation between normative and descriptive arguments. We have to ask for the kind of norms that enable us to discuss the environmental problems appropriately. A formal illustration follows in Figure 3.4.

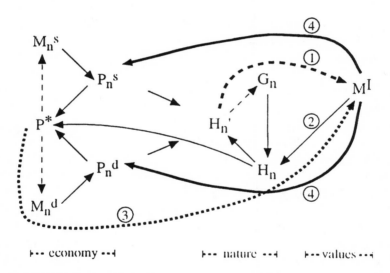

Figure 3.4. Institutions in an economic-ecological model.

By adding to Figure 3.3 the role of "norms," M^I is now considered. Arrows 1 and 2 represent the usual process of cultural evolution as discussed previously and as shown in Figure 3.1; the development of human societies not only depends on their biological "success," but also on their cultural traits passed on via cultural replication. Humans communicate about environmental norms; they pass them on from generation to generation, but also through the media, etc. Moreover, they communicate via election campaigns, elections, and other political mechanisms. As memes change, the quality of life and even the probability of survival will be affected. For the purposes of this chapter, the norms with respect to the environment are of special interest (Norton 1992). Norms cannot be derived scientifically, but natural and social sciences can help to clarify the implications of certain norms so that we can derive general qualitative properties from environmental ethics (Hinterberger 1992): we should not want the impossible.

Stability and flexibility are crucial for evolutionary processes; only a proper combination of both guarantees the conservation of reliable properties as well as the possibility for the progress of the system (which can be a species, an organization, etc.) as a whole. Hence, a sensible norm in this context should ensure both. Both stability and flexibility are highly intertwined and depend on the workability of various natural, social, and economic feedback mechanisms. The relative importance of stability and flexibility will be of special interest in this discussion. Democracies provide positive and negative feedbacks; elections weaken or strengthen certain parties according to their former performance. This is widely discussed within the literature on "public choice." One may say that—regarding all this literature—the negative feedbacks are quite weak and to some extent necessary to guarantee the stability of the political system. Flexibility of the system may be ensured by the openness of the system, so that new aspects are permanently allowed to enter. As both elements, stability and flexibility, may affect each other negatively, certain rules for their interaction may be necessary in order to keep the system workable.

In the context of evolving norms, it is important whether and to what extent the society is willing and able to accept certain changes. A most fundamental normative question in this context refers to the units, which are covered by our norms. Traditional economic norms only cover human individuals. The ability to state norms that give nature its own value is based on the uniquely human property to evaluate the biological process of evolution. Norms become "institutions" as they form patterns. This is the case when individuals relate their behavior to each other. Institutions, in turn, also influence economic variables (demand and supply behavior [arrows 4]). Finally, economic and environmental "outcomes," when perceived as a "manmade" influence, in turn, are the institutions. Certain consumption experiences may induce individual and societal "norms" (arrow 3).[19]

SUMMARY, CONCLUSIONS, AND SOME POSSIBILITIES FOR FURTHER RESEARCH

We identified three stages of evolution. First, because humans are products of biological evolution, their physical appearance, as well as their social attitudes, are naturally determined. Second, some traits are culturally passed on from generation to generation and within generations. Above these two kinds of evolution we have economic processes, which can be described as analogous to the other two kinds. Economic capacities are developed further by economic evolution; they not only give human societies a tremendous evolutionary advantage over other species, but they also lead to differences between and among human societies.

Environmental policy has been analyzed from an evolutionary economic point of view, and two fundamental problems have been identified: (1) the adequate identification of environmental as well as economic "facts," and (2) the choice of appropriate norms. This is complicated by the fact that norms cannot be strictly separated from theoretical and empirical findings. The first problem refers to identifying the appropriate economic theory to describe and explain the underlying economic processes. The evolutionary approach allows us to describe the analogy between the social world and nature, and connections between both can be described more appropriately. The systemic view leads to the type of models that are open to connect the economic system with other systems such as nature. It also allows a discussion of the energetic interrelations between economic and ecological systems. Although interdisciplinary research is needed for such an undertaking, this is fundamentally an economic task. As Savory (1991, 181–2) puts it:

> Today, a bewildering array of success and failure surrounds us. ...All of the successes are in the artificial manmade world of technology which is mechanical in nature....When we look at the areas of failure, already apparent and looming, we find all lie in the area where things are non mechanical—the real or natural world of multi-dimensional relationships.

---

19. German panel studies show, for instance, how individual worries about the state of the environment rose after the accident in Chernobyl and fell again a year later. In our memetic model, this could be shown as a change in preferences as soon as certain environmental changes take place.

Thus we see astounding success in space exploration, communication, computer technology, household comforts, transport, and similar endeavors. But in the natural world, we see mounting failures as deserts expand relentlessly, global weather changes, agricultural practices cause one civilization after another to collapse, wildlife disappears, diseases rise, and forests and lakes die.

Between these two areas we find one field entirely of mankind's making, but which is multi-dimensional in nature and running into increasing problems: economics.

Unlike natural systems, economic systems have a price system, which complements the physical relations systems discussed above. The price system helps the economy to deal with scarcity "better" than nature does. Markets based on a functioning price mechanism evaluate a scarce factor or commodity higher than commodities of which many units are available.[20] Generally speaking, this leads towards a smoother, anticipatory pattern. Georg and Røpke (1992) stress that environmental policy has to deal with "accumulated externalities" rather than simply influencing current processes. Economic and cultural evolution led us into social traps that are even more difficult to escape. We must not only avoid future harmful collective behavior, but we have to compensate the effects of former harmful behavior.

In this chapter I have recommended tackling the problems arising from that necessary intermediation. Such an approach also allows us to analyze political influences to the economy-ecology relationship, so that some practical consequences can be derived. One may see this as a very technical description of natural processes, but I prefer to see it the other way round: the "biological" way to see the economy should help to get a better understanding of the interrelatedness of both systems. Further research has to make the concept more concrete. Synergetic and evolutionary computer simulations could bring about progress in this direction. Moreover, more concrete knowledge from both economics and ecology has to be incorporated.

---

20. This has its limits if one talks about the evaluation from the point of view of future generations.

ACKNOWLEDGMENTS

Thanks to Christoph Berg, Michael Common, William Durham, Matthias Huppmann, Elias Khalil, Richard Norgaard, Thomas Sikor, Peter Söderbaum, and Silke Specht for helpful comments and encouragement. The work on this chapter was financially supported by the Deutsche Forschungsgemeinschaft. It was partly written during a stay at the universities of Roma and Firenze, the institutional support of which is gratefully acknowledged.

REFERENCES

Binmore, K. 1990. Evolution and contractarianism. *Constitutional Political Economy* 1: 1–26.

Boulding, K. E. 1981. Evolutionary Economics. Beverly Hills: Sage Publications.

———. 1991. What do we want to sustain? Environmentalism and human evaluations. In Ecological Economics: The Science and Management of Sustainability, ed. R. Costanza. New York: Columbia Univ. Press.

Boyd, R., and P. J. Richerson. 1985. Culture and the Evolutionary Process. Chicago: Chicago Univ. Press.

Brooks, D. R., and E. O. Wiley. 1986. Evolution as Entropy: Toward a Unified Theory of Biology. Chicago: Chicago Univ. Press.

Clark, N., and C. Juma. 1988. Evolutionary theories in economic thought. In Technical Change and Economic Theory, eds. G. Dosi et al. London; New York: Pinter Publishers.

Costanza, R. 1991. Assuring sustainability of ecological systems. In Ecological Economics: The Science and Management of Sustainability, ed. R. Costanza. New York: Columbia Univ. Press.

Costanza, R., H. Daly, and J. A. Bartholomew. 1991. Goals, agenda and policy recommendations for ecological economics. In Ecological Economics: The Science and Management of Sustainability, ed. R. Costanza. New York: Columbia Univ. Press.

Dardi, M. 1991. The concept and role of the individual in Marshallian economics. In Alfred Marshall's "Principles of Economics" 1890–1990. *Quaderni di Storia dell' Economia Politica* 9: 89–114.

Dawkins, R. 1986. The Blind Watchmaker. New York: W. W. Norton.

———. 1989. The Selfish Gene. Oxford; New York: Oxford Univ. Press.

Depew, D. J., and B. H. Weber, eds. 1985. Evolution at the Crossroads: The New Biology and the New Philosophy of Science. Cambridge, MA; London: MIT Press.

Dietz, F. J., and J. van der Straaten. 1992. Rethinking environmental economics: missing links between economic theory and environmental policy. *Journal of Economic Issues* 26: 27–51.

Durham, W. 1991. Coevolution: Genes, Culture and Human Diversity. Stanford: Stanford Univ. Press.

Ehrlich, P. R. 1992. Der Verlust der Vielfalt. Ursachen und Konsequenzen. In Ende der Biologischen Vielfalt? Der Verlust an Arten, Genen und Lebensräumen und die Chancen für eine Umkehr, ed. E. O. Wilson. Heidelberg: Spektrum Akademischer Verlag.

Faber, M., and J. Proops. 1990. Evolution, Time, Production and the Environment. Heidelberg; New York: Springer.

Foster, J. 1991. The Thermodynamical Approach to Economic Science: Marshall Revisited and Prigogine Reassessed. Paper prepared for the Third Annual Conference of the European Association for Evolutionary Political Economy, Wien.

Georg, S., and I. Røpke. 1992. Facing the Ecological Challenge—Consumer Behavior and Structural Changes. Mimeo. Paper presented at the 1992 Conference of the Society for the Advancement of Socioeconomics, Irvine, CA.

Georgescu-Roegen, N. 1976. Energy and Economic Myths. Institutional and Analytical Economic Essays. Cambridge, MA: Harvard Univ. Press.

Gowdy, J. M. 1993. Georgescu-Roegen's utility theory applied to environmental economics. In Entropy and Bioeconomics, eds. J. C. Dragen, E. K. Seifert and M. C. Dementrescu. Milano: Nagard.

Haken, H. 1977. Synergetics. Berlin; Heidelberg: Springer.

Hayek, F. A. 1967. The results of human action but not of human design. In Studies in Philosophy, Politics, and Economics. London: Routledge and Kegan Paul.

Hinterberger, F. 1992. The Role of Norms and Economic Policy in the Context of Evolutionary Economic Theory. Paper presented at the 1992 Conference of the Society for the Advancement of Socioeconomics, Irvine, CA (revised version).

———. 1993. A note on sociobiology: Schumpeter, Georgescu-Roegen and beyond. In Entropy and Bioeconomics, eds. J. C. Dragan, E. K. Seifert and M. C. Demetrescu. Milano: Nagard.

———. 1994. On the evolution of open socio-economic systems. In On Self-Organization, eds. R. Mishra, D. Maass and E. Zwierlein. Berlin; Heidelberg: Springer.

Hodgson, G. M. 1992a. Thorstein Veblen and Joseph Schumpeter on Evolutionary Economics. Report Nr. 10/92 of the Research Group on Biological Foundations of Human Culture, Bielefeld.

———. 1992b. Optimization and Evolution: Winter's Critique of Fiedman Revisited. Report Nr.11/92 of the Research Group on Biological Foundations of Human Culture, Bielefeld.

Hull, D. 1981. Units of evolution: a metaphysical essay. In The Philosophy of Evolution, eds. U.-J. Jensen and R. Harré. New York: St. Martin's Press.

Kafka, P. 1991. Conditions of Creation: Is There Hope in Spite of the Entropy Law? Paper presented at the First International Conference of the European Association for Bioeconomic Studies, Rome.

Lorenz, K. 1973. Die Rückseite des Spiegels. Versuch einer Naturgeschichte menschlichen Erkennens (Behind the Mirror). München: Piper.

Mayr, E. 1978. Evolution. In Evolution: A Scientific American Book. San Francisco: Freeman.

Mohr, H. 1990. Biologie und Ökonomik—Chancen für eine Interdisziplinarität. In Studien zur Evolutorischen Ökonomik, ed. U. Witt. Berlin: Duncker & Humblot.

Nelson R. R., and S. G. Winter. 1982. An Evolutionary Theory of Economic Change. Cambridge, MA: Harvard Univ. Press.

Norgaard, R. 1984. Coevolutionary development potential. *Land Economics* 60: 160–173.

———. 1992. Der Aufschwung des Welthandels und der Verlust biologischer Vielfalt. In Ende der Biologischen Vielfalt? Der Verlust an Arten, Genen und Lebensräumen und die Chancen für eine Umkehr, ed. E. O. Wilson. Heidelberg: Spektrum Akademischer Verlag.

Norton, B. 1992. Waren, Annehmlichkeiten und Moral. In Ende der Biologischen Vielfalt? Der Verlust an Arten, Genen und Lebensräumen und die Chancen für eine Umkehr, ed. E. O. Wilson. Heidelberg: Spektrum Akademischer Verlag.

Prigogine, I., and I. Stengers. 1984. Order out of Chaos: Man's New Dialogue with Nature. Toronto: Bantam.

Savory, A. 1991. Holistic Resource Management: A conceptual framework for ecologically sound economic modeling. *Ecological Economics* 3: 181–91.

Selten, R. 1991. Evolution, learning and economic behavior. *Games and Economic Behavior* 3: 3–24.

Siebert, H. 1987. Economics of the Environment: Theory and Policy. 2nd ed. Berlin: Springer.

Sraffa, P. 1960. Production of Commodities by Means of Commodities. Cambridge: Cambridge Univ. Press.

Tietzel, M. 1983. Ökonomie und Soziobiologie oder: Wer kann was von wem lernen? *Zeitschrift für Wirtschafts-und Sozialwissenschaften* 103: 107–27.

Verbeek, B. 1990. Die Anthropologie der Umweltzerstörung. Die Evolution und der Schatten der Zukunft. Darmstadt: Wissenschaftliche Buchgemeinschaft.

Wilson, E. O. 1975. Sociobiology. The New Synthesis. Cambridge, MA; London: The Belknap Press of Harvard Univ. Press.

———, ed. 1992. Ende der Biologischen Vielfalt? Der Verlust an Arten, Genen und Lebensräumen und die Chancen für eine Umkehr. Heidelberg: Spektrum Akademischer Verlag.

Winter, S. 1964. Economic "natural selection" and the theory of the firm. *Yale Economic Essays* 4: 225–72.

Witt, U. 1985. Economic behavior and biological evolution: some remarks on the sociobiology debate. *Journal of Institutional and Theoretical Economics* 141: 365–89.

———. 1987. Individualistische Grundlagen der evolutorischen Ökonomik. Tübingen: Mohr Paul Siebeck.

4 ETHICS AND VALUES IN ENVIRONMENTAL POLICY: THE SAID AND THE UNCED[1]

Harold Glasser
Department of Civil and Environmental Engineering
Sustainable Futures Group, College of Engineering
University of California
Davis, CA 95616

Paul P. Craig
Department of Applied Science and Graduate Group in Ecology
Sustainable Futures Group, College of Engineering
University of California
Davis, CA 95616

Willett Kempton
Center for Energy and Environmental Policy
University of Delaware
Newark, DE 19716

INTRODUCTION

While citizens often use non-instrumental arguments to support environmental protection, most governmental policies are justified by instrumental arguments. This chapter explores senior policy advisors' personal and professional views on the role of values in the environmental policy process. The authors interviewed senior policy advisors to four European governments active in global climate change negotiations and the programs of UNCED (United Nations Conference on Environment and Development). In response to the questions, most of these advisors articulated deeply held personal environmental values. They said that they normally keep these values separate from their professional environmental policy activities. These findings are interpreted within the context of

---

1. This chapter is an expanded and revised version of Craig et al. 1993.

the literature on environmental ethics and values. We suggest that environmental policy could be improved if widely held environmental values were articulated, validated, and admitted into the process of policy analysis and deliberation.

INTERVIEWS

Scholars have observed a rift in environmental policy discussion between experts, who tend to speak in "objective" language that emphasizes empirical data and utilitarian aims, and public citizens, who often speak and argue for environmental policies using more heart-felt, wider identifying, and ostensibly "subjective" language that often reveals a belief in the intrinsic value of the environment (Naess 1986a; Kempton 1991). While such values seem to be at the heart of keystone environmental legislation, such as the Endangered Species Act in the United States, they are rarely articulated in policy debates, even by environmental groups.

Similarly, non-use values were rarely mentioned in landmark environmental planning reports such as the IUCN's *World Conservation Strategy* (1980) and the WCED's *Our Common Future* (1987). These documents approach the environment from an enlightened, self-interest perspective. They emphasize the *use value* of nature for humans, arguing the importance of preserving this use value well into the future through "wiser use" and more careful stewardship. The absence of a discussion of non-use value does not mean that the authors of these reports never contemplated non-use values or failed to discuss them among themselves. We know only that, whether for reasons of custom or pragmatic political strategy, they did not incorporate such values into their primary arguments. We return to this point later in the chapter.

The prospect of the U.N. Conference on Environment and Development (UNCED), held in Rio de Janeiro, Brazil, in June 1992, prompted our in-depth examination of how policy advisors to UNCED think about such issues. Their responses lead to the conclusion that the practical requirements of policy advice can and do lead to suppression of concepts and belief structures that are important to the advisors themselves.

The interviewees included policy advisors involved with creating and critiquing legislation and negotiating current treaties. When asked about their environmental values, advisors often advocated ethical stances that extended well beyond a stewardship perspective. In fact, the personal

views of these policy advisors were strikingly similar to wider-identify-
ing views found in previous research to be held by the general public
(Kempton 1991; Löfstedt 1992, 1993). This chapter demonstrates that the
values and ethics that inspire many people's dedication to environmental
concerns should be seen as relevant to policymaking.

Twenty-four senior policy makers from Austria, the United Kingdom,
Sweden, and Germany were interviewed. These are some of the industrial nations that are taking leading roles in the global climate change debate. Interviewees were selected using networking among individuals involved with the Intergovernmental Panel on Climate Change (IPCC) and
with preparations for the 1992 Rio de Janeiro UNCED conference. The
complete set of interviews covered scientific, institutional, political, and
ethical topics. In this chapter discussion is limited to environmental values. Other findings are reported elsewhere (Kempton and Craig 1993).
Anthropological interviewing techniques were used, and all interviews
were recorded and later transcribed. An interview protocol (available
from the authors) was used, but answers were open-ended. Interviews
were scheduled for one hour, but many lasted longer as interviewees often wished to further elaborate and suggested continuing. As with most
interviewing at the level of senior advisors to governments, this was not a
"random" sample, and statistical indicators are not computed from the interview data.

ENVIRONMENTAL VALUES

Interviews opened with background questions and general questions
about familiarity with global climate change. Two questions were particularly productive in eliciting personal and professional environmental
values, the primary focus of this chapter:

Q: Do you have environmental values?

Q: How would you describe those values? [2]

These questions would almost always generate a pause for reflection,
then an often eloquent response. Such responses were generally phrased
in language that emphasized personal association, experience, and insight
rather than abstract or theoretical knowledge. The philosopher Naess
characterizes this emphasis upon direct experience as the language of

---

2 "Q" indicates our question, while "A" indicates the interviewee's answer. Questions
   are italicized to clearly distinguish them from responses.

"spontaneous experience" (Naess 1986a). Some interviewees said that a fundamental question, one virtually never raised in professional policy activities, had been asked. One person responded:

A: Well, how difficult. I don't think I've ever had to describe a value.

He then went on to do so with clarity and insight.

The chance to reflect on the meaning of his work led one interviewee to express thanks for interviewing him and to surprisingly comment at the end of his interview, "Now I understand why I've been working so hard on these problems."[3] This and other responses indicated that questions touched heart-felt values, rather than merely triggering standard responses.

Many interviewees perceived environmental values issues as personal rather than abstract. Many responses appeared to originate from an inner depth, and conveyed significant prior contemplation. For example, when asked if he had environmental values, a Swedish official replied:

A: Oh yes, definitely. Very much. Very much. I would say that my first value is to [apply] the precautionary principle, which we have been fighting so much about. But to apply it *much*[4] more rigorously than it is being applied.... Personally I'm willing to sacrifice quite a lot of my material [well being] in order to protect the environment.

The precautionary principle to which this official makes reference recommends policies that make some effort or investment to prevent possible environmental damages, even in the absence of absolute certainty that damages will occur. The purchasing of insurance serves as an analogy. The precautionary principle is often compared to a "no regrets" strategy, in which actions are pursued only if they have sufficient other benefits that they would be worth doing even if there were no threat of environmental damage. Of the two, the precautionary principle is regarded as the stronger environmental position.

This same official conveyed tension between his personal values and his responsibilities as a public servant and a member of his political party.

---

3. Unlike all other quotations in this chapter, this is a paraphrase of a remark that was made after the interview was concluded.

4. Italic text in quotations from interviews indicates verbal emphasis by the interviewee. Words and phrases in brackets [] have been appended by the authors in order to clarify the tape transcript.

A: As a government official of course, I'd have a much more balanced view than as an individual person. I certainly realize there has to be a balance between the economic interests and the environmental interests.... Actually it is politically unthinkable to sacrifice material well-being in Sweden. It's something we people want, and we have to be nationally competitive.... Within that formula there are of course enormous possibilities for protecting the environment.

Similarly, a British Department of Environment official replied that she had environmental values, but "They aren't supposed to come through in my work." A treasury official, who did not work primarily on environmental issues, was more direct: "We try to give good economic advice rather than taking a bias on nature. We're not attempting to build any of our values into that at all."

When a German environmental official was asked, *"Why would you say that environmental protection is important?"*, she responded with a carefully crafted, three-part argument that clarified her personal views on the value of nature, while conveying a well-tempered awareness of the complex of issues associated with trying to mitigate environmental degradation:

A: [Y]ou can't answer that question with one small and short sentence. [First, there are] a lot of immediate problems. You can see [from] East Europe that if you ignore the ecological impacts—[by] very egoistic and [immediate] economic-oriented argumentation—you destroy your economic basis.... Not only the macroeconomic, but also the microeconomic costs of neglecting ecological concerns are very high. [Better accounting of costs] is one traditional way of [arguing for environmental protection].

The second [perspective], which is perhaps more long-term oriented, is the global, the political, and the social point of view.... In the third world we have an increasing number of catastrophes that are caused by neglecting the local natural situation: desertification,... [flooding in] Bangladesh,... and erosion problems in mountain areas. And I know from the newspapers that California, perhaps in the future, will not... be the agriculture paradise that it was.... [The catastrophes happen] because of neglecting ecological issues and thinking that technological innovation is able to deal with everything.

The last point—and that is my personal feeling—[is] that mankind has not a right to exploit nature and natural resources to the extent we [have been] doing... [for] the last 100 years or perhaps more.... Biodiversity for me has very, very high value. It has a value in itself, from my personal [view], and also [from my] political and philosophical points of view. [I value] the rarity of not only opinions and things like protection of minorities,... [but also] protection of species. [Without this,] we will come to a very poor and one-dimensional world. Aesthetics and beauty of life are dependent on a variety of landscapes, of animals and so on. That's my personal point of view.

We note her use of the term "egoistic behavior" to illustrate a disjunction between wider values and narrow, self-interested materialism. The authors had not seen this term used in environmental value discussion in the United States, and asked for clarification. She replied:

The egoistic point of view. I want to express by this... the [emphasis on] short-term benefits in monetary terms. So you can calculate. You pay this, and your income is that. This is the egoistic, the materialistic approach.

It is significant that in this response she explicitly identifies questions of value as her personal point of view, clearly implying that these values should not enter into her policy recommendations.

The personal perspective may be placed in a long, historical context. Well over a century ago in *Principles of Political Economy*, John Stuart Mill wrote:

It is not good for man to be kept perforce at all times in the presence of his species.... [T]he presence of natural beauty and grandeur is the cradle of thoughts and aspirations, which are not only good for the individual, but which society could ill do without. Nor is there much satisfaction in contemplating the world with nothing left to the spontaneous activity of nature; with every rood of land brought into cultivation, which is capable of growing food for human beings; every flowery waste or natural pasture ploughed up, all quadrupeds or birds which are not domesticated for man's use exterminated as his rivals for food, every hedgerow or superfluous tree rooted out, and scarcely a place left where a wild shrub or flower could grow without being eradicated as a weed in the name of improved agriculture (Mill 1848, 111).

Mill's position was mirrored by an advisor to the Austrian government who advocated identifying more widely with all life forms:

A: I believe that humanity is a beneficiary and a guardian of nature at the same time. It's a double function. It's benefiting [from] nature, but it is also protecting nature. Not only for the sake of humanity but also for the sake of nature itself.

Not all interviewees answered with such clarity. For example, one U.K. official didn't respond to the question about environmental values. He was then asked, *"Does that question make sense?"* He said, "I'm sure it does." With further prompting, he added:

A: On the personal level,... we all want clean water to drink, and we want a fairly tranquil home life.... We all get a bit tired of pollution from traffic... we all like pretty scenery, clean air. So if that's what you mean by environmental values, then I suppose everybody instinctively is in favor....

Responses to the question on "environmental values" in narrow terms of personal conveniences were rare. Even in the above case, evidence from other parts of the interview suggests he may have simply misunderstood the question.

One obvious question is whether interviewees were providing "canned" answers, saying what they thought was expected. (This question was raised when this study was presented at the Second Conference of the International Society for Ecological Economics, Stockholm, September 1992). While this interpretation is, of course, possible, it seems compelling that a majority of advisors responded so eloquently to these questions, while a small minority failed to make contact with them.

Many advisors discussed the notion of "intrinsic value." In this chapter the term "intrinsic value" is used in an everyday, non-technical sense to reflect the character of the interviewees' responses. In this context, the term refers to two distinct senses of value. The first sense, non-instrumental or "means independent" value, refers to entities that are ends in themselves. The second sense, "objective" value, is a meta-ethical claim. It refers to values, in the sense of properties, that exist independently of the valuations of human valuers. The term "intrinsic value" is not used to suggest that non-relational value exists.

While some environmental ethicists have argued that subtle distinctions between these senses of intrinsic value are crucial for establishing a foundation for obligations towards nature (O'Neil 1992), most of the interviewees used the term without making such distinctions. However, an important observation does arise from these discussions. Some humans may have interests in protecting a species. In contrast, others may subscribe to the idea that the species themselves have interests. These senses of value are in no way mutually exclusive. An animal or a tree may be seen as simultaneously possessing instrumental, non-instrumental, and objective value. Policies based exclusively upon instrumental value are likely to be radically different from those that are justified and rooted in the notion of multiple senses of value.

Interviewees who embraced the intrinsic value notion were often lead to a normative prescription: the well-being of non-human life must be considered along with human life. Such views suggest that conceptions of value be expanded beyond narrowly defined use value to include a wider sense of nature's value. These views frequently associate a certain magic and sacredness with nature's richness and diversity. In fact, conservation biologist E. O. Wilson argues that humans, as a co-evolutionary species, exhibit a built-in affinity for nature, which he refers to as "biophilia" (Wilson 1984). These perspectives view nature as much more than a means to achieve human ends.

We were struck by the contrasts between our interviews, where fundamental values and the concepts found in many professional environmental planning documents were probed. Intrinsic value and issues of multiple and incommensurable senses of value are rarely mentioned in policy documents. When they do appear, it is with the idea of either (1) dismissing them as either too difficult to quantify and therefore not useful for policy analysis, or (2) as being readily integrable into existing tools, such as the contingent valuation techniques of economics. As the economist Herman Daly remarked:

> [T]he intrinsic value of other species, their own capacity to enjoy life, is not admitted at all in economics, and their instrumental value as providers of ecological life-support services to humans is only dimly perceived (1991, 236).

VIEWS OF THE ROLE OF ECONOMIC ANALYSIS

Economics is a key tool for policy analysis. All the interviewees had some familiarity with, and generally strong opinions about, economic techniques. Several also had formal training in the area. The interface between economic values and environmental values proved one of the most fruitful areas of the interviews.

While most interviewees recognized the importance of economic tools, many were also concerned about some economics limitations. A

German economist working on global climate change with the Enquette Commission of the German Bundestag[5] expressed the problem this way:

A: If I were answering as an economist I would have a very different answer than my personal one.... [An economist] would say, "What's the value of nature?" If people won't pay money for it, then they don't really value it. And so you might say that we don't want all these species to die, but if a few species die, it really doesn't affect people. If you ask the average consumer if they're willing to pay more for products in order to keep two or three species from dying, they'll say that they're not; therefore, it has no value.

Q: *That suggests that value is defined by what people are willing to pay for an item.*

A: Well, that's the way an economist defines value, but I don't agree with that myself.

Issues of this type have given rise to a whole sub-field of economics that seeks better ways to include non-market values in economic analysis. Numerous studies show that people routinely admit that they are willing to pay substantial sums for preservation (Goodland 1990; Loomis 1986; McNeeley 1988; Mitchell and Carson 1989). The "contingent valuation method" attempts to measure quantitatively the value of non-market goods by asking consumers what they are willing to pay for a cleaner environment, prevention of species extinctions, etc.

A closely related issue is how economics deals with the future. A Swedish scientific advisor spoke about economic discounting. We pointed out that an economist might argue that sound decisions require applying discount factors to future costs. Since the time periods are very long when one considers inter-generational equity, mainstream economics tends to lead to situations in which the future does not weigh heavily in today's planning. He responded:

A: I know.... That is theoretical.... But the world is finite. When you exploit natural resources—those are limited. I know that some of it is limited because of the cost increase, and it's not truly physically limiting. Nevertheless, that's not to be ignored. What the economists say is

---

5. In October 1987 the German Bundestag (German parliament) established a study commission on "Preventative Measures to Protect the Earth's Atmosphere." This top-level committee, known as the Enquette Commission, was comprised of scientists and members of the Bundestag. It held weekly meetings, reviewed extensive scientific evidence, and issued several detailed policy reports (Bundestag 1989).

that the free market and the optimal use today is best for the future. But why is that so? That's a hypothesis based on [the idea] that if you exhaust [resources], there are other replacements [that will] do equally well or even better. That's an axiom that they base their arguments on. I don't accept that because of the finiteness of the world.

This advisor believes basing environmental decision making upon such hypotheses may be unwise even from an instrumental value perspective. He expressed optimism about a recent movement towards incorporating more realistic assumptions into economic analysis:

A: There is an emerging [field] of ecological economics that is most interesting and addresses these questions. I'm sorry to say that ninety percent of economists just don't know about it. Out of ten, I would say that probably nine think it's silly. This will change over the next decade. I'm absolutely convinced.

A German official in the environmental ministry put the matter far more succinctly, expressing pessimism about the scope and influence of economics:

A: [Economics] is one of these disciplines... that is the most influential because it is so simple and simplistic,... even the most stupid person can understand it.... If you don't change [the] influence of this sort of science, then it will be very difficult to [achieve change].

Q: *You're saying if we don't change economic science, it's going to be hard to formulate good policy because economic science is so influential in policy?*

A: Yes.

Another German advisor expressed concern over the abstraction of value, calling the empiricism of economics artificially narrow:

A: The empiricism of economists.... This deprivation of the human sense.... The more you put the problem off to later generations, the cheaper it is for us today. This is a perversity.... If you have waste problems in... ten thousand years, they cost us nothing? This cannot be right.

He was then asked how he would, as an economist, decide when discounting is appropriate:

Q: *If you took a job for a firm and you were asked to evaluate investment decisions... you would advise the firm as an economist that you're better off with the nearer return because the net present value is greater.*

As an economist you would make such a recommendation. So how do you distinguish these two cases?

A: You can't compare these kinds of systems. You can't compare apples with [oranges]. In one case, the damages are repairable if you want. In global warming we don't have any idea what later generations can do against it. It's a problem of a new quality. We know the problem will be huge and really economically expensive. [We lack] the instruments [to deal with] this huge problem.

COLLAPSING MULTIPLE SENSES OF VALUE INTO A SINGLE NUMERAIRE

These advisors are expressing concern over the built-in tendency for the mainstream economic enterprise to obscure both the distinctions and linkages between natural capital (environmental resources and services), cultural capital (the dynamic stock of information, values, traditions, and intuitions that shape how we perceive and interact with nature as well as influence the process of how we modify and "manage" natural capital), and human-made capital (that which we produce from natural capital using technology, labor, and cultural capital) (Berkes and Folke 1992, 2). Traditional economics, because of its high level of aggregation, makes it nearly impossible to assess the "costs" and extent of reversibility of transformations between different forms of capital. Reliance upon any highly abstracted, single attribute sense of value—money or utility—inexorably leads to decoupling from both physical reality and human values.

Interviewees expressed concern over the possibly irreversible and highly uncertain consequences of prior and current economic activities. An essential concern is that those things that do possess intrinsic value, once lost, cannot be re-created. Even if restoration ecology existed as a highly developed science, restoration would not always be possible. A lost species is an obvious instance. Once lost, money and technological ingenuity cannot bring it back.

It is useful to compare these views with an example of leading work on techniques for achieving economic sustainability. The collaborative work of Pearce, Barbier, Markandya, and Turner (Pearce 1988, 1989, 1992; Pearce et al. 1988, 1989, 1990; Pearce and Turner 1992, 1993) provides one important interface between neoclassical economics and considerations of environmental sustainability. So, too, does the work of Dietz and van der Straaten (1992), Ekins et al. (1992), and Jacobs (1991).

Some British interviewees reported that *Blueprint for a Green Economy*, prepared by Pearce and collaborators in 1989 for the U.K. Department of the Environment, was important in the formation of British environmental policy. An academic policy advisor told us that:

> A: The Pearce report really outlines how you could start tackling environ-
> mental problems through the pricing system.... So that was really the
> point in which Mrs. Thatcher started to turn around and make pro-envi-
> ronmental statements.

Pearce and Turner's approach, however, rejects the concept of intrinsic value:

> If inherent/intrinsic and not just instrumental value exists, what is it and
> how do we discover it? It seems reasonable to conclude that we either
> justify our acceptance of intrinsic value at an intuitive level only, or we
> look for support via appeals to "expert judgment." Both of these forms
> of justification seem problematic (Pearce and Turner 1990, 238).

Rather, to establish an economic justification for environmental protection, they argue that all relevant multiple senses of value can be incorporated into existing tools:

> We have seen that the passing-on of the resource base "intact," (i.e., con-
> stant natural capital stock K_N), over the next few generations is central
> to the concept of sustainable economic development. Such a managed
> growth policy, although directed primarily toward the satisfaction of
> human needs, would also necessarily ensure the survival of the majority
> of non-human nature and its natural inhabitants. Adequate environmen-
> tal safeguards are available, therefore, without the need to adopt any of
> the radical "deep ecology" arguments and ethics. In particular, it is not
> necessary to have to accept the notions of intrinsic value in its widest
> sense, or of equal rights for all species. Our sustainability principle is
> general enough to encompass the environmental ethical concerns of
> consequentialist philosophy, as well as meeting the inter-generational
> equity objective (Pearce and Turner 1990, 238).

The core idea underlying Pearce and Turner's "sustainability principle" is the hypothesis that there exists, in principle, a scalar quantity, K_N, which completely characterizes the "natural capital stock." They argue that keeping this single numeraire constant will ensure that both human and non-human life will thrive. While the symbol is clear enough, the procedure for operationalization is not. Why should it be assumed that a *single scalar* quantity for measuring natural capital stock exists? In what units, and over what time horizon should it be defined? How is one to include the functional integrity of ecosystems? Of more theoretical and philosophical concern, however, is this approach's dependence upon "compensating projects" to mitigate the negative environmental effects of the other projects in the program. Such an approach still allows whole ecosystems to be annihilated as long as the net "natural capital stock" is maintained.

At the same time, Pearce and collaborators accept that many natural resource functions cannot be substituted by man-made capital (Barbier et al. 1990). Nevertheless, they persist in their belief that the cost-benefit analysis (CBA) should be maintained. They argue that alternative objective functions can be chosen that "extend" the CBA framework beyond economic efficiency. Turner and Pearce even argue that "moral" and "cultural" capital can be incorporated into CBA (Turner and Pearce 1993).

In order to accommodate economic sustainability considerations, Pearce at al. modify the usual economic efficiency (positive net benefits) with an additional constraint that requires zero or negative natural capital depreciation. This approach is not intended for the evaluation of single projects; it is oriented towards evaluating an array of projects at the program level. Pearce and his collaborators posit a "weak sustainability" criterion, which aggregates in the time dimension, and only requires the sum of individual damages to be zero or negative (i.e., the present value of the sum of environmental damages is constrained to be nonpositive). A "strong sustainability" criterion is also proposed that constrains the sum of environmental damages to be nonpositive for *each* time period. Thus, they attempt to integrate sustainability considerations into the CBA through the concept of shadow or environmentally compensating projects (Barbier et al. 1990).

The ideas expressed by our interviewees make it clear that many of them hold the position that different forms of capital are not completely fungible. These interviewees believe that accounting and analysis must at least distinguish between natural, human-made, and cultural capital. Reliance upon a single monitized value unit such as Pearce and Turner's "constant natural capital stock" not only obscures distinctions of this sort, but may in fact be conceptually erroneous.

Pearce and Turner do at one point acknowledge this methodological issue: "The long run survival of human society [also] depends on certain functional requirements that are met by a set of social norms (i.e., principles of behavior that ought to be followed). Over time, such norms must be consistent with the natural laws governing ecosystem maintenance if sustainability is the accepted policy goal" (1990, 226).

Our interviewees are, of course, not alone in their reservations of attempts to reformulate economics that do not incorporate more realistic assumptions and deeper values as a means to direct the reformulated analytical machinery. The philosopher Andrew Brennan is dubious about attempts to reformulate economics by using a single, all-inclusive attribute unit:

> Since some... forms of value will forever elude quantification, it would be folly to set up a single order of values, or of corresponding preferences. Much though economics may like to present itself as a rational discipline, commitment to a single order of values and of preferences would be quite the opposite of rationality.... Yet this is precisely what is attempted by those economists who aim to include all values in their calculations. They are pursuing a phantom; for however hard they try, there will be values which forever elude them (Brennan 1992, 20–21).

Brennan also discusses the concept of "transformative" value, the capacity for our preferences to be altered, over time, by new experiences. Brennan argues that transformative values, which can be associated with living things and systems, are nearly impossible to account for within the economic paradigm (Brennan 1992). Mill, in the publication quoted earlier, was referring to just this sense of the transformative capacity of nature.

Brennan's article represents an appeal to consider the limitations of economic rationality in general and cost-benefit analysis in particular. He questions the feasibility of quantification or measurement. He argues that the commensurability assumption, which takes as a given that all forms of value can, in principle, be assigned a single attribute unit and compared, cannot be empirically validated.

These tensions are not limited to the realm of abstract concepts. They show up in the practical world of the policy advisor. In one interview the confusion about the utility of traditional economic tools was particularly clear. An economist familiar with the work of Pearce showed his frustration in trying to reconcile his economic training with the needs of his job. He began optimistically, but soon expressed reservations:

A: Economics offers a lot of very powerful techniques for saying which is going to be a more costly path between two alternatives. But in some cases there seem to be other factors that enter that aren't really easily quantifiable. What's the value of a species, or of transboundary pollution?... We've been thinking very long and hard and deep about these issues.... We do find it extremely difficult to invent a structure of analysis and to put the numbers into the framework, including the economic values.

He was asked about inter-generational equity.

Q: *Can you indicate the kinds of techniques that you're using for thinking about these long-term inter-generational issues?*

He began with cost-benefit analysis, but then turned to its difficulties:

A: The very broad frame work in which we're working is cost-benefit analysis. Where one is setting up structured analysis and calculating all the costs and benefits and quantifying and valuing everything that you can. But in practice it is... extraordinarily difficult to do....

What we often aim for is some sort of intermediate exercise where you measure or quantify as much as you can and you value as much as you can, but you recognize that you can't add up apples and pears necessarily, because you can't actually get the values.

We've discussed inter-generational issues [too].... One of the jobs we have to do in the Treasury is to set a discount rate for calculating the present values.... We have essentially adopted the traditional economic framework, I think it's fair to say. But I would be pained to say that when decisions were presented to politicians... we should not tie up in a single number all the economic... assumptions. I quite see why... politicians might want to make different decisions about... the impacts of different policies on different generations.

He recognized the tension between his training and his job requirements:

A: These are... decisions which are bigger than economics actually. They do raise philosophical discussions... my own view is that... it's very hard for economists not to want to discount.... I think nearly everything points in favor of some sort of belief that the future is worth less than the present.... [However] I don't know a paper that's ever got to administrators that had to use discount rates over fifty years.

> Our economics research council is currently financing a program of re-
> search on global climate change.... Quite interestingly, it comes to the
> conclusion that you shouldn't discount actually. The case for discount-
> ing is weak.... [Our] training leads us to be terribly suspicious of that
> sort of argument of some intrinsic value. But that's the way we look at
> these things....

He was then asked about intrinsic value. He stated by framing the question in terms of marginal costs, but began to recognize the problems with
this approach:

> A: I would tend to regard [the discussion over intrinsic value] as a confu-
> sion between... total utility and marginal utility—that is between...
> some notion of the overall worth of a thing and... what factors actually
> determine the price of the thing.
>
> The classic case is water. Water is obviously intrinsically a very valu-
> able thing but at the margins, it is highly plentiful in some areas of the
> world. So it's value has actually gotten small because of the margin....
> Additional water is not terribly valuable....
>
> We have all of these millions and millions of species and what is the
> value of the additional species? Or losing one species when you've now
> got only 2,999,999 etc. of the species to go. That's the kind of question
> I would ask. That's why I say suspicious.... We really put an infinite
> value on these things.... People do implicitly value things even if they
> don't like doing so.... There comes a point where just about anything
> becomes too expensive for people to accept.
>
> Q: *You mean, if it's value isn't zero and if it isn't infinite, then there must
> be some number?*

He ultimately gave up on a price-oriented approach and considered the
political process as a solution to the problem.

> A: Yes, yes. I'm not saying economists can necessarily arrive [at a price],
> but the political process will arrive at it. And clearly you... are, it seems
> to me anyway, talking about things that are bigger than economics.... I
> don't think economists should pretend they've got the answers [for] ab-
> solutely everything.

He was clearly having problems distinguishing between basic assumptions and technique. This seems to be a systemic problem. However, not
everyone interviewed had such difficulty. One journalist for a major U.K.
business newspaper with a graduate degree in economics had a clear
grasp of the limitations of economics:

A: Economists typically feel more comfortable with things that the market puts a price on. The market will tell me exactly what this tape recorder you are using is worth.... But the market cannot tell me what it's worth to have the panda still on Earth, in existence. I mean there's a price at which people would buy a panda, but that's something rather different. Nor can it tell me what I'm prepared to pay for the continued, healthy, existence of my children or for this lovely view out here, or lots of other things.... Most of the things we value most are actually the things that the market doesn't put a price on. And the environment is often about those things.

The difficulty economists experience in including values is perhaps akin to that to which Daly refers in the introduction to the second edition of *Steady State Economics* (1991). Daly quotes from Daniel Raymond's *Thoughts on Political Economy* (1820). Raymond, an early American economist, was explaining why he omitted consideration of the then current ideas of Malthus:

Although [Malthus's views are]... founded upon the principle of nature, and although it is impossible to discover any flaws in his reasoning, yet the mind instinctively revolts at the conclusions to which he conducts it, and we are disposed to reject the theory, even though we could give no good reason (Daniel Raymond quoted in Daly 1991, pxi).

VALUES IN ENVIRONMENTAL POLICY

How, then, is one to think about incorporating these varied and wider senses of value? There is no single way, but there are means to gain insights. A Swedish advisor to the IPCC acknowledged the complexity of such an endeavor:

A: [We have] a responsibility to nature itself, too, to try to let all different types of animals and other live things flourish, and increasingly [we have responsibility] to people in the third world.

An Austrian diplomat echoed and expanded upon these concerns:

A: For me it's one system.... I see it as an integrated system. Therefore, I would not undertake to separate [it], because then it gives the wrong perception to the people.... First of all, as part of the system, you have... [a] responsibility to keep the system up. It's your share. It's your share because you are part of the system.... Second, as part of the system humanity has much more [impact] than any other part of nature on the system. [Our] responsibility [has] two aspects. The one is a service part of the system. The other...[is] to keep up the possibility for evolution to go on.... That is also a philosophical answer,... to keep up the possibility that evolution takes place.

The philosopher Mark Sagoff expresses a similar outlook, conveying the magnitude and importance of such a realignment of ethics and policy:

> Our environmental goals—cleaner air and water, the presence of wilderness and wildlife, and the like—are not to be construed, then, simply as personal wants or preferences; they are not interests to be "priced" by markets or by cost-benefit analysis, but are views or beliefs that may find their way, as public values, into legislation. These goals stem from our character as a people, which is not something we chose, as we might choose a necktie or a cigarette, but something we recognize, something we are (Sagoff 1988, 28).

Sagoff points out that attempts to shadow-price public values as externalities results in the creation of a category error. He argues that preferences are inherently quantifiable and hence amenable to comparison through numerical techniques like optimization and rank ordering. Ethical values, however, lie deeper and elude quantification. The word "value" is used here in two entirely different ways. The concepts are of different logical types.

> Is it a matter of principle, not merely of methodology, that the beliefs and opinions of citizens are usually listed and treated separately from their consumer preferences? Is it a logical or conceptual truth, in other words, that ideas or convictions that can be supported by reasons in the political process are to be considered by the decision maker as different from consumer wants and interests that may be satisfied in markets? If so, if the limitation is logical, if political and ethical debates are conceptually different from economic analysis, then we must infer that efforts to shadow-price "intangible" or "fragile" values must fail—not for any technical or empirical reason but because they rest on a logical mistake (Sagoff 1988, 92).

Trade-offs necessarily exist in the policy process. Making policy decisions involves values along with preferences. Sagoff contends that because the economic framework purports to incorporate preferences only, and to be "value neutral," it must be inherently incapable of addressing all elements crucial to the decision process.

A political advisor to the Swedish government indirectly reflected this kind of tension in language that he told us he would never imagine using in an official document.

A: [This is] a great dilemma for me. Certainly I realize that the market system [is] best in order to achieve an efficient production. Increased trade between nations is also very important in order to reach a good material standard. The competitive advantages of free trade is certainly crucial and that is one of the main features of the market economy.... *But* on the other hand, the whole idea behind the market economy is to increase the consumption of materials all the time. That is very much contrary to my values. Certain aspects of the market economy are fantastic. Another aspect is working completely contrary to my personal views. And I can't resolve this. I'm probably desperate. I don't know what to do. I can't find a system which could combine the good aspects of the market economy system but not have this bad aspect, which is the consumerism.... It is difficult, very difficult.

Another advisor talked of the need for a comprehensive approach for integrating wider values with tools and policies.

A: But... mankind is one part of an ecologically whole system.... We had in the late seventies and early eighties a very interesting research [project] concerning changes in the [perception] of ecological problems within our population. In the early seventies when you asked people what was the major ecological problem, people said waste or noise. These were problems that they were personally concerned [with]. They could see and touch and hear [them]. In the late seventies and in the eighties the answers were totally different. People said [they] are afraid of the chemicals, of those things that you can't see that are everywhere.... They were more and more aware of the fact that... those problems that are not immediately to be seen are perhaps more important than those that are at the moment on the agenda.

We do not want to leave the impression that all advisors consciously think in terms of intrinsic value, nor that all believe economic analysis is seriously flawed as a tool for dealing with the long run. For example, one British industrial executive was dubious about preservation:

A: [People] often see things at much too local a level.... People live close to it, and they value that local environment more than the sorts of benefits that would come to the global environment.... If we look at the U.K. landscape... the whole of [it] is man-made. There's no *natural* landscape here. It seems to me to be rather hard to want to preserve everything.

There is much he loves about the U.K. landscape, but he recognizes the enormous impact of humanity on it over millennia and finds continued intervention both inevitable and often desirable. In contrast, the environmentalists we interviewed recognize the role humanity has played in changing the environment, but are disturbed about the pace and form of change that exists today. We interviewed no one who "want[s] to preserve everything."

NAESS'S WORK ON VALUES

This disjunction between values and theory has also been addressed by the philosopher Arne Naess (1986a, b; 1989). Our findings are consistent with his work. Naess conducted systematic interviews with so-called "ordinary people" on the rights of animals, plants, and landscapes, and on their intrinsic value.

> In spite of what one would guess from the way they vote (and I am speaking as a Scandinavian), there is a substantial majority with quite far-reaching ideas about the rights and value of life forms, and a conviction that *every life form has its place in nature,* which we must respect (Naess 1986a, 508).

These individuals expressed the feeling that the so-called environmental "experts," in resorting to narrowly utilitarian practices for supporting current environmental policies, had deserted them.

To examine this belief Naess sent a detailed personal letter to 110 people who influence national environmental policy in Norway to clarify their environmental values. He asked for their comments on a series of eight statements (and clarifying commentary) that begin with an assumption of the inherent value of nonhuman life forms and state that this value is independent from its usefulness for human purposes. These statements are known as the Deep Ecology Platform (Devall and Sessions 1985; Naess and Rothenberg 1989; Naess 1986a).

One in three environmental experts replied to Naess's letter. They answered in a very favorable manner, suggesting that at least on a personal level, they are much in line with Naess's "ordinary people." General agreement with the Deep Ecology Platform has also been shared by others outside the deep ecology movement (Daly and Cobb 1989). Naess concludes that more fruitful approaches to policy analysis must attempt to explicitly incorporate fundamental values:

> What is needed is a methodology of *persistently connecting basic value judgments and imperative premises with decisions in concrete situations* of interference or noninterference in nature. What I therefore sug-

gest is that those who are thought to be experts and scientists repeatedly and persistently deepen their arguments with reference to basic value judgments and imperative premises. That is, they should announce their normative philosophy of life and discuss environmental problems in their most comprehensive time and space frame of reference (Naess 1986a, 510).

The following conclusions relate this injunction both to the interviews and to the process of undertaking this research.

CONCLUSIONS

Senior environmental policy advisors to several European governments told us that they hold deep environmental values, which quite often go far beyond instrumental value. While all the advisors we interviewed did by no means hold such values, enough of them did that we are persuaded that many policy advisors, like many citizens, do hold deep and conse- quential environmental values. However, the predominant policy process at the national and international level routinely fails to acknowledge such values.

Instead, analytical tools are used, which are often asserted to be value- neutral, but are not. In our view the problem of embedded values occurs in every area, but the problem is especially severe with techniques that rely heavily on mathematization—particularly in the field of economics (Dasgupta 1992).

All too often even those who employ such techniques are unaware of embedded values and implicit category errors. We are greatly encouraged that many of the policy advisors we interviewed have a clear understand- ing of these matters. Unfortunately, some do not. Unfortunately, too, in- stitutional pressures can and do lead to conflict between personal values and work. Many of the interviewees stated that institutional pressures forced them to separate and sublimate their personal environmental val- ues to satisfy institutional constraints. Such discord has often resulted in the generation of flawed environmental policies—policies that stem from a severe mismatch between evaluation tools and policy instruments. Individuals, society, and the environment are the worse for that.

Naess has recommended that we learn to incorporate fundamental values explicitly into environmental policy analysis and decision-making frameworks. We concur. Recent work in the theory of policy analysis recognizes the role of argument and persuasion (Majone 1989). Indeed, if the research reported here is any guide, a movement toward explicit recognition of values in the policy process would be as welcome to policy advisors as to the general public.

We are encouraged to see a few signs that explicit recognition of the relevance of environmental values is becoming more widespread. This occurred at the Brazil UNCED Conference—especially in the meetings of the NGOs (non-governmental organizations). Legitimation of environmental values would have several positive effects. Members of the public would likely become less reticent about expressing their motivations. Policy advisors and politicians may then feel more comfortable articulating such values. These changes could lead to deeper examination of the values that are embedded in analytical tools, and the articulation of these values when these tools are used in policy evaluation. Such recognition could help to avoid falling into "social traps" (Platt 1973; Cross and Guyer 1980; Costanza 1987), which lead to situations in which decisions based on short-term goals and narrow interests lead to long-term outcomes desired by no one.

ACKNOWLEDGMENTS

We would like to thank our interviewees for their participation and their candid responses. All interviewees were sent a draft of this chapter and were asked to correct our quotes and comment on our interpretations. We are grateful to those who responded. One serious disagreement was noted and, upon reflection, we agreed with it and modified the chapter accordingly.

This work benefited from conversations Harold Glasser had with scholars at the International Institute of Applied Systems Analysis [IIASA] while he participated in the Young Scientists Summer Program in 1992. In particular, we would like to acknowledge the detailed comments of Amanda Wolf. We also thank Ragnar E. Löfstedt, Arne Naess, R. Kerry Turner, and three anonymous referees for reviewing and commenting upon the manuscript.

We are particularly indebted to Mark Levine, Florentine Krause, Gerald Leach, and Irving Mintzer for help in structuring the project and in setting up interviews. Without them the project would have been impossible.

This work was supported by the U.S. Department of Energy through the National Institute on Global Environmental Change. The work reported herein is that of the authors. There is no implication expressed or intended that any of the ideas expressed herein are endorsed by the U.S. government.

REFERENCES

Barbier, E. B., A. Markandya, and D. W. Pearce. 1990. Environmental sustainability and cost-benefit analysis. *Environment and Planning A* 22: 1259–66.

Berkes, F., and C. Folke. 1992. A systems perspective on the interrelations between natural, human-made, and cultural capital. *Ecological Economics* 5(1): 1–8.

Brennan, A. 1992. Moral pluralism and the environment. *Environmental Values* 1(1): 15–33.

Bundestag. 1989. Schutz der Erde: Einen Bestandsaufnahme mit Vorschlägen zu einer neuen Energiepolitik. Bericht der Enquette-Kommission des Deutschen Bundestages "Vorsorge zum Schutz der Erdatmosphäre." Available in English as Protecting the Earth's Atmosphere: An International Challenge. Report of the Study Commission of the 11th German Bundestag, Bundestag, Germany.

Costanza, R. 1987. Social traps and environmental policy. *BioScience* 37(6): 409–12.

Cross, J. G., and M. J. Guyer. 1980. Social Traps. Ann Arbor: Univ. of Michigan Press.

Craig, P. P., H. Glasser, and W. Kempton. 1993. Ethics and values in environmental policy: the Said and the UNCED. *Environmental Values* 2: 137–57.

Daly, H. E., and J. B. Cobb. 1989. For the Common Good: Redirecting the Economy Toward Community, the Environment, and a Sustainable Future. Boston: Beacon Press.

Daly, H. E. 1991. Boundless bull. In Learning to Listen to the Land, ed. B. Willers. Washington, DC: Island Press.

———. 1991. Steady State Economics. 2nd ed. Washington, DC: Island Press.

Dasgupta, P. 1992. Nutrition, non-convexities and redistributive policies. In The Future of Economics, ed. J. D. Hay. Cambridge, MA: Blackwell.

Devall, B., and G. Sessions. 1985. Deep Ecology: Living As If People Mattered. Salt Lake City: Peregrine Smith Books.

Dietz, F., and J. van der Straaten. 1992. Rethinking environmental economics: missing links between economic theory and environmental policy. *Journal of Economic Issues* 26(1): 27–51.

Ekins, P., M. Hillman, and R. Hutchison. 1992. Wealth Beyond Measure: An Atlas of New Economics. London: Gaia Books.

Goodland, R., ed. 1990. Race to Save the Tropics: Ecology and Economics for a Sustainable Future. Washington: Island Press.

IUCN. 1980. International Union for Conservation of Nature and Natural Resources. World Conservation Strategy: Living Resource Conservation for Sustainable Development. Gland, Switzerland: IUCN.

Jacobs, M. 1991. The Green Economy: Environment: Sustainable Development and the Politics of Future. London: Pluto Press.

Kempton, W. 1991. Lay perspectives on global climate change. *Global Environmental Change: Human and Policy Dimensions* 1: 183–208.

Kempton, W., and P. Craig. 1993. European thinking on global climate change. *Environment* 35(3): 16–20, 41–5.

Löfstedt, R. E. 1992. Lay perspectives concerning global climate change in Sweden. *Energy and Environment* 3(2): 161–75.

———. 1993. In press. Lay perspectives concerning global climate change in Vienna, Austria. *Energy & Environment* .

Loomis, J. B. 1986. Assessing wildlife and environmental values in cost-benefit analysis: state of the art. *Journal of Environmental Management* 22: 125–31.

Majone, G. 1989. Evidence, Argument, and Persuasion in the Policy Process. New Haven: Yale Univ. Press.

McNeeley, J. A. 1988. Economics and Biological Diversity: Developing and Using Economic Incentives to Conserve Biological Resources. Gland, Switzerland: IUCN.

Mill, J. S. 1970. The stationary state, chapter 6. In Principles of Political Economy: Books IV and V (reprint of 1848 edition). New York: Penguin Books.

Mitchell, R. C., and R. T. Carson. 1989. Using Surveys to Value Public Goods: The Contingent Valuation Method. Washington, DC: Resources for the Future.

Naess, A. 1964. Reflections about total views. *Philosophy and Phenomenological Research* 25: 16–29.

———. 1986a. Intrinsic value: will the defenders of nature please rise. In Conservation Biology: The Science of Scarcity and Diversity, ed. M. E. Soulé. Sunderland, MA: Sinauer.

———. 1986b. The deep ecology movement: some philosophical aspects. *Philosophical Inquiry* 8: 10–31.

———. 1989. Ecology, Community and Lifestyle: Outline of an Ecosophy (translated and revised by David Rothenberg). Cambridge: Cambridge Univ. Press.

O'Neil, J. 1992. The varieties of intrinsic value. *The Monist* 75(2): 119–37.

Pearce, D. W. 1988. Economics, equity, and sustainable development. *Futures* 20: 598–605.

———. 1989. Sustainable Development: an Economic Perspective. London: International Institute for Environment and Development; London Environmental Economics Center.

———. 1992. Green economics. *Environmental Values* 1: 3–13.

Pearce, D. W., E. B. Barbier, and A. Markandya. 1988. Sustainable Development and Cost-Benefit Analysis. London: London Environmental Economics Center.

Pearce, D. W., A. Markandya, and E. B. Barbier. 1989. Blueprint for a Green Economy. London: Earthscan.

Pearce, D. W., E. B. Barbier, and A. Markandya. 1990. Sustainable Development: Economics and Environment in the Third World. London: Earthscan.

Pearce, D. W., and R. K. Turner. 1990. Economics of Natural Resources and the Environment. Baltimore: Johns Hopkins Univ. Press.

Platt, J. 1973. Social traps. *American Psychologist* 28: 641–51.

Sagoff, M. 1988 The Economy of the Earth. Cambridge: Cambridge Univ. Press.

Turner, R. K. 1992. Speculations on Weak and Strong Sustainability. Working paper GEC 92-2, Centre for Social and Economic Research on the Global Environment (CSERGE).

Turner, R. K., and D. W. Pearce. 1993. Sustainable economic development: economic and ethical principles. In Economics and Ecology: New Frontiers and Sustainable Development, ed. E. B. Barbier. London: Chapman and Hall.

Wilson, E. O. 1984. Biophilia. Boston: Harvard Univ. Press.

WCED (World Commission on Environment and Development). 1987. Our Common Future. Oxford: Oxford Univ. Press.

PART II

METHODOLOGY AND TECHNIQUES

5 SPATIAL ECOSYSTEM MODELING IN A DISTRIBUTED COMPUTATIONAL ENVIRONMENT

Thomas Maxwell and Robert Costanza
Maryland International Institute for Ecological Economics
Center for Environmental and Estuarine Studies
University of Maryland
P.O. Box 38
Solomons, MD 20688

INTRODUCTION

Spatial systems modeling is essential if one's modeling goals include developing a relatively realistic description of past behavior and predictions of the impacts of alternative policies on future behavior. Development of these models has been limited in the past by data requirements, conceptual/computational complexity issues, and insufficient computational resources. These limitations have begun to erode with the increasing availability of remote sensing data, and the development of faster processors and parallel computer systems. Intelligent development environments can help alleviate the model complexity limitations if linked with appropriate supercomputing platforms. The architecture and applications of an intelligent, user-friendly environment for ecological/economic model development in a parallel, distributed computational environment are presented in this chapter.

We have developed a spatial modeling workstation, which combines hardware and software tools that allow development, implementation, and testing of spatial ecosystem models in a convenient desktop environment. In this system the unit model development and testing is done on a Macintosh computer using the STELLA™ or EXTEND™ dynamic simulation development packages. A simple configuration step allows the user to link data resources and generate spatially or nonspatially articulated models for parallel or serial computers. The system automatically generates code for several different distributed computing environments and types of parallelism, alleviating the need for scientists to invest time in computer programming. A Hypercard interface guides the user through the model development process. An application of these techniques involving simulations of the Barataria basin in southern Louisiana is presented later.

SPATIAL ECOSYSTEM MODELING AND SUSTAINABLE DEVELOPMENT

Ecological systems play a fundamental role in supporting life on Earth at all hierarchical scales. They form the life-support system without which economic activity would not be possible. In the long run a healthy economy can only exist in symbiosis with a healthy ecology. There are many signs that the collective global economic activity is dramatically altering the self-repairing aspects of the global ecosystem. Our ability to change the economic and the ecological systems, and the rate of spread of the impacts of these changes, far exceeds our ability to predict the full extent of these impacts. Protecting and preserving our natural life-support systems requires the ability to understand the direct and indirect effects of human activities over long periods of time and over large areas. Computer simulations are now becoming important tools to investigate these interactions.

Spatial modeling of ecosystems is essential if one's modeling goals include developing a relatively realistic description of past behavior and predictions of the impacts of alternative management policies on future ecosystem behavior (Risser et al. 1984; Costanza et al. 1990; Sklar and Costanza 1991). Development of these models has been limited in the past by the large amount of input data required and the difficulty of even large mainframe serial computers in dealing with large spatial arrays. These two limitations have begun to erode with the increasing availability of remote sensing data and GIS systems to manipulate it, and the development of parallel computer systems that allow computation of large, complex, spatial arrays. Improved computational capabilities (both in terms of raw speed and ease of use) can enhance many aspects of spatial modeling and landscape ecology. In efforts to describe landscapes, many new, computationally intensive indices have been developed (Colwell 1974; Mandelbrot 1983; Weins et al. 1985; Gardner et al. 1987;

Krummel et al. 1987; Urban et al. 1987; Costanza 1989; Turner et al. 1989), which could benefit from computer systems that are faster and easier to use. This chapter describes how far these computer developments have come and how they may now be used in building and running dynamic spatial ecosystem models.

In order to be effective management tools, spatial models with adequate resolution require the use of supercomputers or parallel processors. This class of models is a near-ideal application for parallel processing, since a typical model consists of a large number of cells that can be simulated semi-independently. Each processor can be assigned a different subset of cells, and most interprocessor communication is nearest-neighbor only. Although parallel processing in some form has become nearly universally available, the conceptual complexity involved in applying these architectures has prevented scientists from utilizing this resource. This chapter will describe our attempt to bridge this gap by linking intelligent computer modeling environments with automatic parallel code generators.

Spatial Ecosystem Modeling

A dynamic spatial model can be defined as any formulation that describes the changes in a spatial pattern from time t to a new spatial pattern at time t+1, such that

$$\mathbf{X}_{t+1} = f(\mathbf{X}_t, \mathbf{Y}_t)$$

where $\mathbf{X}(t)$ is the spatial pattern at time t and $\mathbf{Y}(t)$ is a set of array, vector, or scalar variables that may affect the transition (Sklar and Costanza 1991). There are four major disciplines that use spatial models within the broad topic of ecology: geography, hydrology, biology, and ecosystem science. Within geography, spatial models can be further subdivided into geometric, demographic, and network models. In hydrology, there are basically two types of spatial models of fluid dynamics: finite element models, or hydrodynamic models, and finite difference models, or general circulation models. Spatial models in biology include growth models, population models, and point-averaged ecosystem models. Spatial ecosystem models can be classified as stochastic landscape models or process-based landscape models. For a recent review of spatial modeling, see Sklar and Costanza (1991).

Although all of the forms of dynamic spatial modeling described above are highly amenable to parallel processing, the primary focus of this chapter is on process-based landscape models. These models simulate spatial structure by first compartmentalizing the landscape into some geometric design and then describing flows within compartments and spatial processes between compartments according to location-specific algorithms. Examples of process-based, spatially articulate landscape models include wetland models (Sklar et al. 1985; Costanza et al. 1986; Kadlec and Hammer 1988; Boumans and Sklar 1991; Costanza et al. 1990), oceanic plankton models (Show 1979), coral reef growth models (Maguire and Porter 1977), and fire ecosystem models (Kessell 1977). The general structure of a process-based landscape model is shown in Figure 5.1.

The Coastal Ecological Landscape Spatial Simulation (CELSS) model, for example, is a process-based spatial simulation model consisting of 2,479 interconnected cells, each representing 1 km^2, constructed for the Atchafalaya/Terrebonne marsh/estuarine complex in southern Louisiana (Sklar et al. 1985; Costanza et al. 1990). Figure 5.2 shows the location of this study area and of the Barataria study area referred to later. Each 1 km^2 cell in the CELSS model contains a dynamic, nonlinear ecosystem simulation model with seven state variables similar to the one shown in Figure 5.3. The model is generic in structure and can represent one of six habitat types by assigning unique parameter settings. Each cell is potentially connected to each adjacent cell by the exchange of water and materials. The volume of water crossing from one cell to another is a function of water storage and connectivity. Connectivity is a function of landscape characteristics, including habitat type, drainage density, waterway orientation, and levee height. Habitat succession occurs in a cell when its environmental variables (i.e., salinity, elevation, water level, productivity, etc.) fall outside the ranges for its designated habitat type. Succession means that the cell habitat type and all the associated parameter settings are switched to a set more adapted to the changed conditions. For example, if salinity in a cell that was initially fresh marsh goes beyond a threshold value of 3 ppt and remains at this high level for more than 45 weeks then the cell is converted to brackish marsh with all its associated parameters, including a habitat specific function for primary production. The CELSS model, when applied to the Atchafalaya-Terrebonne area of coastal Louisiana, explained about 90% of the 1978

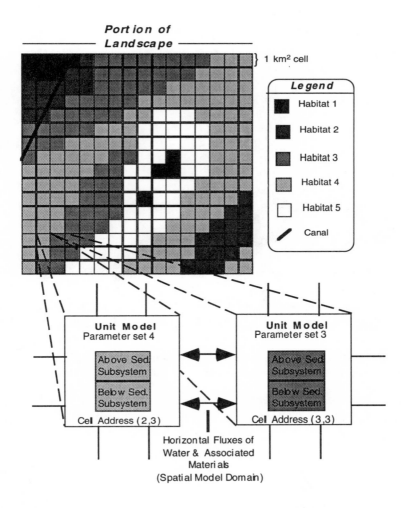

Figure 5.1. The basic structure of a spatial ecosystem model. Each cell has a (variable) habitat type, which is used to parameterize the unit model for that cell. The unit model simulates ecosystem dynamics for that cell in the above-sediment and below-sediment subsystems. Nutrients and suspended materials in the surface water and saturated sediment water are fluxed between cells in the domain of the spatial model.

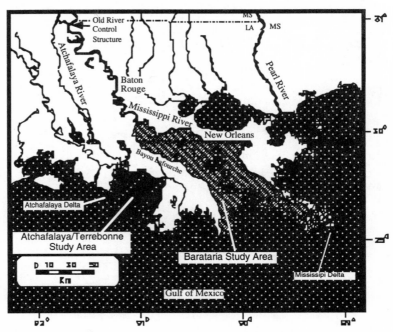

Figure 5.2.   Map of southern Louisiana showing the Atchafalaya/Terrebonne
and the Barataria study areas in Louisiana.

ecosystem type calibration data and predicted about 79% of the 1983
verification data (Costanza et al. 1990). Figure 5.4 shows some sample
output indicating the real and simulated habitat changes from 1956 to
1983, along with nitrogen and water predictions from the model. Table
5.1 indicates the range of management options, as well as past and future
climate scenarios that the model has been used to analyze.

The CELSS model was written in standard FORTRAN (3,021 lines of
code), and was run with a time step of 1 week on a variety of computers
including a VAX 11/780, IBM 3034, and CRAY X/MP. A typical 22-
year run at a weekly time step (1,144 total time steps) for all 2,479 cells
with 8 state variables each (19,832 total simultaneous difference equations) takes about 24 hours of CPU time on the VAX, 2 hours on the
IBM, and 15 minutes on the CRAY. Most of the full-scale runs of the
model were done on the CRAY, with the other computers used primarily
in the early model development stages. The original CELLS model took

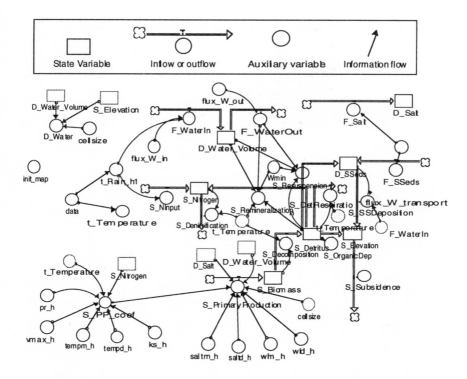

Figure 5.3. STELLA diagram of the generic unit model used for both the
Atchafalaya/Terrebonne and the Barataria modeling studies.

four people about four years (sixteen-person-years) to fully develop and
implement using a supercomputer. The model has proved to be very effective in helping us understand complex ecosystem behavior and in
guiding policy and research (Costanza et al. 1990). We are now working
on reducing the time involved for both developing and running this type
of model, and moving the modeling to smaller, less expensive computers.
Toward that end we have developed the integrated spatial modeling
workstation described in the next section.

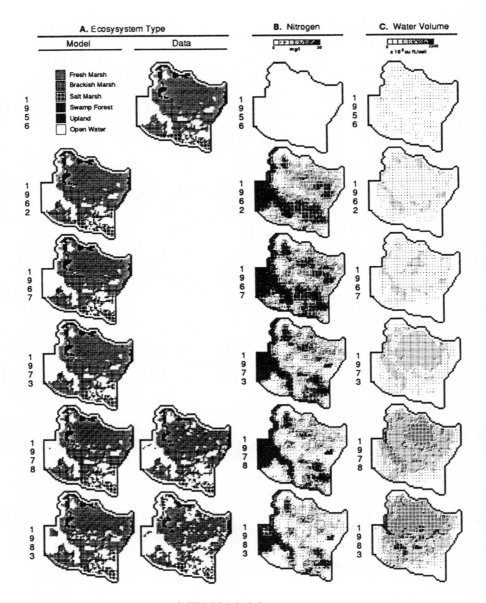

Figure 5.4.   Sample output of CELSS Model.

Table 5.1. Number of Square Kilometers of Each Ecosystem Type for the Three Years for which data is available, and for the year 2033 for various scenarios from the CELSS model (changes from the base case in sq. km are indicated in parentheses) (Costanza et al. 1990).

	Swamp	Fresh Marsh	Brackish Marsh	Saline Marsh	Upland	Total Land	Open Water
1956	130	864	632	98	13	1737	742
1978	113	766	554	150	18	1601	878
1983	116	845	347	155	18	1481	998
2033 SCENARIOS [1]:							
CLIMATE SCENARIOS [2]:							
Climate run 3 (climate base case)	84	871	338	120	10	1423	1056
Climate run 1	79 (-5)	874 (+3)	337 (-1)	127 (+7)	10 (0)	1427 (+4)	1052 (-4)
Climate run 4	85 (+1)	900(+29)	355 (+17)	130(+10)	10 (0)	1480 (+57)	999 (-57)
Climate run 5	83 (-1)	891(+20)	332 (+6)	126 (+6)	10 (0)	1442 (+19)	1037 (-19)
Mean Climate	94(+10)	974(+103)	402 (+64)	136(+16)	11(+1)	1617 (+194)	862 (-194)
Weekly Average Climate	128(+44)	961(+90)	813(+475)	300(+180)	11(+1)	2213 (+790)	266 (-790)
MANAGEMENT SCENARIOS:							
No levee extension (Base Case)	100	796	410	123	15	1444	1035
Two reach levee extension	98 (-2)	804 (+8)	399 (-11)	123 (0)	15 (0)	1439 (-5)	1040 (+5)
CLF Marsh Management	102 (+2)	798 (+2)	409 (-1)	123 (0)	15 (0)	1447 (+3)	1032 (-3)
Falgout Weir	104 (+4)	799 (+3)	403 (-7)	122 (-1)	16(+1)	1444 (0)	1035 (0)
Full six reach levee extension	103 (+3)	790 (-6)	362 (-48)	122 (-1)	15 (0)	1392 (-52)	1087 (+52)
Fresh water diversion (FWD)	103 (+3)	803 (+7)	404 (-6)	123 (0)	15 (0)	1448 (+4)	1031 (-4)
FWD and Palmetto Wier	102 (+2)	802 (+6)	407 (-3)	123 (0)	15 (0)	1449 (+5)	1030 (-5)
FWD and Superior Wier	104 (+4)	799 (+3)	404 (-6)	123 (0)	15 (0)	1445 (+1)	1034 (-1)
FWD, Superior & Palmetto Weirs	104 (+4)	792 (-4)	407 (-3)	123 (0)	15 (0)	1441 (-3)	1038 (+3)
FWD, Superior & Falgout Weirs	104 (+4)	803 (+7)	407 (-3)	122 (-1)	15 (0)	1451 (+7)	1028 (-7)
BOUNDARY SCENARIOS [3]:							
EPA low sea level rise	104 (+4)	800 (+4)	411 (+1)	124 (+1)	15 (0)	1454 (+10)	1025 (-10)
EPA high sea level rise	89 (-11)	794 (-2)	396 (-14)	131 (+8)	15 (0)	1425 (-19)	1054 (+19)
HISTORICAL SCENARIOS [4]:							
No original Avoca Levee	84	951	350	126	13	1524	955
No impacts	130	863	401	144	12	1550	929

1. The summary maps and this table indicate the "dominant" habitat type for each cell (i.e., the ecosystem type that was present in the cell for the largest amount of time during the year). Alternately, we could have added the total number of cells of each ecosystem type for each week of the simulated year and divided the totals by 52. While this gives a somewhat more accurate picture of the habitat distribution, it is inconsistent with the totals from the maps.

2. The climate analysis scenarios used a slightly different set of parameters for the model than the other scenarios. See text for details.

3. EPA low scenario is 50 cm rise by the year 2100. We used 0.46 cm/yr which is double the historical rate of eustatic sea level rise in the study area of 0.23 cm/yr. Subsidence in the study area varies horizontally from 0.57 to 1.17 cm/yr, giving historical rates of *apparent* sea level rise (eustatic rise plus subsidence) of 0.8 to 1.4 cm/yr. EPA high scenario is 200 cm rise by the year 2100 (1.67 cm/yr eustatic or 2.24 to 2.84 cm/yr apparent). Base case for comparison was the no levee extension case.

4. No comparisons with a base case are given for the historical scenarios since these runs started in 1956 rather than 1983.

COMPLEX SYSTEMS MODELING

Three forms of complexity can be identified that limit the implementation of complex systems models: conceptual complexity, computational complexity, and data complexity. Different approaches are required to address these three issues, but any computational environment designed for complex systems modeling should address all three.

Conceptual complexity arises in the process of formulating models with many state variables and processes. In the traditional approach (implementing models as large FORTRAN programs) debugging, calibrating, and understanding the model become very difficult as the model becomes very complex. It is very difficult for anyone other than the model's creator to understand it, and even the creator may run into difficulties if he/she leaves the model for a period of time and then tries to resume work. Collaborative work becomes difficult or impossible. Communicating the structure of the model to others can become an insurmountable obstacle to the acceptance of the model. Policymakers are less likely to trust a model if they don't understand how it works.

These problems can be at least partially alleviated with graphical, hierarchical, "intelligent" modeling environments (IMEs). In an IME the structure of the model at each hierarchical level is represented graphically so that viewers can recognize the major interactions at a glance. Viewers can easily shift hierarchical levels, allowing them to "zoom out" to see the big picture, or "zoom in" to investigate the fine structure of the components. Inherent constraints and "intelligent" error checking make it much easier to generate bug-free models. Built-in tools for display and analysis facilitate understanding and calibration of the model dynamics.

The second form of complexity (computational) refers to the tremendous computational resources required to integrate the equations of a large model in a reasonable amount of real time. Large models typically require supercomputers for efficient execution. Advances in computing architectures have allowed handling of increasingly larger models. One advance that has had particular impact on modeling is the development of parallel processing architectures, which allow a separate processor to be assigned to each component of a model, greatly increasing simulation speed. Despite their great promise and increasing availability, these advanced architectures have not found much usage in the life sciences. The major barrier to wide acceptance of these techniques has been reluctance on the part of scientists to invest time in learning new languages and architectures.

The third form of complexity (data) refers to the tremendous amount of data required to build and calibrate a large model. Even the most detailed, carefully articulated model running on the world's fastest supercomputer is subject to the "garbage in, garbage out" principle. In many cases the data required to properly outfit a model is simply not available. In this case the model-building process can provide hypotheses and specific data demands to spur further field research. However, with the increasing concern for the fate of the planet driving new research, and with the increasing availability of inexpensive remote sensing data, calibration of large, highly spatially articulated ecosystem models is becoming feasible. Parallel advances in GIS systems and intelligent databases are providing better methods for storing and manipulating large quantities of data. These tools must be packaged in a form that is accessible to the life scientists who are building and using the models, or they will not be used.

As discussed above, addressing the first two forms of complexity seems to require divergent techniques. Alleviating conceptual complexity requires extremely user-friendly intelligent interfaces that are generally implemented on micro-computers. However, addressing computational complexity requires advanced supercomputers and/or parallel processing architectures that are generally not user friendly. Even learning to program these platforms in "traditional" style (i.e., in extensions of FORTRAN or C) requires a considerable time investment. This chapter will describe our spatial modeling package, which addresses all three types of complexity simultaneously, by linking an "intelligent" graphical modeling environment with GIS systems and a selection of parallel supercomputers.

SPATIAL MODELING WORKSTATION DEVELOPMENT

Computer systems are much more effective tools for research and education if they are easy to use. In order to be effective management tools, spatial models with adequate resolution (like the CELSS model) have, until recently, required supercomputers. Our goal was to utilize new developments in parallel computer architectures to bring useful spatial ecosystem modeling to an easy-to-use microcomputer platform, allowing scientists to utilize advanced computer architectures without having to invest time in computer programming or learning new systems.

Toward this end we developed a spatial ecosystem modeling system to run on Apple Macintosh II™ computers (with the possibility of exporting code to run on supercomputers for very large problems). The system consists of three major software components, corresponding to the major phases of model development, linked together using Hypercard™. The system is illustrated in Figure 5.5.

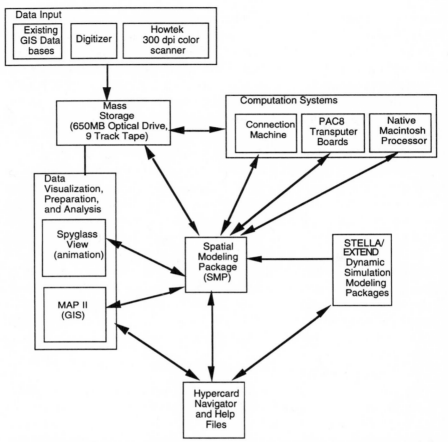

Figure 5.5. Diagram of major hardware and software components of the spatial modeling workstation.

The major phases of developing a spatial model are: (1) unit model development and testing, (2) data assembly and manipulation, and (3) linkage of the data and unit models to run in space and time. In our system the unit model development and testing is done using STELLA™[1] (Costanza 1987), or EXTEND,[2] both of which are commercially available dynamic simulation model development packages that are very easy to learn and use. The data assembly and manipulation is done using MAP

1.   High Performance Systems, Inc., Lyme, NH. (603)–643–9636.
2.   Imagine That, Inc., San Jose, CA. (408)–365–0305.

II™,[3] an easy-to-use Geographic Information System (GIS) for the Macintosh. These elements are linked together with a Spatial Modeling Package (SMP) that we have developed. The SMP automatically generates code to be run on the Connection Machine parallel computer, Pacific Parallel transputer boards installed in the Mac II,[4] a Sun Workstation, or the native Macintosh II series 680x0 processors. The model drivers for other platforms, such as Hypercube and CRAY supercomputers, are currently being developed. These systems generate output files that can be read and manipulated using one of the GIS systems.

The system can be used either as four separate software modules, or through a Hypercard™ front end. Hypercard allows easy navigation through the system and online help and explanation. Using the Hypercard™ front end, even first-time users can gain access and effectively use the system.

Intelligent Modeling Environments

Use of intelligent modeling environments is essential for the development of large, complex, error-free models within a reasonable amount of time. The ideal modeling environment has not yet been developed. However, some of the features one would expect to find in such an environment are listed below:

1. *Graphical display.* The environment should be icon-based, with symbols representing major stocks, flows, and relationships. The viewer should be able to see the structure of the model at a glance, without having to read or understand equations.

2. *Modularity.* The separate components of the model should exist as self-contained modules so that specialists can develop different modules at remote sites and then mix-and-match components to form full-scale models. A modeling environment with this feature can provide a universal modeling language to promote worldwide collaborative model building.

3. *Hierarchical structure.* The graphical interface should exist at several levels; high level icons should expand to show the more detailed interactions at the next lower hierarchical level. Through this mechanism,

---

3. Available from ThinkSpace, Inc. (519)–661–4006.
4. Available from Pacific Parallel Research, Inc., Cardiff by the Sea, CA. (619)–481–8427.

the viewer can "zoom out" to see the big picture or "zoom in" to see the detailed structure of the components of the model.

4. *Conceptually simple interface.* Scientists unfamiliar with the environment should be able to begin building and running models almost immediately—the interface should be largely self-explanatory. Viewers unfamiliar with the modeling environment should be able to understand the graphical display of a completed model with little or no explanation.

5. *Modeling toolbox.* The modeling environment should include tools for integrating differential equations, performing sensitivity analyses, and displaying the model output graphically in various forms, as well as providing math tools to support model building.

6. *Modeling database/GIS link.* The modeling environment should be seamlessly linked to a database containing all currently available relevant data in the field of interest, and to a GIS system for manipulation and analysis of spatial data.

7. *Supercomputer link.* The modeling environment should be seamlessly linked to a network of supercomputers so that the completed unit model can be exported to a more powerful platform for fully articulated production runs.

8. *Accessibility.* The modeling environment should run on an inexpensive desktop microcomputer so that it is easily accessible to a wide range of scientists with limited budgets and network access.

The environments that we have chosen for initial development are STELLA (Costanza 1987) and EXTEND, software packages for the Macintosh designed to facilitate model building. STELLA does not incorporate all the features mentioned above; its main strengths are in areas (1), (4), (8), and to a lesser degree, (5). Augmenting STELLA with our SMP translator gives the combined package some capacity for modularity (2). The EXTEND package supports modularity and hierarchy, and contains many other features, such as support for discrete event programming, which go far beyond STELLA's stock and flow formalism. To make the power of EXTEND more accessible, much of the STELLA environment has been recreated within EXTEND.

STELLA uses symbols that are based on Jay Forrester's systems dynamics language (Forrester 1961), which has become popular among modeling practitioners as a way to define and communicate a model's structure. These icons, representing stocks, flows, and functional relationships, are manipulated with the mouse to graphically build the model structure. Once the structure is established, the initial values for the state variables and the form of the rate equations are defined by clicking on the appropriate icon to generate a dialog box. The defining equations can then be typed in analytically, making use of numerous built-in functions, or entered graphically, using either a graph pad or a data table. When the definitions are complete, the model can be run. STELLA will scale the variables automatically and plot up to four variables simultaneously on each output "page." As many pages as necessary can be used to view as much of the model output as desired. In addition, there is the option to plot the change over time of one variable against the change of another variable. STELLA greatly increases the ease with which one can change the model and see the effects of those changes on the model's behavior. It allows the computer to handle the computational details (which is, we think, as it should be) and frees the user to concentrate on modeling, greatly reducing model development time.

The STELLA (or EXTEND) models represent local ecosystem site models that can be linked through horizontal flows of nutrients, sediments, etc. to form spatial ecosystem models. The modeling package will generate an output file containing a set of difference equations that describe the model. This equation file includes initial conditions, model structure equations representing the dynamics of the state variables, and auxiliary equations describing the parameters. These files serve as input to the SMP translator, which integrates the various local models into a spatial ecosystem model.

GIS Systems

Geographic Information Systems (GIS) are software systems used to collect, store, and manipulate spatially referenced data. The development of spatial ecosystem models requires access and manipulation of large quantities of spatial data, such as land use, habitat, and climate maps. These maps will typically be collected from many different sources and come in widely different formats. The GIS component of the SMP handles the crucial tasks of translation, manipulation, and storage of this data.

The SMP can utilize several GISs, including MIPS (Map and Image Processing System), GRASS (Geographic Resource Analysis Support System), and MAP II (Map Analysis Package II). MIPS, which runs on the IBM PC, and GRASS, which runs on the Sun Workstation, are large scale systems capable of data digitizing, data read-in and read-out conversions, image processing, data analysis, and data presentation. These two systems have the advantage of being powerful, versatile, programmable, and capable of performing translation between various map formats. GRASS is capable of reading data in the digital line graph, digital terrain elevation, digital elevation models, and several other formats. Their disadvantages are that they are difficult to learn and use, and are not directly accessible from the Macintosh Operating System (Mac OS).

MAP II, which runs under the Mac OS, is a simple, easy-to-use, raster-based GIS. It is adequate for most applications but lacks (in the current version) the flexibility and extensibility of GRASS and the other systems. In general, we have tried to make the Spatial Modeling Workstation work with a number of GISs so that the user is not limited to those mentioned above, but can take advantage of new developments as they arise.

Parallel Computers

Most existing computers are "serial" in that they have one central processor, and all operations must be done one after the other, in a series, using the single processor. There are inherent speed limitations with this kind of computer architecture, even with the fastest processors. However, many operations (but not all) can be separated into a number of tasks that can all be performed simultaneously. The CELSS spatial ecosystem modeling process (Costanza et al. 1990), image processing, neural networking processes, and GIS systems processing (Burrough 1986) are good examples. For these kinds of problems, much faster solutions on much less expensive hardware are *theoretically* possible by using "parallel computers" with many processors. While this idea has been around for some time, it was hindered in the past by the high cost of central processors and the increased complexity and lack of availability of software for parallel machines. With the advent of microcomputers and low-cost processors, the parallel approach is now being implemented. Several parallel computing options are currently available, and there is much work in progress on parallel software systems.

We have investigated two basic approaches to parallel computer implementation of spatial ecosystem models:

1. The Connection Machine, manufactured by Thinking Machines Inc., which is a large, massively parallel (up to 64,000 processors) "mainframe" parallel computer. We have used two versions—the CM2 and the CM5. The CM2 is a "fine-grained" parallel machine with 16–64 thousand processors, each with approximately the computational power of an IBM PC. The CM5 is a "coarser" grained parallel machine with more powerful (but typically fewer) processors. The CM behaves as an extra processor linked to a front-end serial computer. All code development and user interaction occurs in the UNIX environment of the front end. The CM programming languages are parallel extensions of FORTRAN, Lisp, and C.

2. Transputer-based microcomputer systems—we have used the Pacific Parallel Pac8 ™ system, which consists of Pac8 cards that plug into the slots of a Macintosh II computer (similar boards are also available from other manufacturers for IBM PC compatible computers). Each card can hold up to four Inmos™ Transputers, each with 256KB, 1MB, or 4MB of memory. The Transputer (transistor-computer) is a 32-bit high speed reduced instruction set computer (RISC), based on VLSI technology manufactured by Inmos, Ltd. in the U.K. The Pac8 system operates as an extension of the native Macintosh system. The transputer code is written in C with parallel extensions and developed under the Macintosh Programming Workshop (MPW). Most of the code in the parallel program is identical to the serial version.

When working in the SMP environment, the steps of the parallelization process (described below under *SMP Grid Manager*) are, for the most part, handled automatically. For the fine-grained parallelism of the CM2, each cell of the model is simulated on a separate processor. For the coarse-grained parallelism of the transputers, the spatial grid is divided into sub-areas, and each sub-area assigned to a separate processor. The CM5 falls between these two architectures in the mid-grained range.

According to Pacific Parallel documentation, "Programs that have little or no vector code,[5] that can be made to run in parallel, and that require little communication between processes like: finite state analysis, Monte-Carlo simulation, ray tracing, image processing, differential equations, etc., would require 6-8 modules on 2 Pac8 cards to match the power of

---

5. Vector code refers to computations that can be converted into vectors and operated on in a "psudo-parallel" way by treating the elements of the vectors as being in a "pipeline." Serial elements in the pipeline can be manipulated simultaneously. Most non-linear models and those with discontinuties do not vectorize well.

the CRAY in these instances." CELSS-type spatial simulation models (Costanza et al. 1990) fit this definition perfectly. One should therefore be able to run spatial ecosystem models on a suitably equipped Macintosh II in about the same amount of CPU time as on the CRAY XM/P. Actual timing results are reported in Table 5.4. Since a local microcomputer would eliminate time-intensive communication with the CRAY, the real time necessary to do the job would be significantly less on the microcomputer. The total cost of an 8-transputer system (about $13,000 excluding the Mac II itself) is modest indeed for a system with such capabilities.

Spatial Model Development

The process of spatial model development using the Spatial Modeling Workstation is illustrated in Figure 5.6. This process can be summarized in seven steps:

1. *Unit Model Development.* The ecosystem cell model is developed using the STELLA modeling package. We have developed a generic ecosystem model (GEM) (DeBellevue and Costanza 1990), illustrated in Figure 5.7, which we are using in models currently under development. Figure 5.8 shows a simple hydrologic model implemented in STELLA with the associated STELLA equations for comparison. This model will be used as an example later.

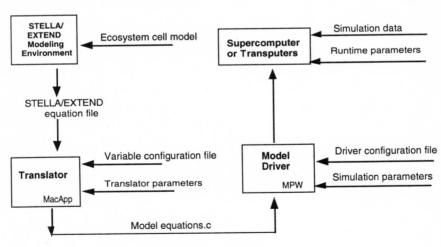

Figure 5.6. The process of translating STELLA models.

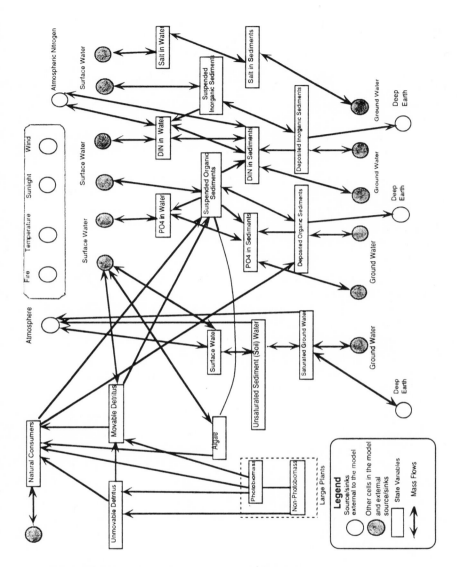

Figure 5.7. Diagram of the Generic Ecosystem Model.

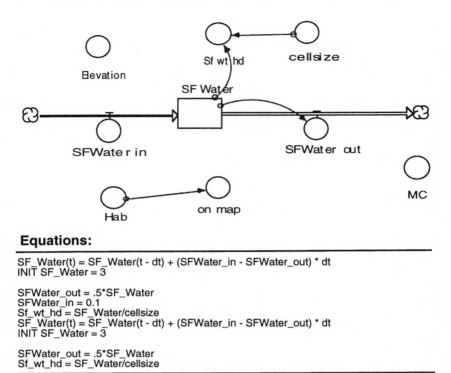

Equations:

SF_Water(t) = SF_Water(t - dt) + (SFWater_in - SFWater_out) * dt
INIT SF_Water = 3

SFWater_out = .5*SF_Water
SFWater_in = 0.1
Sf_wt_hd = SF_Water/cellsize
SF_Water(t) = SF_Water(t - dt) + (SFWater_in - SFWater_out) * dt
INIT SF_Water = 3

SFWater_out = .5*SF_Water
Sf_wt_hd = SF_Water/cellsize

Figure 5.8.   The diagram and equations for a simple hydrologic model in
STELLA.

2. *Data Assembly.* The maps and time series data that will be input to the simulation must be assembled in the proper format. We are currently using Map II interchange format for all input maps, but may soon implement other formats (such as the National Center for Supercomputing Application's HDF format).

3. *Spatial Model Configuration.* This step provides the configuration information that is required in the process of translating from a single cell model in STELLA to a spatially articulated model implemented in C code. At this point the information is provided by editing a text file (Table 5.2), but soon a menu-driven interface will be available.

4. *Automatic Code Generation.* The system automatically generates the C code for the spatially articulated model customized for the specified platform. A sample of translated STELLA equations is shown in Table 5.2.

Table 5.2. A Sample of the Translated STELLA Equations for the Simple
Hydrologic Model of Figure 5.8

```
float *SF_Water, *SFWater_out, *SFWater_in, *Elevation, MC, cellsize;
float *Sf_wt_hd;
unsigned char *Hab, *on_map;

void cell_dyn0(step)
 int step;
 {
int ix, iy;

 for(ix=1; ix<=s0; ix++) {
          for(iy=1; iy<=s1; iy++) {
            if(on_map[T(ix,iy)]) {
                     Sf_wt_hd[T(ix,iy)] = SF_Water[T(ix,iy)]/cellsize ;
            }
          }
 }
 link_maps0();

 for(ix=1; ix<=s0; ix++) {
          for(iy=1; iy<=s1; iy++) {
            if(on_map[T(ix,iy)]) {
                     SFWater_out[T(ix,iy)] =
flux_SW_out(Sf_wt_hd,Elevation,MC,ix,iy);
                     SFWater_in[T(ix,iy)] = flux_SW_in(Sf_wt_hd,Elevation,MC,ix,iy);
                     SF_Water[T(ix,iy)] = SF_Water[T(ix,iy)] +
                              (SFWater_in[T(ix,iy)] - SFWater_out[T(ix,iy)]) * dt;
            }
          }
 }
 }

void init_vars() {
int ix,iy;
  read_map_file("Elevation_map",Elevation,'f',255.0,0.0,0.0);
  MC = .5;
  cellsize = 1;
  for(ix=1; ix<=s0; ix++) {
          for(iy=1; iy<=s1; iy++) {
                   Hab[T(ix,iy)] = 1;
                   on_map[T(ix,iy)] = Hab[T(ix,iy)];
                   SF_Water[T(ix,iy)] = 3;
          }
  }
 }
```

5. *Model Driver Configuration.* This step provides the configuration in-
    formation that is required in the process of running the simulation and
    generating output. At this point the information is provided by editing a
    text file, but soon a menu-driven interface should be available.

6. *Running the Simulation.*

7. *Analyzing Output.* Several built-in methods can display the model's
    output: (1) real-time display of raster maps in a Macintosh window, (2)
    spatial time series output to a folder for animation via a visualization
    tool such as Spyglass View™, (3) output to the Map II GIS application
    for display and analysis, and (4) non-spatial and windowed output
    printed to a set of text files for import into a spreadsheet application.

The spatial model configuration step, which involves editing a configuration file, can be broken down into three components, listed below.
A sample configuration file with some further explanation is reproduced
in Table 5.3.

Table 5.3. Configuration File for the Simple Hydrologic Model of Figure 5.8

* SF_Water		v	0 0		
* SFWater_out	f		0 0		flux_SW_out Sf_wt_hd Elevation MC
* SFWater_in	f		0 0		flux_SW_in Sf_wt_hd Elevation MC
* Hab		c		0 0	NULL
* on_map		c		0 0	NULL
* Elevation		d		0 100	Elevation_map 0.0000 255.0000
* MC		v		0 0	
* cellsize		v		0 0	
* Sf_wt_hd		v		4 4	Surface_Water 0.000000 5.000000

Legend:

The data listed on each line above includes the variable name, the variable type
(VType), how often (in timesteps) to print (outstep) or plot (plotstep) the variable, and
extra data, which depends on the variable type. The table below lists the variable types
and the extra data required for each type.

VType	Meaning	Extra data required on line
v	regular	none
t	timeseries	Data file base name
		Number of points to be read in at once
f	flux function	Name of flux function
		Arguments to flux function
m	map dependent	Map file base name
	parameter	data file name
c	class map	Map file base name
d	surface map	Map file base name
		max value (for rescaling)
		min value (for rescaling)

Also, if plotstep or outstep are set >0, then the map file base name, and maximum and
minimum values for scaling must be listed.

The spatial model configuration process involves several steps:

1. *Define driver platform.* At this step users specify which of the currently supported platforms they intend to use to run the model.

2. *Link input maps with STELLA variables.* Each input map (i.e., elevation, land use, etc.) is linked with a variable in the STELLA model so that when the map is read into the running application, it is stored in the memory allocated to the associated variable.

3. *Link flux variables in STELLA to predefined fluxes.* The model driver supplies a library of predefined intercellular fluxes such as simple diffusion, surface flux based on Manning's equation, etc. Manning's equation (Manning 1890) is one method used to calculate the velocity of water movement across each cell boundary as a function of the slope of the water surface across the boundary and the water depth in the cell. In order to access these fluxes, a flux variable in the STELLA model must be linked with one of the predefined fluxes, and appropriate arguments specified. For example, the surface water flux variable in STELLA is linked with the predefined Manning's equation intercellular flux. The next step in the linking process specifies the arguments elevation, surface water head, and Manning's coefficient, which are variables in the STELLA model.

The model driver configuration step allows model and simulation parameters to be reset at the beginning of each run without requiring recompilation. At this step the following functions are performed:

1. *Set simulation parameters.* The user can set simulation parameters such as timestep, number of iterations, amount of debugging information printed, etc.

2. *Set model parameters.* The user can reset parameters in the STELLA model.

3. *Define model output.* The user can define the output format and frequency for each variable in the STELLA model.

The SMP consists of three components: (1) a *translator* for converting STELLA equations into parallel C code, (2) a *grid manager* for setting up and running the spatial array on the appropriate parallel computer, and (3) a *GIS interface* for handling input and output from the GIS systems. Detailed descriptions of these components can be found in Costanza and Maxwell (1992).

At present, all of the configuration steps listed above are performed by editing text files. We are currently developing a game-like, menu-driven user interface that will link the various component applications of the SMP in a single, user friendly environment. This interface will incorporate several levels of interaction customized to the user's needs. Thus the users, who may range from scientists to policy makers, will be exposed to a level of articulation that is appropriate to their purposes in running/developing the model.

BARATARIA BASIN EXAMPLE APPLICATION

To further test the system described here, we are developing a spatial ecosystem simulation model of the Barataria marsh/estuarine complex in southern Louisiana (Figure 5.2). Our approach is essentially the same as the one described earlier for the CELSS model application to the nearby Atchafalaya/Terrebonne area. The modeled area is divided into seven habitats: fresh marsh, brackish marsh, salt marsh, swamp, open water, upland, and agriculture. Some simulated and actual habitat distributions are shown in Figure 5.4. The same basic cell ecosystem model was used for all habitats, with the parameters of the model varying as a function of habitat. As in the CELSS model, certain physical conditions such as water level rise or fall, change in salt or suspended sediment concentration, etc. were capable of driving cellular habitat succession. The buildup of land or the development of open water in a cell depended on the balance between net inputs of sediments and local organic peat deposition on the one hand, and outputs due to erosion and subsidence on the other hand.

As in the CELSS model, the water flux between neighboring cells was calculated as the difference in water levels between the two cells times a flux constant that depends on the habitats of the two cells. All dissolved materials were assumed to be transported by the water flux alone so that the amount of salt leaving a cell was calculated as the concentration of salt in the cell times the water flux out of the cell. This outflux was balanced by influx from neighboring cells calculated in a similar manner. Time series data for external forcing functions (such as wind, rain, temperature, pumping stations, tides, etc.) were used.

The model is constructed on a 169 by 113 grid of 1-square-kilometer cells that cover the Barataria basin. Only 5,355 (about 1/4) of the 19,097 cell rectangles actually fall within the basin and are considered "active"; the rest are defined to be "void." Within each cell is a local ecosystem model that calculates the state of the system at the next timestep as a function of its current state and inputs (Figure 5.3). The cell unit model is essentially the same one used for the CELSS model (see earlier discussion and Costanza et al. 1990). Changes in physical parameters drive habitat changes within the cells.

Timing comparisons for simulations on the various machines used for the CELSS-type model are shown in Table 5.4, reproduced from White et al. (1992). The CELSS model is highly amenable to parallel processing, but it does not vectorize well on the Cray. The simulation execution time per iteration for this model running on a Macintosh enhanced with 12 transputers falls within an order of magnitude of the time required to run this model on the Cray XMP.

Table 5.4. Comparison of the Time Per Iteration of the CELSS Model Using Various Computers

computer utilized	MacIIx + 12 TP	Vax 11/780	IBM 3033	IBM3090	CRAY X/MP
# cells	5355	2749	2749	2749	2749
# iterations	6126120	3144856	3144856	3144856	3144856
time/simulation (hr)	1.5	24.0	2.0	0.14	0.08
time/iteration (normalized)	9.24	288	24	1.66	1.0

CONCLUSIONS

Parallel computer hardware and software are now well developed enough to allow their use in ecosystem modeling. Parallel systems are particularly well-suited to spatial modeling, allowing relatively complex unit models to be executed over a relatively high resolution spatial array at reasonable cost and speed. When combined (on a user-friendly microcomputer like the Macintosh) with dynamic model development software (like STELLA) and GIS software (like MAP II and GRASS), one has a powerful yet easy-to-use spatial modeling workstation. We have demonstrated these techniques by applying them to a spatial modeling application involving simulations of the Barataria basin in southern Louisiana. These simulations have demonstrated that a Macintosh desktop computer enhanced with relatively inexpensive parallel processing hardware can rival the CRAY supercomputer in speed of computation for some (highly-parallelizable but non-vectorizable) problems. The desktop environment is far superior in terms of ease of use. The spatial modeling workstation we have developed (Figure 5.5) should allow the application of advanced computer modeling techniques to a much broader range of problems, especially those involving detailed, spatially articulate ecosystem and landscape modeling.

In addition, the widespread use of intelligent modeling environments (IMEs) linked transparently to state-of-the-art distributed computing resources could result in a fundamental paradigm shift in computer modeling. The IMEs impose the constraints of modularity and hierarchy in program design. General usage of linked IMEs will support the development of libraries of modules representing reusable model components that are globally available to model builders, as well as making advanced computing architectures available to users with little computer knowledge. Scientists will then be able to build on the work of others instead of starting from scratch each time a new model is initiated. It is possible that the adoption of this paradigm will represent a revolution in computer modeling as fundamental as the invention of standardization and the assembly line process was to the industrial revolution.

ACKNOWLEDGMENTS

This research was supported by the National Science Foundation, Grant #BSR-8906269 titled, "Landscape Modeling: the Synthesis of Ecological Processes Over Large Geographic Regions and Long Time Scales," R. Costanza and F. H. Sklar, Principal Investigators, and by the U. S. Fish and Wildlife Service under purchase order #84110-89-00682 titled, "Parallel Processor Computer Modeling System Development," R. Costanza, Principal Investigator. We would like to thank E. DeBellevue, S. Tennenbaum, and two anonymous reviewers for helpful comments on earlier drafts.

REFERENCES

Boumans, R. M. J., and F. H. Sklar. 1991. A polygon-based spatial model for simulating landscape change. *Landscape Ecology* 4: 83–97.

Braat, L. C., and I. Steetskamp. 1991. Ecological economic analysis for regional sustainable development. In Ecological Economics: the Science and Management of Sustainability, ed. R. Costanza. New York: Columbia Univ. Press.

Braat, L. C., and W. F. J. van Lierop. 1985. A Survey of Economic-Ecological Models. Laxenburg, Austria: International Institute for Applied Systems Analysis, A-2361.

Burrough, P. A. 1986. Principles of Geographic Information Systems for Land Resources Assessment. Oxford: Clarendon Press.

Colwell, R. K. 1974. Predictability, constancy, and contingency of periodic phenomena. *Ecology* 55: 1148–53.

Costanza, R. 1987. Simulation modeling on the Macintosh using STELLA. *BioScience* 37:129–132

————. 1989. Model goodness of fit: a multiple resolution procedure. *Ecological Modelling* 47: 199–215.

Costanza, R., and T. Maxwell. 1992. Spatial ecosystem modelling using parallel processors. *Ecological Modelling* 58: 159.

Costanza, R., F. H. Sklar, and J. W. Day, Jr. 1986. Modeling spatial and temporal succession in the Atchafalaya/Terrebonne marsh/estuarine complex in south Louisiana. In Estuarine Variability, ed. D. A. Wolfe. New York: Academic Press.

Costanza, R., F. H. Sklar, and M. L. White. 1990. Modeling coastal landscape dynamics. *BioScience* 40: 91–107.

DeBellevue, E., and Costanza, R. 1990. UGEALUM: a Modelling Approach for Simulation and Evaluation of Landscapes. New Perspectives in the Chesapeake System: A Research and Management Partnership. Conference proceedings, Chesapeake Research Consortium Publication No. 137.

Forrester, J. W. 1961. Industrial Dynamics. Cambridge, MA: MIT Press.

Gardner, R. H., B. T. Milne, M. G. Turner, and R. V. O'Neill. 1987. Neutral models for the analysis of broad-scale landscape pattern. *Landscape Ecology* 1: 19–28.

Kadlec, R. H., and D. E. Hammer. 1988. Modeling nutrient behavior in wetlands. *Ecological Modelling* 40: 37–66

Kessell, S. R. 1977. Gradient modeling: a new approach to fire modeling and resource management. In Ecosystem Modeling in Theory and Practice, eds. C. A. S. Hall and J. W. Day, Jr. New York: Wiley.

Krummel, J. R., R. H. Gardner, G. Sugihara, and R. V. O'Neill. 1987. Landscape patterns in a disturbed environment. *Oikos* 48: 321–4.

Maguire, L. A., and J. W. Porter. 1977. A spatial model of growth and competition strategies in coral communities. *Ecological Modelling* 3: 249–71.

Mandelbrot, B. B. 1983. The Fractal Geometry of Nature. San Francisco, CA: W. H. Freeman.

Manning, R. 1890. Flow of Water in Open Channels and Pipes. Transactions of the Institute of Civil Engineers, Volume 20. Ireland.

Risser, P. G., J. R. Karr, and R. T. T. Forman. 1984. Landscape Ecology: Directions and Approaches. Special Publication No. 2. Champaign: Illinois Natural History Survey.

Show, I. T., Jr. 1979. Plankton Community and Physical Environment Simulation for the Gulf of Mexico Region. Proceedings of the 1979 Summer Computer Simulation Conference. San Diego: Society for Computer Simulation.

Sklar, F. H., R. Costanza, and J. W. Day, Jr. 1985. Dynamic spatial simulation modeling of coastal wetland habitat succession. *Ecological Modeling* 29: 261–81.

Sklar, F. H., and R. Costanza. 1991. The development of dynamic spatial models for landscape ecology: a review and prognosis. In Quantitative Methods in Landscape Ecology, eds. M. G. Turner and R. Gardner. Ecological Studies Vol. 82. New York: Springer-Verlag.

Turner, M. G., R. Costanza, and F. H. Sklar. 1989. Methods to compare spatial patterns for landscape modeling and analysis. *Ecological Modelling* 48: 1–18.

Urban, D. L., R. V. O'Neill, and H. H. Shugart. 1987. Landscape Ecology, a Hierarchical Perspective. *BioScience* 37: 119–27.

Weins, J. A., C. S. Crawford, and J. R. Gosz. 1985. Boundary dynamics: a conceptual framework for studying landscape ecosystems. *Oikos* 45: 421–7.

White, M., D. Day, T. Maxwell, R. Costanza, and F. Sklar. 1992. Ecosystem modelling utilizing desktop parallel computer technology: the contributions of freshwater and sediment to habitat succession in the wetlands of Louisiana. In Hydraulic and Environmental Modelling: Estuarine and River Waters, ed. R. Falconer. Aldershot, Hampshire, U.K.: Ashgate.

6 THE NATURAL PHILOSOPHY OF NATURAL CAPITAL: CAN SOLAR ENERGY SUBSTITUTE?[1]

Jane King and Malcolm Slesser
Centre for Human Ecology
University of Edinburgh
Buccleuch Place 15
Edinburgh EH 9 LN
Scotland

INTRODUCTION

There are three types of natural capital: depletable, recyclable, and renewable. At present all economies depend on a sustained, and often growing, rate of supply of depletable natural capital. We pose the question of whether it is possible for the world's economy to build the systems to capture solar energy on a scale sufficient to replace depletable natural capital sources, before these become seriously depleted. The question is addressed through a dynamic natural capital accounting procedure known as ECCO, to create a model of the world expressed as two regions—developed and developing countries. The procedure demonstrates that the dynamics of substitution are, in certain circumstances, feasible for the Developed (First) World, but not so for the Less Developed (Third) World, due to the latter's low capacity for wealth creation and its higher population growth. Some alternative solutions are explored. The interim conclusion of this study is that, given the data base and solar capture technologies currently available, *the transition from a*

---

1. A list of abbreviations and symbols is provided in Appendix A. Note especially that "HMC" stands for Human-Made Capital, i.e., physical (artificial) capital stock; and "DNC" for Depletable Natural Capital, i.e., non-renewable energy resources. Note also that *fuels* are energy vectors available on the market for immediate effective use, whereas *energy* is considered to represent primary sources yet to be transformed to useful forms.

world economy based on the depletion of natural capital to one that is truly sustainable is only possible if both coal and nuclear energy continue to be used as energy sources for at least the next fifty years.

NATURAL CAPITAL DEPLETION

In our optimistic moments we like to think that human potential is boundless, and so it is in spirit. It is, however, constrained by the reality of the physical universe. Nevertheless, we humans have managed to exploit the earth's *natural capital* to create a vast human-made physical capital stock (HMC), whereby we provide food, fuel, clothing, and shelter for the majority of the Earth's inhabitants. In doing so we have damaged the environment and dissipated much of what we have inherited.

Since the stock of natural capital is finite, how long can this depletion and erosion continue? With what do we replace it in order to maintain our economic systems? This chapter explores in a quantitative manner the potential to substitute solar energy for one particular type of natural capital, namely depletable natural capital.

In order to proceed, we need to distinguish between different types of natural capital, and understand the nature of Human-Made Capital (HMC) and what factors determine the viability of solar energy capture systems.

Types of Natural Capital

The term "Natural Capital" embraces Nature's gifts to humankind: physical resources, and what we like to refer to in a qualitative manner as "the environment." Natural capital occurs in three fundamental forms:

- depletable (i.e., non-renewable energy resources),
- recyclable (i.e., non-energy minerals resources), and
- renewable or potentially renewable (i.e., soils, the environment—which is often irretrievably degraded).

The demands on Depletable Natural Capital (DNC) are many and determine to a great extent, in conjunction with Human-Made Capital (HMC), the potential for recycling and renewing other forms of natural capital.

Quantifying the amount of DNC required to achieve any particular economic activity has been the objective of *energy analysis*, whose fundamental conventions were laid down at a workshop in Sweden in 1974 sponsored by IFIAS (1975), and which have formed the basis of our work since then.

Human-Made Capital

Production, as Georgescu-Roegen (1972) and others (e.g., Roberts 1982) have observed, is (from a thermodynamic point of view) a procedure in which chaos is reduced and order is increased. One may use the thermo-dynamic term *entropy* as a measure of disorder.

Manufacturing a product like a motor vehicle is not wrought in one magic process, but is the result of fabricating many components, which when assembled, become a product capable of doing a job. Disorder, in the form of many separate components, becomes order in the form of a vehicle—so, too, for the photo-voltaic cell, the wind-generator, the wave-capture device, etc.

We can also consider the production of the components themselves. For example, iron ores are converted to iron, then steel, then stamped into forms used in the assembly of the vehicle. Each stage is a reduction in entropy, and thus an increase in order, often called *negentropy*. In well-defined processes, these changes may be precisely computed (using the concept underlying the Second Law of Thermodynamics) with data found in physics-chemical tables.

As applied to production, the Second Law may be paraphrased as fol-lows:

> In order to achieve a reduction in entropy in one part of the system, elsewhere, at the same moment, there has to be a sacrifice of order into chaos of at least equal magnitude, i.e., at least an equal increase in en-tropy. In other words, the decrease in entropy (negative entropy = ne-gentropy) of one part must be matched by an equal or greater consump-tion of negentropy elsewhere.

Thus production in negentropy terms is a zero sum game. Virtually the only practical sources of negentropy are fossil fuels on combustion, fissile fuels on fission, and solar energy captured and converted into bio-fuels, or into thermodynamic work through solar capture devices like wind-generators or photo-voltaic cells.

Depletable Natural Capital

The fact that most negentropy is drawn from finite energy resources suggests that it should be incorporated into economic assessment. Since DNC is consumed in production of HMC, one may say of that capital stock that it "contains" embodied energy. If this is true, then the total amount of capital stock in any sector of the economy can be quantified as the total energy embodied in its manufacture, and consider its growth and depreciation in the same terms.

Human-Made Capital and Development

HMC stock has many uses, some essential for life-support, such as the provision of food, fuel, water, etc., and some, which though not essential for survival, play a considerable role in enhancing the quality of our lives. HMC is unevenly divided among the world's people, though on average there is enough for all. The conventional solution to this inequity is to stimulate economic growth and thereby create development everywhere without sacrificing any regional levels of welfare already attained. This solution, applied unthinkingly, will merely exacerbate the depletion of DNC.

Development, essentially a process of creating ever more HMC, stems from production. Energy analysis techniques calculate the amount of DNC embodied in the production of any HMC. It is then but a short step to constructing a macro-economic model in which HMC and DNC are related through the systems and technologies used, a procedure called *natural capital accounting*. It can be accomplished through the simulation modeling system known as ECCO (RUI 1992)

Technological development hopefully reduces the DNC requirement per unit of HMC produced, as well as the rate of its depletion. Technological development calls for new HMC, and underlines the fact that we must invest to become more energetically efficient.

The Solar Breeder

Solar energy may be a free good, but to capture and deliver it as a useful fuel to the market requires human-made devices, that is HMC. To make this HMC, which will be composed of machined metals, glasses, and many esoteric inputs, requires the prior dissipation of high-grade fuels in its manufacture.

If the device can deliver over its lifetime more fuel of same quality than is consumed in its manufacture, then we have an energy-breeding device, at least so far as the Earth is concerned (Slesser 1976). It is then, in principle, possible to substitute solar energy for depletable natural capital. Clearly the higher the capture efficiency of the device, and the smaller the embodied DNC per unit solar flux captured and usefully transformed, then the faster one can substitute solar energy for DNC.

Dynamics of Substitution by Solar Energy

The question then arises as to whether sufficient HMC can be built to capture solar energy before one of the following events occurs:

- fossil energy sources become seriously depleted,
- carbon dioxide reduction become mandatory, or
- per capita global wealth production goes into decline.

There is, of course, no unique answer to any of these questions. Much depends on the environmental and economic policies adopted by countries of the world in the interim. However, it is important to appreciate that this question is not a simple one of exchange of technology, but involves the dynamics of building up an entirely new energy capture and transformation infrastructure. Thus a subsidiary question is whether the world's productive capacity has the means to do it, even if people have the creativity and the will.

Creation of Wealth

To provide a quantitative answer to this question, we need to determine whether the burden of investing in solar energy capture and transforming it into a physical capital stock will undermine or enhance the rate of global wealth production. A robust way to do this is to measure the amount of DNC required to produce a unit of HMC devoted to the capture of solar energy and compare it with that required to operate the economy on fossil and fissile fuels. In other words, we need to know the amount of DNC embodied in the creation of all forms of HMC. If this is done not merely for the energy system, but the entire economy, a model of the economy can be created in physical terms, in which wealth creation and wealth consumption (in all sectors) can be quantified.

Where We Are Going?

Before considering the model used and results obtained, it may be useful to consider a current perspective on future energy consumption

There are two conflicting views of the long-term world energy situation. The optimistic one, as reflected in Keyfitz (1982), is that world energy use is but a fraction of a percent of incident solar radiation, so that all we need to do is apply our technological skills to capture it. A less optimistic view is that reflected in the writings of Georgescu-Roegen (1972), who pointed out that sooner or later, the rate of supply of the world's sources of negative entropy (negentropy, i.e., depletable natural capital) may not match the rate of entropy increase dictated by the nature of the human-made capital system that has been created and upon which we have based our life-style. Thereafter, economic decline is inevitable.

Both are right, and both are wrong. The optimists are right as to potential, but naive as to dynamics. Georgescu-Roegen's analysis is correct for a closed system, but not if we include the ability to harness solar energy as a replacement for DNC.

There is a still a great deal of DNC in the Earth. However, not all of it is highly accessible. Consider our 1992 estimate (using our GlobEcco model) that to drive the world's economy will require a rate of depletion of DNC of 259 EJ/y in the Developed (First) World and 128 EJ/y in the Developing (Third) World—387 EJ/y in all, not including solar capture through photosynthesis. Though this rate of consumption of DNC is a small proportion of the total stock believed to exist in the Earth (McLaren 1987), by 2015, 80% of the easily accessible (i.e., economic at current prices), and 35% of ultimate oil and gas resources will have been tapped *if* current economic and population policies persist. Table 6.1 summarizes the prospect by 2015 if current policies continue. Note that although there is a massive capture of solar energy by photosynthesis (estimate 3000 EJ/y by Hall and De Groot reported in McLaren and Skinner 1987, 487), all of this is recycled within the biosphere. Capturing a surplus requires land- and energy-based inputs. The net energy per hectare of such systems does not justify their use beyond a limited scale.

Table 6.1. World Energy Resource Base in 1992 and Predicted in 2015

Resource base	oil	gas	coal	uranium
Present (total)	14.3	13.7	259	2.2
(easily accessible)	4.3	3.7	238	1.3
cumulative use 1992–2015	4.2	3.1	5.4	879E3[*]
2015 resource base	10.1	10.6	254	NONE

[*]However, there is 10E12 tonnes of uranium in sea-water.
Data in 1000 EJ (E9 GJ).
Sources: Depletable natural capital base (reserves+resources) in 1992 (from 2015 forecast from McLaren and Skinner 1987), and natural capital consumption based on GlobEcco model (Slesser and Saraph 1991) assuming 1992 policies persist to 2015.

The Sustainable Alternatives to Depleting Natural Capital

There would appear to be only three physically sustainable alternatives to natural capital depletion:

1. fast breeder reactors, which can extend the existing stocks of uranium-238 by a factor of fifty—very long term but not ultimately sustainable;

2. fusion reactors, making use of huge reserves of deuterium; or

3. use of solar flux or its derivatives.

Option 1 requires only the extension of existing tested technology. It must be said that many people have grave doubts about its desirability on grounds of safety, waste fuel storage, and potential for terrorism. There is, however, an enormous stock (in the sense of its energy potential) of already mined and purified U-238 on hand in many countries.

Option 2 is still a technological dream. There are those who believe it will come to pass within the next 25 years. Even so, penetration of this technology will take much time. It is, nonetheless, a nuclear technology, with all the disadvantages of the fast-breeder option, except that the fuel supply is so large as to put back the "entropy" issue beyond conceivable time horizons. It can be argued that if fusion is to be used, why not use a rather large and successful reactor—the sun—situated a safe 150 million kilometers away.

Option 3, *the Sun*, is widely canvassed. As yet the total world investment in solar capture (outside photosynthesis for food production) is trivial compared to that used for tapping DNC. The arguments in its favor are that it is benign, renewable, and falls upon the entire world as a flux almost 10,000 times greater than the current global rate of depletion of natural capital. It is a free good. Unfortunately, the most obvious method of capture, photosynthesis, offers no way forward for two reasons. First, averaged over a year, photosynthetic capture is rarely above 0.1% of incident solar energy, and is usually much lower. Second, there is simply not enough land in the world to produce a surplus over the output required from crops and forests. If solar energy is to be used, then it must be through direct technical intervention, using human-made devices like wind generators, photo-voltaics, wave generators, and other devices yet to be invented.

All these technologies have one advantage over fossil energy in that they form neither carbon dioxide, sulfur dioxide, nor nitrogen oxides. However, they have one weakness in common. They cannot easily produce a valuable fuel vector like liquid hydrocarbons. Nuclear heat can be used to turn coal into gas and liquid fuels. They can all produce electricity, and so can electrolyze water to produce hydrogen, either as an alternative fuel vector or in conjunction with coal to produce hydrocarbons. Whether the coal option is acceptable renews the carbon dioxide/greenhouse gas issue. For the moment, given the results of the Rio de Janeiro conference, one must assume that all steps possible will be taken to diminish carbon dioxide output.

High Quality Solar-Sourced Energy

HMC stock consists of many components made with high quality energies, often at high temperatures. The capture of solar heat at low temperatures (as in hot water generators or space heating), while a valuable contribution to the world's energy needs, is not of a quality that can turn ores into metals or fabricate structures. Of course one can add further technology to upgrade the temperature of the solar heat, but this is also capital-intensive and less efficient. Such processes are likely to be net energy sinks (Slesser 1980). If solar energy is to replace DNC, then it must deliver to the economy a high-grade energy source, (i.e., be a good solar energy breeder).

With current solar technologies, it is only through electricity generation that high quality energy can be produced. Hence, for the purposes of focusing on the dynamics of replacing DNC with solar energy, we shall here consider only the production of electricity and its use to provide an energy vector like hydrogen as a partial replacement for fossil fuels. Table 6.2 provides a reference profile for a "Business-as-Usual" world that continues 1992 policies. It shows our estimate (from GlobEcco, Slesser and Saraph 1991) of the contribution of various fuel sources to the world electricity supply in 2015 (13.36 E43 TWh/y).

Table 6.2. Estimated Means of Electricity Generation in 2015

solar		nuclear			fossil
hydro-power	other	thermal	fast fission	fusion	
20	8	11	3	0	58

Global demand = 13.36 e3 TWh/y in 2015.
Data as percentage.
Source: GlobEcco

Solar Energy

Solar energy is a high quality energy source reaching the Earth in a rather diffuse form. At its most intense, it provides about 3.6 MJ/h.m2. Such is the situation in the Egyptian desert at noon in summer. By way of sens-ing the scale involved, to replace 100% of the world's energy demand in 1992 at 100% capture and transformation efficiency would therefore re-quire the dedication of a mere 1.23 million hectares of desert land. However, taking into account inefficiencies, other geographical loca-tions, load factors, and transformation losses, the area required cannot be less than 400 million ha. To put this in perspective, that is 22 times the present urban land area, but only 4.5% of the world's cultivatable land area. In the present study dealing only with electricity, much less area, of course, would be required (see below).

Investment for Solar Capture

In order to consider the substitution of solar technologies for DNC, one needs to know the capital intensity of solar energy capture systems in terms of the embodied DNC in HMC per kWh delivered. At the moment, virtually all such HMC is made by processes depleting DNC. However, as solar substitution takes place, the embodied DNC in HMC will de-cline.

The capital investment to create a device to capture solar energy and deliver it as a high quality energy supply (e.g., as work, electricity) is about the same per installed MW as that for thermal nuclear, and is somewhat cheaper than fast-fission breeder reactors. Hydro-electricity is, however, generally much cheaper, but limited in availability. There the similarity ends. Nuclear can attain higher load factors—80% has often been achieved. Solar driven systems can be expected to attain between 13% and 21% depending on location. This is because the wind does not always blow, and the sun does not shine 24 hours a day.

On the other hand, solar systems, apart from their construction, require no fuels—or very little. However, except for wave generators, solar systems require significant land areas. Worldwatch (1990) estimates 66 ha/GW for wind generators and 280 ha/GW for photo-voltaics. However, in the case of wind, it is possible for crops to be grown in much of the area required.

If one made the assumption that half of the world's electricity were to come from solar in 2015, and of this half, half again from photo-voltaic and half from wind, then 776,000 ha would be required for electricity generation. This is a tiny portion (.00087%) of the world's cultivatable land area, none of which must be arable. Thus, at first sight, the area factor does not seem significant, providing we are only dealing with electricity provision. If we can create an essentially electrically driven economy, or use solar electricity to electrolyze water in a hydrogen-driven economy, then both the investments and areas would be no more than one order of magnitude greater.

The Dynamics of Change

There is a further factor. Proceeding along the path of depletion of natural capital requires no revolution, only evolution. Retrofit, energy conservation, rationalization, movement toward economies of scale, and proven technologies all conspire to maintain the structure of fuel supply along well-trodden paths. The question we must ask of ourselves is whether there is enough time for a transition to renewable energy systems before the scarcity crunch comes. Moreover, there may be another important factor—carbon dioxide emissions. Will the world have to cut back on fossil fuels? If so, coal is the obvious candidate for elimination, for it produces on combustion 88kg CO_2 per GJ of heat, as opposed to 65kg for natural gas. By 2015, if no steps are taken to deal with the problem, the world's CO_2 output could be 31 billion tonnes/y, 20% more than today. Yet coal is twenty times more abundant than oil and gas, and so it is the obvious candidate to use with nuclear heat to create synthetic hy-drocarbon fuels.

METHODOLOGY: NATURAL CAPITAL ACCOUNTING

The Role of Energy in Production

As Weissmahr (1991) has pointed out, the traditional factors of produc-tion—land, labor, and capital—have not provided a coherent evolution-ary theory of wealth creation or of economic growth. We now understand that production potential depends, inter alia, on the ability to develop sustainable energy resources. The missing ingredient in the production function has been energy. With the inclusion of energy, one can explain not only the evolution of the economy from the times of hunter-gatherers to the present day, but the decline and fall of many civilizations (White 1949).

In a modern economy human beings make decisions. Energy is used to do work, for the thermodynamic work potential of a human being is trivial. It amounts to about 0.6kWh–0.8kWh per day, which may be pur-chased for about 1/400 of the average European daily wage. One does not employ workers merely for their physical effort, but for their ability to make decisions, no matter how simple these may be. Human capital thus includes not only people and their ability to create ideas and make decisions, but the stock of existing knowledge—theirs and that of their predecessors.

To drive an economy, physical capital stock, human capital, and en-ergy are all needed. Land plays a vital role. Land area is a surrogate for the lithosphere, wherein lie the minerals we exploit, and upon whose surface we find that which we loosely call the visible environment. Land is important not only for cultural reasons, but because the natural pro-cesses of solar energy capture are area dependent. Moreover, land area is finite. It cannot be increased (except where the sea area is decreased, but these are trivial variations). Natural capital embraces the many complex factors of land.

Models of Development

In a qualitative sense, development is always desirable, and the processes of economic growth must be related to the nature and level of develop-ment desired. For a successful outcome, much depends on how our wealth creation is partitioned between investment and consumption. This is not purely an economic issue, but also a social and moral one. Nonetheless, for progress, HMC must be created and for that, output must exceed consumption.

Any useful model of development must take into account how stocks of DNC decline and stocks of HMC increase. Where there is change in stocks, there are necessarily rates to account for those changes and driving forces to stimulate them. Nothing changes without stimulus. It can be argued that such stimuli are human creativity, will, or even greed. Whatever they are, they result in changes in the stock of knowledge, human-made physical capital, and natural capital. Such changes may be both quantitative and qualitative. Only in the case of physical capital is it easy to measure those changes.

Rate Processes and Stocks

It follows that two of the elements of economic evolution are rate processes—energy supply and human creativity (or knowledge creation), and three of the elements of economic evolution are stocks—knowledge, Human-Made (physical) Capital (HMC), and DNC. There is, however, a third rate factor that plays a significant role—the rate of change of population.

The stock of knowledge is changed by education and research, both of which require investment of HMC. That stock is increased through industrial output, itself requiring investment in HMC and fuels for its operation. The stock of DNC is depleted by the consumption of energy and minerals and the destruction or alteration of the environment. The stock of people is changed by birth and death rates.

The ECCO Model

This way of looking at the economy offers a way of identifying physically feasible futures. This is not without value, for if a process is not physically feasible, it cannot be economically possible.

This may be done if one recognizes that at all times, the fuel (as opposed to the primary energy, DNC, from which it is derived) required to drive the system and the appropriate HMC must be in place. The fact that fuel, unlike money, cannot be borrowed sets a rigorous physical rate constraint on the economic system that may not surface when quantifying in monetary units. If, then, the fuel used to create HMC (i.e., the embodied DNC in capital stock) is linked to the ability of the economy to release further DNC, one can measure the surplus available for further investment and thus assess the physical potential of the system to expand.

Clearly this potential depends on the resource base, the population density, the policies in play, and the technologies in use, not to mention the impact of humanly devised constraints of management quality or environmental concerns.

In order to identify the physical potential, a macro-economic modeling procedure called ECCO (Evolution of Capital Creation Options) has been devised (RUI 1992), whose objective is to assess the potential for economic development at the national or global level in the context of the consequent rate of depletion of the Earth's DNC and/or its substitution by renewable energy sources.

Sector by sector it computes rates of capital formation, energy requirements by type, pollution, and the economic and physical effects of imposing environmental constraints. ECCO computes the DNC embodied in capital stock and the operational fuel required to create the necessary outputs or exogenously imposed environmental constraints.

Thus the rate of change of the economy is set by both the rate of creativity and the rate at which energy can be efficiently used. In consecutive rate processes, the limiting rate is always the slowest (as in a single lane road).

ECCO is designed to take account of DNC, fuel, capital, and land. It regards labor as human capital. Since human ingenuity is boundless, the limiting rate of change of the system is the rate at which energy can be *usefully* absorbed by the economy. This in turn means that it depends on the nature and quality of the HMC available to use it, and whether that HMC is applied to consumption or capital investment. Investment can be for good or ill, wise or foolish.

Such a modeling procedure is not a scenario-driven set of assumptions in which the user is left to choose from a range on offer. Rather the user selects the policies to be explored, the technologies on offer, and the environmental constraints to be imposed. This done, ECCO ascertains the potential growth rate of the system. The criteria of growth are left to the user. Some may see it as GDP, others as capital stock, others as welfare, etc.

Many ECCO models have been constructed dealing with developing countries, the U.K., and the E.C. The model used here to explore the solar option is a global model, GlobEcco.[2]

GlobEcco Applied to the Penetration of Solar Energy Capture

GlobEcco (Slesser and Saraph 1991) is a world model, disaggregated into two economic groups—the developed (First=FW) world and developing (Third=TW) world. As with any aggregated model, it deals with averages. For example, nuclear energy is to be found only in some TW countries, but the total capacity of the nuclear sector is attributed to the entire TW region in the model.

The economy is divided into 23 sectors. Some of these are energy supply sectors comprising coal, oil, gas, nuclear, conventional thermal, hydro, and biomass. Agriculture is partitioned as arable, grazing, non-cereal food crops, non-food crops, animal protein, and fish. Irrigation needs are taken into account. There is a three age group demographic module. Births and death are moderated by a material standard-of-living indicator.

Environmental concerns are reflected in indicators of industrial, municipal, and human wastes; nuclear inventories; and sulfur dioxide and carbon dioxide emissions. In the last two, a module for reducing them via technical fixes is available to the user. Conventional indicators like GDP provide a comparison with traditional econometric model outputs.

The model has 850 statements, half of which are in array form, and are thus equivalent to a model of 1,600 statements.

SOLAR ENERGY SUBSTITUTION OF NATURAL CAPITAL

Reference Profile: Business-as-Usual (BAU)

Business-as-Usual (BAU) is a catch phrase for the continuation of current policies. A BAU (reference) profile of the two world regions makes the assumption that such policies will continue. In reality this is unlikely.

---

2. GlobEcco is a proprietary model that can be run on a PC. It can be adapted readily for use in national studies. A program listing and description is available from the Resource Use Institute, 12 Findhorn Place, Edinburgh, EH9, Scotland. It was developed in 1991–92 by M. Slesser with the expert assistance of Anupam Saraph (see also RUI 1992).

Indeed, the BAU profile is not encouraging (Figures 6.1 and 6.2), and one would imagine that in due course, it would become obvious that BAU will lead to global instability. However, as we know, business does tend to be "as usual" in the short term, at least in government circles, which tend to favor the status quo. Nonetheless, a model "run" with BAU is useful as a basis for comparison with "runs" where other polices and technologies have been tested.

In BAU, all energy systems compete for a share of the market on the basis that penetration favors those requiring the least investment per unit output. The higher load factor of nuclear energy gives it a competitive edge over solar. Nonetheless, non-hydro solar electricity rises to 14% by 2042 due to a steady reduction in its capital intensiveness as a result of anticipated technical innovation.

Population increases by 6% in the developed world (FW) and by 77% in the developing (TW) world. In Figure 6.1 the following indicators (criteria) are exhibited:

- Index of industrial output (world), 1992=1: INDEXW;
- Index of material standard of living, 1992=1: MSOLF(FW) for the Developed World; and MSOLF(TW) for the Developing World.

Figure 6.2 shows the world growth in electricity demand and carbon dioxide output:

- carbon dioxide output, t/y : CO_2
- electricity demand, GWh/y : EEDW

With BAU, the global economic system peaks in about 40 years (2030). The material standard of living (MSOL) continues to rise in the Developed World (FW), but peaks in the Developing World (TW) in 2010 and then declines steeply. Global carbon dioxide rises to over 30 billion t/y. By 2042, 81% of the world's easily ("economically") accessible oil and gas has been consumed.

The reason for the eventual decline is that the demand for capital investment to maintain the economic infrastructure, and to provide food, fuel, and services by 2030 exceeds the ability of the industrial system to furnish it due to the earlier emphasis in BAU on producing consumer goods at the expense of capital goods.

In the results reported hereafter, the BAU profiles are included for comparison.

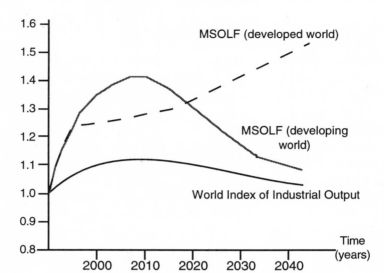

Figure 6.1. Business-as-Usual indices of change.

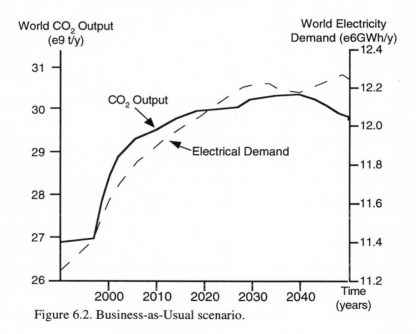

Figure 6.2. Business-as-Usual scenario.

Accelerated Penetration of Solar Electricity

In this study only three solar-electric technologies were incorporated: hydro-power, wind energy, and photo-voltaics. The capital intensity of wave energy is thought to be higher than other solar-driven technologies, even if its load factor is greater. This option remains to be tested when better data is at hand. The technical data required for each technology, such as investment costs, load factor, and land area requirements have already been entered into the GlobEcco program and used in the BAU reference profile.

The procedure is to explore the accelerated introduction of these technologies with the aim of replacing DNC as a source of fuel for the economy. In these policy tests, the user prescribes the proportion of total electricity production from non-fossil sources desired (EPNONFOS) at future time periods for both FW and TW. The policies tested are summarized in Table 6.3. In the policies mentioned there, the word "deliberate" implies a decision enforced by government that overrides free market forces. This chapter will not cover how this may be done.

Table 6.3. Policies Tested

Run Name	Policy Pursued
BAU	Business-as-usual from 1992 to 2042. Ignores impending energy resource scarcity.
Solar 1	Deliberate, but modest additional penetration of solar electricity in both FW and TW. Nuclear energy continues.
Solar 5	Deliberate high investment in solar electricity in FW and TW: nuclear energy continues.
Solar 7	As with Solar 5, but further nuclear construction ceases in 1995 in FW and TW.
Solar 10	As Solar 7, but curb on consumption in FW to permit higher investment in capital goods.
Solar 13	As Solar 10, but with AID to the TW from FW increased by a factor of six.
Solar 16	As Solar 13, but with deliberate high investment in energy conservation in FW.
Solar 17	As Solar 16, but with significant additional family planning in TW.
Solar 18	As Solar 17, but with nuclear energy option available at all times in FW and TW.

Solar 1: Enhanced penetration of solar electricity. The policy here is a deliberate phased introduction of solar electricity with the object of reaching 100% by 2042 in FW, and 80% in TW. These targets are not ac-

tually achieved for two reasons: (1) nuclear energy still takes a sizable fraction of investment in non-fossil energy because it has much the same capital cost, and (2) system growth induces lags. The heavy investment costs of solar capture systems in relation to output (low load factors) eventually undermines investment in the productive manufacturing sector, and causes the world economy to decline even sooner than in BAU (Figure 6.3). As a result, electricity consumption scarcely grows, and although by 2042, CO_2 output is back to 1992 rates, this is largely due to economic decline. Cumulative consumption of natural capital is barely changed from BAU. Moreover, by 2015, 80% of the easily accessible Uranium has also been used. Perhaps a more aggressive policy of solar penetration would pay off.

Solar 5: Fast penetration of solar electricity. Here, the policy sets a target of 100% in FW by 2002 and in TW by 2012. This achieves a solar electricity fraction of over 50% by 2042. This brings down CO_2 rates to 23 billion t/y by 2042, but the high investment required for solar erodes world industrial output (Figure 6.4), and though MSOL in FW is not seriously affected, in TW it falls to 42% of the 1992 figure by 2042.

Solar 7: Fast penetration of solar with no further nuclear. In this policy, nuclear construction world-wide ceases in 1995 (existing plants remain, but depreciate), and a high rate of solar electric penetration is sought. By 2042 the result is disastrous. Industrial output falls to 64% of the 1992 output, MSOL scarcely rises in FW, and falls to 44% in TW. The only good outcomes are that solar electric now provides 73% of all electricity, and CO_2 rates are down to 19.6 billion t/y. Also, there is a slight drop in the consumption of natural capital. Clearly there is no future for the world along this path, with or without nuclear electricity.

Solar 10: Reduced emphasis on consumption goods. Here the policy is to stimulate investment goods at the expense of consumption goods (by taxing consumption?) so that consumption grows 3% slower than the growth of industrial investment. This policy quickly pays off at world level. Industrial output grows 35% between 1992 and 2042 (Figure 6.5a). As to material standard of living (MSOL) after an initial 10-year period of modest penury in FW, it is enhanced, but not in TW. Unfortunately, this switch to solar is too expensive for the Developing World, whose MSOL declines to 70% of the 1992 value. Although solar electricity is now 75% (Figure 6.5b), the more buoyant economy means that even more

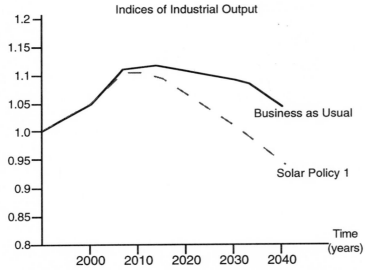

Figure 6.3. Solar Policy 1: Slow planned penetration of renewable electricity.

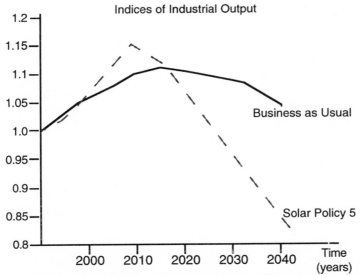

Figure 6.4. Solar Policy 5: Planned high rate of penetration of renewable electricity.

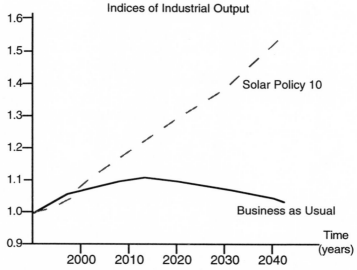

Figure 6.5a. Solar Policy 10: Planned high rate of penetration of
renewable electricity with policy of constrained
consumption.

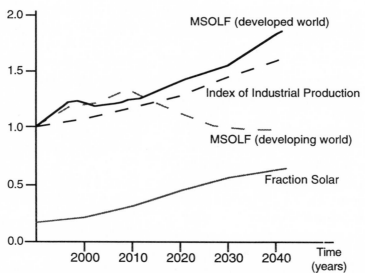

Figure 6.5b. Solar Policy 10: Planned high rate of penetration of
renewable electricity with policy of constrained
consumption.

natural capital has been lost—78% of accessible oil and gas resources have been dissipated by 2042. CO_2 output is now 34 billion t/y.

Solar 13: Reduced consumption and shared wealth. What happens if FW decides to share more of its wealth with TW? In this policy, aid to the Third World is increased by a factor of 6 over that of BAU. MSOL falls less in TW, but still falls. In the FW, economic growth is pulled back sharply from the previous case, and no gains have been made in preserving natural capital nor in accelerating its substitution by solar energy.

Solar 16: Fuel conservation. Are there any other policies that might rescue the world from physical penury? In addition to the above policies, a policy of massive energy conservation is introduced in FW. While this is beneficial to the world economy, it does not cut down the rate of consumption of natural capital. After a few years, economic growth picks up, and fuel use increases.

Solar 17: Family planning enhanced. An additional policy of significant family planning is now introduced for the TW, while in the FW, a major program in energy conservation is implemented. This has two significant consequences. World industrial activity climbs throughout the period, providing wealth for investment, and MSOL now rises in both the FW and TW. However, the price to be paid is that during the period 1995–2012, there is no improvement in FW material standards of living. This would be politically difficult to handle, given popular expectations.

Solar 18: Policy solar 17 + nuclear energy option. In this policy test, family planning in TW, major energy conservation in FW, a high rate of solar penetration, and aid from FW to TW at six times BAU is used, but with nuclear energy still an available option, taking its place in response to market forces. In addition, there is a curb on the use of private transport, thereby reducing hydrocarbon use.

For the interest of modelers, Table 6.4 gives an account of the changes to the reference profile in Solar 18. Note that RCFIND = rate of capital formation in industry (embodied DNC, GJ/y).

Figure 6.6a depicts world industrial output that is restored to a rate of growth of 1.4% annually by 2042. Figure 6.6b shows the fraction of solar and nuclear electricity, the sum adding very nearly to 100%. In spite of this, the very fact of continued growth in the world economy, now largely in the TW due to a high level of aid from the FW (in this set of policies), results in oil and gas reserves being depleted almost as fast as in BAU, while carbon dioxide, which initially falls somewhat, rises to a rate of 32 billion tonnes/y by 2042. Material welfare in both TW and FW rise, though the disparity remains enormous. The required area for solar capture now rises to 1.68 million hectares, and 11% of total world capital investment is now in the energy sector.

Table 6.4. Changes to the Reference Profile in Solar 18

Energy:	Industry: additional	15% of RCFIND(FW);	5% RCFIND(TW)
Conservation:	services:	15%	5%
	domestic:	15%	5%
Consumption:		-3% of RCFIND(FW);	-1% RCFIND(TW)
Investment in service sector:		-1% of RCFIND(FW);	-1% RCFIND(TW)
Birth rate reduction:		0 in FW;	30% in TW
Aid from FW to TW:		6* that in BAU	
Reduction in fossil fuel for private transport: 50% in FW and TW			
Penetration of solar electricity 100% desired by 2011 (75% achieved)			

INTERIM CONCLUSION

There are five interim conclusions to be drawn from these policy studies using GlobEcco. They must necessarily be interim, because the data base on solar technologies, especially the possibilities for technical change, call for further detailed studies.

1. Were current economic policies and population trends to persist, then 50 years from now, not only will material welfare globally have passed its peak (about 2010), but 80% of the world's easily accessible oil, gas, and uranium will have been depleted.

2. Were the present consumption-oriented society to persist, then any attempt to stem the depletion of natural capital by massive investment in renewable (hard solar) energy supply systems will simply result in inadequate wealth generation in both the First World and the Third World, and would soon cause declining material standards of living, thus defeating society's own objectives.

3. If carbon dioxide reduction becomes mandatory, then even a crash program of solar investment will be insufficient. It may then be necessary to restrict people's rate of use of fossil energy. During the next fifty years at least, nuclear energy is indispensable if material standards of living are to be maintained AND carbon dioxide reduced.

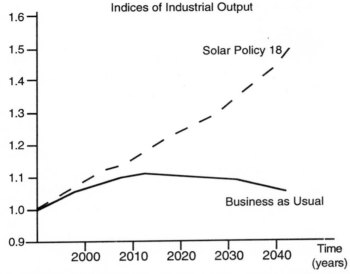

Figure 6.6a. Planned high rate of penetration of renewable electricity plus a range of restraints on consumption, plus major energy conservation investment.

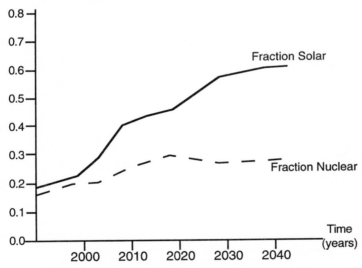

Figure 6.6b. Planned high rate of penetration of renewable electricity plus a range of restraints on consumption, plus major energy conservation investment.

4. In the long term, increasing levels of material welfare do seem possible if:

    •   Consumption growth, as a proportion of investment, is reduced, particularly in the First World;

    •   Population growth in the Third World is significantly reduced;

    •   Energy conservation on a massive scale is introduced everywhere;

    •   Substantial increases in aid from the First to the Third world are enacted, or debts are canceled. These actions, however, will result in an even higher rate of natural capital depletion than in Business-as-Usual. They must therefore be accompanied by:

    •   A massive program of R&D in solar capture technologies plus an immediate crash program of construction of solar-powered, high quality energy systems. Solar energy must be captured not merely to replace electricity, but also to provide liquid fuel vectors like gasoline.

5. Permitting the model to allocate investment in energy sources on the basis of least cost produces a result in which it is too late to invest in alternatives without significant material penury. That is to say free market forces do not drive substitution of natural capital fast enough towards a sustainable world. Hence, deliberate wise intervention at government and international level will be necessary. It has to be said that in the near future, this is most unlikely. If the approach in this chapter is to have any value, it must be to offer one means of alerting decision makers at a high level to the issue facing the world and its economies. There are no easy solutions at hand.

ACKNOWLEDGMENTS:

We are grateful to Dr. John Peet of Canterbury University, New Zealand, and Joseph Weissmahr of Zurich for helpful criticism in the preparation of this chapter. We should also like to thank the Royal Society of London for providing funds for Malcolm Slesser to attend the Stockholm Conference.

APPENDIX: ABBREVIATIONS

BAU	Business-as-usual
CO_2	Carbon Dioxide
DNC	Depletable Natural Capital, direct usage
DNC	Depletable Natural Capital, embodied

EEDW	World electrical energy demand in TWh/y
EJ	exa-joule
FW	First World
GJ	giga-joule
HMC	Human-Made (artificial, manufactured) Capital stock
INDEXW	Index of world industrial output, 1991=1
kWh	kilowatt-hour
MSOL	Material standard of living
MSOLF	Material standard-of-living factor, 1991=1
RCFIND	Rate of capital formation in industry, GJ/y embodied energy
TW	Third World
TWh	Terawatt-hour

REFERENCES

Georgescu-Roegen, N. 1972. The Entropy Law and Economic Process. Cambridge, MA: Harvard Univ. Press.

IFIAS. 1975. Energy Analysis Report, No 6. International Federation of Institutes of Advanced Study, Geography Department, Toronto University.

Keyfitz, N. 1982. Report to the UN Expert Group Meeting on Population, Resources, Environment and Development, April 25–29, Geneva.

McLaren, D., and B. Skinner. 1987. Energy resources. In Resources and World Development. Chichester, New York: Wiley-Interscience.

RUI. 1992. ECCO User's Manual, Parts I & II (3rd ed.), with associated instructional software. Edinburgh: Resource Use Institute.

Roberts, P. 1982. Energy and value. *Energy Policy* 10: 171–80.

Slesser, M. 1976. Solar energy breeders. *Nature* 262 (July 22.): 244–45.

———. 1980. Can solar energy replace fossil-fissile energy sources? *Solar Energy* 25: 425–28.

Slesser, M., and A. Saraph. 1991. GlobEcco software. Edinburgh: Resource Use Institute.

Weissmahr, J. 1991. An Evolutionary Theory of Technical Change and Economic Growth and Development. European Study Group for Evolutionary Economics, Department of Economics, Univ. of Freiburg, Germany.

White, L. A. 1949. The Evolution of Culture. New York: McGraw-Hill.

Worldwatch. 1990. Beyond the Petroleum Age. Paper 100. Washington, DC: Worldwatch Institute.

7 SUSTAINABILITY AND THE LIMITS TO PSEUDO MARKET VALUATION

R. K. Blamey and M. Common
Centre for Resource and Environmental Studies
Australian National University
P.O. Box 4
Canberra, ACT 2601 Australia

INTRODUCTION

While the definition of sustainability generates debate, the basic nature of the concept is reasonably clear. The pursuit of sustainability or sustainable development, involves trying to avoid creating economic problems for future generations arising from current degradation of natural assets. The functions of natural assets in relation to economic activity are:

1. to provide the basis for resource flows into production,

2. to assimilate the waste products arising in production and consumption,

3. to provide the basis for flows of services direct to consumption (i.e., amenity services), and

4. to provide those services that maintain the total global system in a condition to support human life, such as the reduction of ultra-violet radiation reaching the earth's surface or the maintenance of the potential for evolutionary change in the biosphere.

The demarcation between the last of these and the other three is not always clear and exact. A concern for biodiversity conservation, for example, relates to the fourth function, and can be regarded also as relating to one, two, and three. However, it appears useful to distinguish "life support" services from the first three functions; not all natural asset functions can be captured in terms of flows across a national boundary between the economy and the natural environment.[1]

Few would now wish to argue that the management of natural assets can be left entirely to market forces. There are four distinct bases for the position that social action is required to modify the operation of market forces in regard to natural asset management.

First, it is widely recognized that "market failure" problems are, especially in regard to the environmental asset functions of waste assimilator and amenity service base, the rule rather than the exception. Market failure means that allocative efficiency is not attained. Mainstream environmental economics can be regarded as the study of the causes of and means to correct market failure with regard to environmental assets. We label this the *Efficiency School.* It is well represented in the pages of the *Journal of Environmental Economics and Management*. The elimination of market failure does not, of course, itself ensure distributional justice, which both intra- and inter-generationally is a major component of the idea of sustainability or sustainable development as expounded in the Brundtland Report (WCED 1987).

The second basis for not leaving things to the market arises directly from this last point. Intratemporal allocative efficiency is consistent with current injustice, and intertemporal allocative efficiency is entirely consistent with current welfare levels exceeding future welfare levels. Hence, market failure correction is not sufficient for sustainability. An explicit position on justice and asset transfers across people and through time is argued to be necessary for sustainability. We label this the *Equity School*: a representative contribution, focusing on intertemporal transfers, is Howarth (1991).

Both of these positions can be located in fairly standard economic concerns for efficiency and distributional justice. A third basis for the conclusion that matters cannot be left entirely to markets originates in a concern for the integrity of the natural systems where natural assets are located. Sustainability is seen as being about the preservation of such integrity as a necessary condition for levels of future welfare comparable to

---

1. There are now many explicit representations of economy-environment linkages available in the literature. That in, for example, Common and Norton (1992) represents environmental services that do not involve flows across a notional economy-environment boundary.

current levels. Common and Perrings (1992) have argued that consumer sovereignty is not necessarily consistent with the requirements of sustainability thus conceived. To reject consumer sovereignty as the basis for the determination of resource allocation represents a more fundamental departure from standard economic thinking than either of the two positions sketched above. We label this the *Ecological School*.

The fourth position, which would not leave natural asset management entirely to markets, also rejects consumer sovereignty. However, this position is not based directly on consideration of the requirements of ecosystem integrity maintenance. It originates in questioning the normative role of consumer sovereignty in resource allocation generally, or in regard to natural assets particularly, on an ethical and/or behavioral basis, rather than an ecologically instrumental basis. We label this the *Philosophical School*, and discuss it later—a representative contribution is Sagoff (1988).

Each of these positions raises questions of valuation in relation to natural assets. The efficiency school position is that which gives rise to what we call here *pseudo market valuation*. To the extent that market prices do not properly reflect natural asset values, they are to be replaced by pseudo market prices, (i.e., prices reflecting what willingness-to-pay would have been had competitive markets existed). The other three positions all involve some departure from pseudo market valuation. The equity school notes that efficiency prices are conditional upon current distributional settings, and argues that unless such settings are considered appropriate, the prices arising should not guide allocation. The ecological school position is that the consumer-sovereignty-driven outcomes need to be modified by the observance of biophysically specified constraints deriving from system integrity requirements: critical natural assets would then be implicitly valued in a constrained optimization problem. The philosophical school limits the domain of consumer sovereignty on the basis of ethical and/or psychological considerations: individuals are seen as comprising (at least) two choosing entities, and the consumer entity is regarded as of limited relevance to social choices affecting natural assets.

This chapter offers a critical appraisal of the use of *the Contingent Valuation Method* for valuing the amenity and life support services provided by the natural environment. It is, in regard to those services, the dominant methodology employed by the efficiency school. Our appraisal of the methodology is driven mainly by issues raised by the philosophical school, though its reliability is judged against the criteria of the efficiency school.

First, we review the main features of the efficiency school approach to natural asset valuation. Then we consider some aspects of experience to date with this approach. In the next section we draw upon some of the literature from the philosophical school to question the appropriateness of that research agenda in relation to the problem of valuing natural assets. The fifth section then argues that a *prima facie* case can be made for an alternative approach to the valuation of at least some natural assets that would be consistent with considerations raised by the philosophical school. Even if these considerations cannot provide the basis for an alternative approach, they do suggest caution in accepting and interpreting results derived from the efficiency school approach. The chapter concludes with some observations on possible directions for further research on natural asset valuation.

MARKET AND PSEUDO MARKET VALUATION

The literature of the efficiency school that addresses natural asset valuation is predominantly concerned with ascertaining the valuations of environmental assets and services by individuals or households. These valuations are generally understood to relate to function three above, (i.e., to amenity services). However, in some contexts the individual/household valuation of a particular asset or service may include an element relating to function four. Thus, for example, the valuation of a species by a household/individual may reflect both actual or anticipated pleasure from seeing representatives of it and/or knowledge of its existence, and some assessment of the role of the species in maintaining system functioning.

In regard to function one, nonrenewable resource inputs to production are taken generally to be valued in markets, property rights being well-established. The problem of free access in regard to many renewable resource stocks is widely recognized. This implies that there is no market price for the *in situ* resource stock. A pseudo market price can be derived from the value of the marketed product based on the resource via the production function. This would naturally be done within an optimization framework, with the pseudo price emerging as the shadow price of the resource, (see, for example, Ellis and Fisher 1987).

The valuation of assets and associated services in regard to waste assimilation, (function two in the list above), appears to have received virtually no attention. This may be because of the apparent difficulty of defining a particular relevant asset or associated service flow. It is not, however, the case that waste disposal and its consequences have not been of interest to the efficiency school. There is a substantial literature on valuing the benefits of reduced environmental pollution of various kinds, and the methodologies employed overlap with those employed in the environmental amenity context, which will be discussed below.

The valuation of life-support services, function four in the list above, has received rather little attention. Again, this may be due to the apparent difficulty of identifying a particular distinct natural asset or associated flow. Costanza et al. (1989) derive a figure for the "storm protection value of wetlands" by figuring the increases in property value damages that would result if the buffering wetland area were reduced in size. This "damage avoidance valuation" approach would appear to have some general applicability to life-support services provided by the natural environment; for example, flood protection afforded by tree cover in river catchments.

A variant of this approach is the "substitute service" approach, in which a natural asset would be valued according to the costs of the inputs required to provide the same service by means of human production. Repetto et al. (1987) use this approach to soil erosion costs in Indonesia. It would appear that it could be used to provide a value for biotic species *in situ* by way of estimating the costs of *ex situ* preservation. For many species, such an estimate would presumably represent a lower bound for *in situ* existence value in so far as that serves functions additional to those of genetic diversity per se. A variant of this approach would be via the cost of replacing an environmental asset rather than substituting for it. On this basis, a particular wetland area, for example, would be valued at the cost of creating a replacement rather than at the cost of establishing a fish farm, storm protection facilities, etc.

Residual value, damage avoidance, and substitute service approaches all involve deriving values for environmental assets from existing market prices, where prices are taken as given. They are examples of the class of pseudo market valuation techniques. They are not the techniques on which the efficiency school literature has predominantly focused, nor have they been used for the environmental function—amenity services (function two in the list above)—on which efficiency school literature has mainly focused.

The efficiency school literature on non-market environmental valuation is now almost entirely about inferring the willingness-to-pay or -accept of households/individuals for variations in the quantity or quality of directly consumed environmental "commodities." The research agenda involved can be described as the extension to environmental services of the apparatus of consumer demand theory. It is this theory, and associated technique, which is to be used to make the valuation inferences required, because environmental services do not, typically, pass to households/individuals through markets. Indeed, the way in which environmental services have been classified as commodities has been largely dictated by the requirements of this research agenda, rather than on the basis of biophysical considerations. This has implications for the alignment of valuations generated by pseudo market valuation and information relevant to allocation problems arising in the natural sciences, and the requirements of natural asset managers such as forestry agencies (see, for example, Gregory et al. 1989), where it is argued that in existing Contingent Valuation studies, the focus of the questions has not been sufficiently well designed to yield answers to managers and decision makers.

To identify the major concerns of this chapter, we now provide a very brief overview of the way in which pseudo market valuation typically arises and is dealt with in the economics literature.[2] Consider some development project for a wilderness area, and social decision making as to whether or not it should proceed. Let B_d be the measure of the value of all of the project outputs, and C_d be the measure of the value of all of the project inputs. Assume that for aggregation to B_d and C_d market prices are satisfactory, and that B_d and C_d are present values (or annuity equivalents). Over and above inputs captured in C_d, going ahead with the project would involve impacts on the wilderness area. Denote the present value of such as EC, for environmental or external cost. Then, the decision rule is to go ahead with the project if

$$B_d - C_d > EC$$

Clearly, the major problems with this Cost-Benefit Analysis decision rule are the identification and measurement of the impacts on the wilder-

---

2. For a more extended overview, with particular reference to species preservation, see Randall (1986).

ness area, and then their valuation and aggregation to arrive at EC, the environmental amenity benefits of not going ahead with the project.

Assuming that the impacts involved are limited to those affecting what we have called amenity services to households, and that these can be identified and measured, the basic strategy for valuation is as follows. Let x be a vector of ordinary marketed commodities, and q a vector of environmental conditions. Then assume that for the affected individuals the utility function U(x,q) exists. It is then possible to use the standard apparatus of demand theory to establish the existence of monetary measures—consumer surplus, compensating variation, equivalent variation, etc.—of the utility implications of variations in the vector q (Johansson 1987; Mitchell and Carson 1989). The research problem for implementation of this approach to social decision making is then the estimation of the sizes of the appropriate monetary measures for affected individuals and their aggregation to obtain total willingness-to-pay, (WTP), or willingness-to-accept, (WTA), measures from which EC can be computed. The problem has been brought within the ambit of consumer demand theory by virtue of the assumption that U(x,q) exists.

There are two basic approaches to the estimation of WTP/WTA for individuals—the Indirect and the Direct. Both derive from the fact that markets do not exist for elements of q due to non-excludability and/or non-rivalry. The former involves recovering estimates from the observed behavior of individuals in regard to marketed commodities; the latter involves asking individuals about their WTP/WTA. The major operational version of the Indirect approach is the *Travel Cost Method,* (TCM), in which WTP for use of the area affected by the project would be inferred from costs incurred in visiting it. Another indirect approach, sometimes used in conjunction with TCM, is the *Hedonic Pricing Method,* where the basic idea is to use market prices of commodities with different bundles of characteristics to value particular, non-marketed characteristics. The major operational version of the Direct approach is the *Contingent Valuation Method,* (CVM), so called because individuals are asked about their WTP/WTA contingent upon a scenario concerning the affected area. Indirect methods require the assumption of (weak) complementarity between the relevant element of q and some element(s) of x. Direct methods do not require this assumption, and this is why they alone can address existence value questions.

It is conventional to sub-divide EC into four classes of benefit, or value, to individuals:

- Use Value, (UV), arises from the individual's planned use of the area, (for recreation, for example).

- Existence Value, (EV), arises from knowledge that the area exists and will continue to exist, independently of any actual or prospective use by the individual.

- Option Value, (OV), relates to willingness-to-pay to guarantee availability for future use by the individual.

- Quasi-option value, (QOV), relates to willingness-to-pay to avoid an ir-reversible commitment to development now, given the expectation of future growth in knowledge relevant to the implications of develop-ment.

Then,

$$EC = UV + EV + OV + QOV = UV + NUV,$$

where NUV stands for Non-Use Value. The practical difficulties of sepa-rating NUV into its three component parts are widely recognized. Note that OV and QOV arise on the basis of incomplete knowledge of future conditions, whereas UV and EV can arise independently of any uncer-tainty. Note also that the existence for an individual of EV would imply some kind of altruism. EV is itself sometimes sub-divided on the basis of the object of the altruism: see, for example, Randall (1986), where a phi-lanthropic motive relating to contemporaries is distinguished from a be-quest motive relating to future generations. In so far as CVM respondents are concerned about the life-support functions of the assets/services that they are asked about, any WTP arising would presumably be regarded as a component of EV on the basis that it would mainly involve an instru-mental altruism. This would involve WTP to preserve environmental functions instrumental to the well-being of self and very many others, rather than WTP to confer direct use benefits on others. Any WTP to avoid, for example, global climate change would presumably reflect mainly such instrumental altruism. As noted above, explicit consideration of such instrumental altruism is rare in the literature, where altruism is generally seen as relating to use by others. Randall (1986) does consider "intrinsic" altruism, where "the individual human cares about the well-being of nonhuman components of the ecosystem" (85), but does not re-late this to a concern for system function. Common and Norton (1992) consider a model that introduces a purely instrumental basis for species valuation.

The TCM can address only the estimation of use values. The CVM can, in principle, address the estimation of all four of the above classes of benefit/value separately. Of these classes of value distinguished in the economics literature, it appears that it is existence value that is particularly, but not solely, relevant to sustainability questions. The major reason for this is that the sustainability problem is seen as being essentially about problems of intergenerational equity arising from current impacts on the natural environment. It relates to the state of the environment to be passed on to future others. Of the four classes distinguished above, only existence value aligns directly with this concern. Use and option value relate to use by a current individual. Quasi-option value clearly does have some relevance to intergenerational equity. Applications of this extended consumer demand theory approach that are generally considered most directly relevant to sustainability issues are those relating to species preservation. Randall (1986) discusses the approach in just that context. An example of such an application is Samples et al. (1986), where it was WTP for preservation as such that was investigated by the CVM.

Given all this, it appears that the methodology regarded as relevant to sustainability by the efficiency school is CVM.

THE ACCURACY OF PSEUDO MARKET VALUATION

The next section presents some arguments to the effect that it is inappropriate to use CVM to inform environmental decision making. First, however, we consider the accuracy of CVM when assessed within the conceptual framework from which it has emerged. If CVM results are not, on their own terms, very reliable, abandoning the approach involves no great sacrifice. The question to be addressed here then is—Supposing that CVM is appropriate, how well does it perform?

There is a very short answer to this question—nobody knows. The fundamental problem is that there is, special cases apart as noted below, no information on the "truth" against which CVM outcomes can be tested. Further, it is in the nature of the case that this is not a transitory situation to be remedied by further research. Where environmental "commodities" to which existence values attach are non-rival and non-exclusive in use, there cannot exist actual markets in which "true" valuations could be manifest.

Considerable technical virtuosity has been deployed in efforts to assess the reliability of CVM by other means. Several approaches and arguments have been used. Our assessment of the results arising is that CVM cannot reasonably be regarded as sufficiently reliable for the incorporation of sustainability-relevant valuations in project appraisal. The rest of this section briefly presents the main approaches to the reliability question, with examples, in order to support this assessment.

Mitchell and Carson (1989) review results from a number of studies designed to test for various kinds of bias in CVM responses by comparing them with experimental outcomes. These experiments do not involve environmental existence values, and relate to individual WTP revelation, rather than to the aggregate relevant to decision making using the project appraisal methodology outlined above (see below). In their conclusion, Mitchell and Carson pose the question, "...can CV surveys actually measure values that are sufficiently reliable and valid for use in benefit estimation?" (295). They note an "emerging consensus...that CV studies are able to measure meaningful values for 'familiar' goods such as local recreational amenities" (296); "meaningful" is not quantified. In regard to "less familiar goods, such as air quality improvements...," it is recognized that "we cannot test the accuracy of CV surveys against a criterion." Mitchell and Carson express sympathy with those who are skeptical about CV in these contexts, and respond by changing the rules of the game somewhat. In this context, they consider the market model "inappropriate," and state that:

> in our view, the appropriate model for CV surveys of pure public goods—goods that citizens are least likely to have direct experience in valuing—is the referendum, by which citizens make binding decisions about the provision of public goods. From this perspective, instead of falling short of the relevant market model, well-conducted CV surveys offer significant improvements over actual referenda as a means of measuring consumer preferences (296).

However well-founded this view, if this is to be understood as the basis for the evaluation of CV studies of existence values, then the results cannot properly be regarded as appropriate for use in cost-benefit analysis.[3]

---

3. In the light of the discussion in the next section of Sagoff's consumer/citizen distinction, it does not appear that these terms should here be interpreted in the sense of Sagoff. Certainly, Sagoff is not cited in Mitchell and Carson.

Cummings et al. (1986) define "reference operating conditions" that they regard as necessary if an individual CV response is to be accurate within 50% of the true value of WTP. The first two of the conditions are: (1) understanding of and familiarity with the "commodity" to be valued; and (2) prior valuation and choice experience with respect to consumption levels of the "commodity." Clearly, it would be unlikely that these conditions are generally satisfied in respect to existence value "commodities."

In some circumstances, CVM results can be compared with outcomes in which actual money transactions take place. Bishop et al. (1983) report results relating to permits for geese hunting. The CVM results for permit value ranged from $11 to $101. In an experiment involving actual purchases of permits, the price established was $63. Bishop et al. comment that "our contingent valuation mechanism seemed to provide meaningful—albeit inaccurate—economic information." The permits are, of course, in the nature of private goods and have little connection with existence values.

An alternative approach is to elicit responses from the same set of individuals in repeat surveys. Evidence that individual valuations are constant across repetitions is taken as evidence for the reliability of CVM. This is a weak test, as any systematic biases in responses will simply be repeated. Loomis (1989) reports repeat survey results for two samples, of visitors and of the general population, in regard to water quality at a California lake. The results obtained were mixed according to the precise formulation of the test for constancy, and Loomis concluded that they "support the contention that the contingent valuation method provides reliable estimates" of individuals' willingness-to-pay. It appears that on the basis of the results reported, this assessment is overly strong. Loomis notes that one might expect responses to be non-constant if individuals acquire new information between repetitions of the survey. Samples et al. (1986) examined this issue in relation to species preservation. Statistically significant response differences were found according to the information on which they were based, giving rise to "the fact that information, appropriately selected, can influence the outcome of valuation studies." Clearly, this gives rise to problems for the use of CVM results in project appraisal. Crocker and Shogren (1991) consider individuals learning about their preferences, concluding that this too has implications for the interpretation of CVM results.

A number of studies have compared CVM results with corresponding TCM results, with the idea that convergence demonstrates reliability. Actually, of course, it demonstrates only convergence unless replicated over many studies, or unless it is taken as given that one result is known to be reliable. The implicit assumption in most of these studies appears to be that the TCM result is the more reliable, and that some validity is conferred on the CVM result if it is "close" to the TCM result. It should be noted that in so far as TCM can address only use values, this approach can assess the reliability of CVM only in regard to use values. An example of a study of this genre is Hanley (1989), where, on the basis of a CVM figure of £   181,250 and a TCM figure of £160,744 (pounds Sterling) for aggregate annual consumer surplus, it is stated that, "This might seem to indicate that the two methods do produce similar outcomes." Actually, Hanley gives, in Table 8, TCM results ranging from, according to the functional form used in the visits demand equation, £73,948 to £1,497,858. Given standard statistical tests, there is no basis for discrimination between the £160,744 result "preferred" by Hanley and the upper limit of this range. The CVM figure of £181,250, therefore, could equally be compared with a TCM figure of £1,497,858. The basis given by Hanley for preferring the TCM figure of £160,744 is that the £1,497,858 figure "seems inconsistent with other travel cost work on U.K. sites." Hanley is somewhat unusual in that he reports and discusses his results in terms of the aggregates that are relevant to decision making rather than in terms of individual consumer surpluses (see also Willis and Garrod 1992).[4]

This is important in that if CVM or TCM results are to be used in project appraisal, it is necessary to aggregate the estimated individual valuations. Clearly, over and above any potential for error at the level of individuals, there is large potential for error in the aggregation procedure. Most fundamentally, it is often not clear at the level of principle what the relevant population for sampling is. In practice, even if the relevant

---

4. We note that TCM does offer an advantage over CVM, where both are applicable, in regard to reliability assessment. In the case of TCM, it is not true that there is no external reference for reliability assessment. In order to calculate consumer surplus, it is necessary to fit a trip-generating equation to the data. This equation can be, and routinely is, subjected to the standard tests for goodness of fit, etc. Also, an estimated equation on data for one year, for example, could be used to predict visits for another year. It seems this is rarely done.

population is agreed, it is not necessarily the case that it is sampled in its entirety. Consider species preservation, for example. Presumably, for a relevant project in one country, the relevant population is that of the world, though, of course, in many countries individual WTP might, in fact, be vanishingly small. But suppose a conservation area threatened by development in Australia is considered as an example, and suppose in all countries except it and the United States, average individual WTP is, in fact, zero. For reasons of expediency, a CVM is confined to a sample of Australians for whom average individual WTP is found to be x. Since the population of the United States is some thirteen times that of Australia, if average individual WTP there is x/10, aggregation over only Australian individuals will give less than 50% of true preservation benefits. There is often some ambiguity as to whether CVM responses should be interpreted on behalf of an individual or a household. Clearly, to the extent that errors arise in this respect, aggregation has the potential to introduce large errors into the project appraisal-relevant result.

The potential magnitude of aggregation problems in a decision context can be illustrated using results from Common and McKenney (1992), where Monte Carlo methods are used with a simple hedonic travel cost model. The problem considered is whether or not a unique stand of timber should be harvested. The value of a decision to harvest is known to be a perpetual annuity of $2,500,000. Conveniently, it is also known that there exists, as well as the forest in which the stand is located, a forest identical in all respects save that it does not have such a stand. Then, the preservation value of the stand of interest can be determined by a very simple application of the hedonic travel cost method, as the difference between aggregate consumer surplus for visits to the two forests. The computer model of visits to the two forests was specified so that the difference between the expected values of the two consumer surpluses was an annuity of $2,683,344. This preservation value is 7.3% greater than the harvest value, so that the correct decision is not to harvest the stand.

The computer model generated the data to be used for estimation so that there were none of the problems that usually arise, such as errors in reported travel costs, for example, confronting estimation of individual consumer surpluses at the two forest sites. As well as assuming that the true values of the parameters in the trip-generating equations were not known, the model was set up to allow for errors in the estimation of the

number of visitors from each point of origin. Specifically, 5 identical individuals actually visited each forest from each of 50 origins. Individual
consumer surpluses were computed using $5e_j$ as the estimated number of
visitors from each of the 50 origins, where $j=1,2$ indexes forests and e_j
gives the error in the estimation of visitor numbers when e_j is not equal to
unity, with e_j constant across the 50 origins. For e_j equal to unity there is
no such error. On this basis, for 50 replications of the estimation and decision-making exercise, the number of incorrect decisions classified by
the values used for the e_j was:

e_2	e_1 0.9	1.0	1.1
0.9	50	0	0
1.0	50	0	0
1.1	50	50	0

The pattern of decision-making errors here is as would be expected,
with the benefit of hindsight perhaps, and the incidence depends on the
numerical specification, of course. It is nonetheless salutary that a 10%
error in total visitor assessment at one forest site can produce a 100%
wrong decision-making performance. Common and McKenney (1992)
report results for some variants of this basic model situation. If travel
cost reporting errors correlated with true travel costs are introduced,
giving rise to heteroskedasticity as well as errors in variables, the results
corresponding to those above are:

e_2	e_1 0.9	1.0	1.1
0.9	17	13	7
1.0	28	11	8
1.1	25	21	18

For some e_1/e_2 combinations, performance improves; for others it de-
teriorates. Presumably the former is counter-intuitive. In any case, even
where the estimation of behavior at the individual level is well-founded
and reasonably accurate, as it is in the first case above, small errors in
aggregation can have severe implications for decision making. This point
receives little attention in the literature and applies to CVM as much as to
TCM.

Our position on the accuracy of CVM for sustainability-relevant valuations is, then, that in relation to the decision-making framework that it is intended to inform, it is inaccurate. Abandoning it would not involve great loss.

THE APPROPRIATENESS OF PSEUDO MARKET VALUATION

This section briefly reviews the nature of a number of contributions to the literature that have raised questions about the model of human behavior which serves as the basis for the pseudo market valuation approach reviewed in the previous section. These contributions are representative of the previously mentioned Philosophical School. It is contributions from this school that question most directly the appropriateness of using CVM to derive environmental valuations for social decision making.

Sagoff (1988) attacks the approach to environmental decision making based on neoclassical economics, (i.e., that involving pseudo market valuation and cost-benefit analysis). He argues that in regard to the making of "hard" decisions, which include decisions about the environment, individuals act as *citizens* rather than *consumers*. The distinction is put as follows:

> As a citizen, I am concerned with the public interest, rather than my own interest; with the good of the community rather than simply the well-being of my family.... As a consumer...I concern myself with personal or self-regarding wants and interests; I pursue the goals I have as an individual. I put aside the community-regarding values I take seriously as a citizen, and I look out for Number One instead (Sagoff 1988, 8).

In the citizen role the individual considers the benefits of a proposal to the nation as a whole. This involves consideration of sentimental, historical, ideological, cultural, aesthetic, and ethical values. Thus, the "individual as a self-interested consumer opposes himself as a moral agent and concerned citizen" (67). Sagoff refers to this consumer/citizen dichotomy as "the conflict within us."

Sagoff sees environmental decision-making problems as falling within the provenance of what he calls "social regulation" and therefore matters for citizens rather than consumers. Social regulation is to be guided by "ethical rationality" that emphasizes the need for highly informed deliberation rather than choice on the basis of given, and most likely, poorly informed preferences. It follows that in such contexts aggregated individual willingness-to-pay is an inappropriate measure of "worth," and that decision making is to involve a process of political representation and majority voting. The role for economics is largely limited to that of cost-effectiveness analysis, i.e., determining the least costly means to the accomplishment of goals set on the basis of ethical and moral arguments and emerging from the political process. Economics would have some role in goal setting in so far as the costs of alternative goals will have some implications for the desirability of those goals. In relation to the issues addressed in this chapter, it is Sagoff's view that it is a "category mistake" to expect individuals to behave as consumers rather than citizens in regard to hard decisions such as environmental protection. The question is whether the observable needs of the political process for information on individuals' views on environmental matters, over and above those capable of being expressed through the processes themselves, are properly addressed in the context of individuals as citizens or of individuals as consumers. The pseudo market valuation approach assumes that the answer is "consumers." Sagoff asserts that it is "citizens."

Some economists have taken positions similar to that of Sagoff in that the standard representation of the individual in terms of a single preference ordering is seen as inadequate. Thus, for example, according to Sen:

> purely economic man is indeed close to being a social moron. Economic theory has been much preoccupied with this rational fool decked out in the glory of his one all-purpose preference ordering...we need a more elaborate structure (Sen 1977, 336).

Sen refers to the work of Harsanyi (1955), where a distinction is made between an individual's ethical and subjective preferences. Harsanyi, commenting on then emerging trends, notes that:

> our individual utility concept has come logically nearer to a social welfare concept. Owing to a greater awareness of the importance of external economies and diseconomies of consumption in our society, each individual's utility function is now regarded as dependent not only on this particular individual's economic (and noneconomic) conditions but also on the economic (and other) conditions of all other individuals in the community (Harsanyi 1955, 315).

He considers taking this further by viewing the individual as having an individual social welfare function, ISWF, as well as a utility function. In order to maintain a clear distinction here, Harsanyi requires the ISWF to express what the "individual prefers (or rather would prefer) on the basis of impersonal social considerations alone," and the utility function to "express what he actually prefers, whether on the basis of his personal interests or on any other basis" (1955, 315). The first set of preferences is "ethical," the second is "subjective." For Harsanyi, the ethical preferences

> express what can only in a qualified sense be called his "preferences": they will, by definition express what he prefers only in those possibly rare moments when he forces a special impartial and impersonal attitude upon himself (315).

It is argued that this impersonality requirement will be satisfied if preferences are expressed from behind a (what would now be described as Rawlsian) "veil of ignorance."

This dual self envisaged by Harsanyi clearly has affinities with the consumer/citizen duality espoused by Sagoff. In regard to the claim by Harsanyi that the ISWF self, Sagoff's citizen, will only be manifest in "rare moments," it is interesting to note the work of Maslow in the field of behavioral psychology. Maslow (1954) suggested that human needs satisfaction proceeds from the material through the social to the moral. The last are also referred to as self-actualizing needs, and it is argued that they are self-perpetuating so that there is in respect to them non-satiation. Within this view, self-actualization, addressing moral needs, would await the satisfaction of the lower order needs, consistently with Harsanyi's view of only rare references to the ISWF. However, in later work Maslow (1968) modified this view somewhat, stating that self-actualization is not

> some far off distant goal at the end of a long series of steps, but is present as a possibility all the time, even when the lower needs are still operating (Lutz and Lux 1988, 16)

This view is closer to Sagoff's in that higher and lower needs are presenting themselves to the individual simultaneously. There is a continuous interplay between lower and higher needs (Maslow), ethical and subjective preferences (Harsanyi), and citizen and consumer (Sagoff). It would not be expected that the boundaries involved in these distinctions would be the same for all individuals, given different experiences in terms of social conditioning as well as genetic endowments, nor constant over time for a given individual, given changing circumstances. This does not render the distinctions useless, of course. On the contrary:

the dual self conception is what economics needs in order to break out of its overly narrow and distorted image of what people are and how they operate (Lutz and Lux 1988, 18).

Etzioni (1988) also rejects the single "self" represented as a single set of preferences, which is the foundation of the standard economic approach to the understanding of human behavior, and to normative prescription. He focuses on conflicts between a morally committed self and a plea-sure-maximizing self, arguing that "people's behavior is systematically and significantly affected by moral factors that cannot be reduced to considerations of personal gain" (Etzioni 1988, 22). It follows that there are, for an individual (at least), two distinct sources of value. Etzioni characterizes his approach as one of co-determination: "people do not seek to maximize their pleasure, but to balance the service of two major purposes—to advance their well-being and to act morally" (83).

The idea that individuals and preferences are not one-dimensional may have a long history. Lutz and Lux (1988) note that Plato distin-guished two categories of human motives—passions and reason. More recently, Boulding (1969) has noted the relevance for observed human behavior of what he calls the "heroic ethic," to be distinguished from al-truism, which he considered to be more readily accommodated within the conventional economic view of an individual (see below). Boulding re-gards recognition of this as necessary to explain (voluntary) military service and some religious behavior. In Boulding's view:

> man requires both heroic and economic elements in his institutions, in his learning processes and in his decision making and the problem of maintaining them in proper balance and tension is one of the major problems of motivation, both of the individual person and of societies (Boulding 1969, 10).

It has long been recognized that on the standard view of the individual as solely a maximizer of utility, it is difficult to explain participation in democratic voting exercises. For example, Downs (1957) drew attention to the fact that the probability of casting a decisive vote is so small that a "consumer" would not vote, even if the costs involved were small, and sought to explain voting on the basis of "each citizen's realization that democracy cannot function unless many people vote" (274).

Margolis (1982) develops a model of dual rational choice in which individuals are seen to pursue (1) self-interested activities (where altru-ism is not ruled out), and (2) activities that benefit some larger collectivity of which they are part, independently of any personal benefits arising. The two are linked by an allocation rule based on equalization of utilities at the margin. Margolis uses Darwinian survival considerations to place restrictions on the roles for self and group interests for individuals. Individuals who are purely group-interested would be vulnerable to the activities of self-interested individuals within their group. On the other hand, a group comprised of solely self-interested individuals would be vulnerable to other groups where some group interest was the norm, with implications for individual members of the group. Margolis also discusses altruism, which will be discussed below.

The foregoing is an overview of a literature that demonstrates that Sagoff is by no means unique in questioning the concept of a unified self with a single preference ordering that underpins mainstream economic analysis generally. Clearly, the issue is important for the appreciation of the use of CV studies, and consideration of alternatives in relation to non-use environmental amenity valuation. This is covered later in the chapter. Next, some other issues logically distinct from but of relevance to an interest in the dual (or multiple) self-hypothesis are considered. Some of these have been raised in the literature in a general way, and some are specific to consideration of the appropriateness of the pseudo market approach to environmental valuation.

The pseudo market approach depends on acceptance of consumer sovereignty as the foundational normative criterion. Sagoff (1988) rejects consumer sovereignty in the area of hard environmental decision making. Most economists accept it unreservedly, and the standard approach to environmental valuation is but one example of efforts to extend the domain of the technical apparatus developed on its basis. However, it has been questioned at the general level, a notable recent example being the work of Penz (1986). There are four main bases for the critique:

1. individuals may be inadequately informed as to the consequences for themselves of the alternatives they face,

2. individuals may be insufficiently deliberative in assessing the consequences of alternative choices,

3. individuals may lack self-knowledge in the sense that they cannot properly relate the consequences of alternative choices to their preferences, and

4. individuals' preferences may not reflect their true interests due to "preference shaping" arising from socialization processes and advertising.

Clearly, number one is likely to be relevant in the context of consideration of the consequences for the individual of alternative states of the environment. The problem of knowledge is not avoided by the introduction of a citizen-self in addition to a consumer-self, and the question of deliberation has already been raised above. However, it appears to be at least implicit in Sagoff's position that proper recognition of the citizen role would work to increase citizen deliberation and knowledge.

Economics does not insist that the individual as consumer is purely and narrowly selfish; altruism toward other human individuals in various forms is admitted.[5] As noted in the previous section, some form of altruism is necessary for the existence of existence benefits. However, both generally and in regard to such benefits, problems arise in dealing with altruism within the standard conception of the individual. For example, participatory altruism is defined as a situation where satisfaction is derived from an act of giving in and of itself (Margolis 1982). This is closely related to the "warm inner glow" idea introduced by Andreoni (1990). Kahneman and Knetsch (1992a, b) have attempted to use this idea to explain the embedding phenomenon often observed in CVM studies of non-use values.[6] Their paper has evoked strong reactions from CV practitioners (see, for example, Smith 1992). If participatory altruism is at work when individuals respond to WTP questions in CVM studies, it would, in terms of the response that it is intended to elicit, be likely to produce some upward bias. This would be the case to the extent that individuals respond with their WTP for the subject of inquiry and their WTP for the purchase of a "warm inner glow."

So-called "deep-ecology" would attribute "intrinsic value" to non-human biological entities, claiming that they have value independently of any human interest in them. It is difficult to see how value can exist independently of a valuer, and it seems more reasonable to regard claims for intrinsic value as claims that altruism be extended to embrace non-humans. Goodin (1990) seeks to develop a "moderately deep" green

---

5. See Collard 1978, for a useful overview.

6. Embedding arises "when the same good is assigned a lower value if WTP for it is inferred from WTP for a more inclusive good rather than if the particular good is evaluated on its own" (Kahneman and Knetsch 1992a, 58).

theory of value. He suggests that ultimately "what is especially valuable about the products of natural processes is that they are the products of something *larger* than ourselves" (69). Norton (1986) arrives by a different route at what appears to be, operationally, an essentially similar position. According to Norton, "each species should be accorded substantial value and that, when a species has particular, identified uses, the values derived from those uses should be added to that original, general value" (132). The general value arises from interdependencies between species, which are poorly understood.[7] For both Goodin and Norton, as we understand them, species are to be valued not simply on the basis of consumer preferences, but in recognition of the processes which support them and humans. According to the terminology presented at the beginning of this chapter, life-support, as well as amenity services, should be accounted for.

In a paper on "Sustainability and the Problem of Valuation," Page (1991) notes that "from the perspective of evolutionary biology we can say that the concept of an individual human being becomes less 'individuated'"(61). Page is referring here to the fact that related human beings share common genes, and he cites the work of Dawkins (1978). While some of the conclusions and speculations arising in sociobiology are controversial, it seems clear that we are genetically programmed to be social animals, rather than purely selfish individuals. Dawkins discusses altruism from this perspective. Page argues that studies of non-human primate groups support the observation that "society creates the individual, the individual does not create society" (61), and suggests that a response to emerging knowledge in these fields should involve "a search for a value theory that does not rely foundationally on the *predefined (exogenous) individual*" (62). Thus, there seems to be some biological basis for the individual as citizen; cultural conditioning would operate on this genetic base.

Some of those who have entertained the dual-self hypothesis have considered whether the dual utilities are reducible to one (Etzioni 1988; Lutz and Lux 1988; Margolis 1982; Collard 1978). The consensus here would appear to be that while some forms of morally committed behavior are explainable in terms of *consumer*-maximizing behavior, given due

---

7. Common and Norton (1992) discuss an approach to the valuation of species/populations that takes account of interdependencies in relation to human interests.

allowance for altruism, there remains a significant component of behavior that cannot be so explained.

Standard economics does assume reducibility. In the context of the particular concern of this chapter, CVM, and environmental valuation, its application requires, as noted previously, that for the individual there exists a utility function, which has as arguments ordinary marketed commodities and states of the natural environment. Here, it is assumed, for sharpness and brevity, that the latter comprise only arguments that take the value one or zero according to whether a corresponding species exists or not. Denote a vector of ordinary commodities by x and of species existence indicators by s. Then the assumption required for pseudo market valuation is that $U(x,s)$ exists. The conditions on preferences that are necessary for the utility function to exist are discussed in demand theory texts,[8] whose treatment we follow here. Let the alternatives to be considered by the consumer be bundles Q_i, where

$$
\begin{array}{lll}
Q_1 & Q_2 \cdots\cdots\cdots\cdots Q_n \\[4pt]
x_{11} & x_{21} \cdots\cdots\cdots\cdots x_{n1} \\
x_{12} & x_{22} \cdots\cdots\cdots\cdots x_{n2} \\
\;\cdot & \;\cdot \cdots\cdots\cdots\cdots \\
\;\cdot & \;\cdot \cdots\cdots\cdots\cdots \\
x_{1m} & x_{2m} \cdots\cdots\cdots\cdots x_{nm} \\
s_{11} & s_{21} \cdots\cdots\cdots\cdots s_{n1} \\
s_{12} & s_{22} \cdots\cdots\cdots\cdots s_{n2} \\
\;\cdot & \;\cdot \cdots\cdots\cdots\cdots \\
\;\cdot & \;\cdot \cdots\cdots\cdots\cdots \\
s_{1p} & s_{2p} \cdots\cdots\cdots\cdots s_{np}
\end{array}
$$

The condition, or axiom, of Completeness is that for any Q_i and Q_j

Either	$Q_i P Q_j$
Or	$Q_j P Q_i$
Or	$Q_j I Q_i$

where P stands for "is preferred to" and I represents a relationship of indifference. This condition requires that the individual be able to

---

8 . See, for example, Deaton and Muellbauer (1980, 26–30).

compare *all* bundles in such manner as to be able to make a definite statement as to a preference/indifference relation.

The axiom of Transitivity is that

If $Q_i PQ_j$ and $Q_j PQ_k$ then $Q_i PQ_k$

These two axioms, together with the trivial axiom of Reflexivity, define a preference ordering. To go from a preference ordering to a utility function, the fourth axiom of Continuity is required. This is that for Q_i,

the set $A(Q_i)=\{Q|Q \geq Q_i\}$
and the set $B(Q_i)=\{Q|Q_i \geq Q\}$
are closed sets

This axiom rules out discontinuities in the preference ordering. An example of a discontinuous preference ordering is the Lexicographic. An ordering is lexicographic if Q_i is preferred to Q_j because it contains more of, say, food than Q_j, regardless of what else Q_i and Q_j contain, and so on. Bundles are ordered as with words in a dictionary, in which case a complete set of indifference relations does not exist.

These four axioms are sufficient for the representation of a preference ordering by a utility function. Two further axioms are required to yield the "well-behaved" utility functions usually employed in pseudo market valuation, but they will be ignored here. However, a lacuna in the pseudo market valuation literature does exist. The plausibility of extending the domain of the axioms of completeness, transitivity, and continuity from the vector x to include with it the vector s, in the above notation, does not appear to have been examined in that literature. The matter is discussed here in terms of s as a vector of elements relating to species existence, but the same point applies in regard to the more general vector q with elements relating to environmental conditions used in an earlier section. The existence of $U(x,q)$ is simply asserted. It is not obvious that the extension is self-evidently plausible, either in general, q, or in particular in regard to species existence, s. Completeness requires that individuals find all elements of x and of q/s "commensurable." Continuity rules out, for example, situations where individuals prefer all Q_i in which all s elements take the value one to all other Q_j. We do not wish to assert that $U(x,q)$, cannot exist. It seems that it is not self-evident that it does. Given that, it is surprising that the question of its existence has apparently not been raised, analytically or empirically, in the pseudo market valuation literature. In the next section of the chapter we report on some of our own work that indicates how the question might be addressed. The assumption that U(x,q) exists is crucial to the whole of the elaborate methodologies for environmental amenity value estimation that economists have developed in the last three decades.

This is important because, as noted in the previous section, there is, except in special cases, no external reference against which to evaluate the results arising from applications of CVM. Over the domain of marketed commodities, an approach which eschewed any interest in the direct testing of the conditions necessary for the existence of a utility function could, perhaps, be justified by appeal to the methodological position of Friedman (1953). According to this position, briefly, the validity of assumptions need be of no interest so long as the predictions to which they lead are accurate. For marketed commodities, it could be argued, a utility function can be assumed, and demand functions can be estimated and used to generate predictions testable against independently derived observational data. For environmental "commodities," there is generally no independent observational data against which WTP/WTA measures arising from CVM can be evaluated for accuracy.[9] Hence, and particularly if those inferences are to be used as inputs to social decision making, there does need to be some interest in the validity of the assumptions that permit the measures being made.

This section has reviewed some contributions that raise questions about the existence of the individual utility function that pseudo market valuation by CVM requires, and/or question its relevance to social decision making in relation to the environment. It does not appear that any of these contributions would support the proposition that citizens' views on matters particular or general in regard to environmental decision making should not be sought by interview or questionnaire. It would appear entirely consistent with the views of Sagoff, for example, that there is an important role for surveys of citizens' views. As noted above, Harsanyi maintains that an individual's "ethical" preferences are likely to come to the fore "only in those possibly rare moments when he forces a special impartial and impersonal attitude upon himself." Participation in an interview, or the act of completing a questionnaire, could be one way of prompting the reflection and deliberation associated with such "rare moments." If there is anything in this, it has implications both for the inter-

---

9. But, with respect to TCM, see footnote 3.

pretation of CVM responses, and for alternative approaches to using surveys of individuals to inform environmental decision making.

AN ALTERNATIVE BASIS FOR VALUATION?

It is now appropriate to propose what might be called the Sagoff hypothesis: With regard to their non-use relationships with the natural environment, individuals consider questions arising in citizen, as opposed to consumer, mode. A different hypothesis could be proposed, perhaps a variant Sagoff hypothesis: If asked questions about their non-use relationships with the natural environment, individuals consider that they *should* respond as citizens rather than consumers. It would likely be difficult to test these as competing hypotheses, but both have implications for the conduct of and interpretation of the results from CV surveys conducted on the basis of the assumption that individuals respond as consumers. Some aspects of this are considered in the next section. We discuss here some evidence bearing directly upon the two hypotheses put forward here. The evidence is very limited. This is in itself interesting.

Sagoff (1988, 50–51) reports a classroom exercise with students taking an environmental ethics course. In relation to a proposed ski resort development in the Mineral King Valley, he found that what the students wanted for themselves differed greatly from what they thought was best for society as a whole. Sagoff takes this as supportive of his consumer-citizen distinction.

In May and June 1992, we conducted two small-scale experiments with students taking an environmental economics course at the Australian National University. At the first lecture the students, who had not done any previous work in environmental economics, were given a questionnaire. An introductory paragraph explaining that this was a survey and not a class test was followed by five questions on academic background and interest in environmental matters. Use was then made of a scenario originally prepared by Bennett (1984) for a CVM exercise intended to estimate the existence benefits of a nature reserve in New South Wales. The original scenario was slightly modified by adding to the verbal and visual description of the area a statement that a major tourist development was proposed there, the prevention of which, to ensure the "conservation of the biodiversity that it contains," would require that the area be purchased from its current owners.

The students then came to:

Question 7. There are two options in regard to the purchase of this land:
EITHER

a   Depending on the recommendation of a commission of inquiry, which would hold public hearings, the government could buy the land. This would require increased taxation or reduced government expenditure. If the land were taken into public ownership, it would be managed as a nature reserve with access restricted to scientists.

OR

b.   The matter could be left to market forces, with a conservation organization opening a subscription to try to raise enough money to buy the land. The outcome would depend on the willingness of individuals to contribute to the subscription. If the conservation organization could raise enough money, it would manage the land as a nature reserve with access restricted to scientists.

Which do you consider the appropriate way of deciding the future of this area? Please circle one:

              a   b

There were 67 students present at the lecture, 63 of whom returned usable responses. Of these, 70% had circled "a," indicating that they thought the matter should be handled by government rather than left to market forces. If the null hypothesis is that students chose on the basis of tossing a fair coin, it can be rejected in favor of the alternative that the proportion of "b" responses is greater than 50% at the 1% level of significance. This can be interpreted as evidence consistent with the Sagoff hypothesis: a majority of the respondents were opposed to leaving matters to market forces. It can be noted that as economics students, these subjects would not be unaware of the case for leaving things to markets where possible.

If it is accepted that individuals consider questions about their non-use relationships with the natural environment as matters to be considered by them as citizens, rather than consumers, a further question arises. Do citizens have preferences that can be used to inform social decision making that go beyond the capability to provide answers to "either/or" type referendum questions? That is, is there any prospect of eliciting from individual citizens preference information that could be used to determine relative social values? This is an important question, as democratic political processes appear to require this kind of information. While the precise role of cost-benefit-type analysis in actual social decision making on environmental issues is frequently unclear, it is very often the case that it is felt necessary to have some kind of TCM/CVM exercise conducted. A proposal that development projects with adverse environmental implications be approved or rejected on the basis of a "yes/no" referendum question would appear not to meet the needs of the political process in countries like Australia.

There, in 1989, the federal government established the Resource Assessment Commission (RAC) to advise it on resource use matters. The legislation requires the RAC in conducting an inquiry to take account of the alternative uses of a resource and the "environmental, cultural, social, industry, economic, and other values involved in those uses." It is made explicit that "use" is to cover both conservation and development, and the legislation lays down policy principles according to which competing claims are to be resolved. One of these is that:

> Resource use decisions should seek to optimize the net benefits to the community from the nation's resources, having regard to efficiency of resource use, environmental considerations, economic and ecological sustainability, ecosystem integrity and sustainability, the sustainability of any development, and an equitable distribution of the return on resources.

In an early statement on procedures, the RAC chairperson stated that "we will constantly need to address the problem of how to ascribe sensible values to the intangible or non-marketed benefits of natural resources." In both of the RAC inquiries that have so far been completed, CVM was used, though in neither case do the results arising appear to have greatly influenced the report submitted to government. The RAC would seem to be representative in considering it necessary to attempt to assess relative social values. Some aspects of one of these attempts are discussed in the next section.

Given such considerations, we took the student survey described above further to investigate the existence of citizen preferences as follows. According to their answer for Question 7, respondents were directed to either Question 8 or Question 9. These were covered and not readable, provided that instructions were followed, until after Question 7 had been answered. Those who opted for "a" at Question 7 (citizens) were presented with:

> Question 8. Government purchase would require increased taxation or reduced expenditure. The government is committed to not increasing

taxation. It will not decide where expenditure will be cut until after the purchase is made. The purchase price is $A million, which for example represents AA% of the education budget or AAA% of spending on de-fence. Do you think that the government should purchase at this price? Please indicate yes or no.

Those who opted for "b" at Question 7 (consumers) were presented with:

Question 9. Would you be willing to subscribe $B to the conservation organisation's appeal for the purpose of buying this land? Please indi-cate yes or no.

The total set of questionnaires had been split into three subsets of equal sizes according to the values given for A and B (Table 7.1).

Table 7.1. Subsets by Price

	A	AA	AAA	B
1	150	1	2	10
2	750	5	10	50
3	1500	10	20	100

Of the students handing back usable responses, 19 (14 citizens/5 con-sumers) had received subset 1, 20 (11/9) subset 2, and 24 (19/5) subset 3. Table 7.2 gives the percentages responding "yes."

Table 7.2. Percentages of "Yes" Responses

	Citizens	Consumers
1	92.7	60.0
2	63.6	66.7
3	57.9	60.0

The citizen respondents were apparently more responsive to "price" than the consumer respondents. Testing for the significance of the differences in the proportions for the citizens, the 1/2 difference is significant at 5%, the 2/3 difference is not significant at 10%.

At the time of this experiment the students could be assumed ignorant of CVM. A second experiment was conducted after they had attended a lecture on CVM. It was intended to test for the existence of $U(x,s)$. It in-volved giving the students a sheet of paper, headed with the statement that "This is not a test; it is a survey," with three questions on it. The first was:

1. Below are specified three alternatives open to you, in terms of the levels of consumption of commodities and the existence or non-existence of some anonymous species of Australian mammal. As between the alternatives the consumption levels of the many commodities indicated by dots remain constant. Only beer and wine vary: if you do not like beer and/or wine, substitute mentally for them with things you do like—chocolate bars and/or Coca Cola, for example. Think of these alternatives as relating to daily consumption rates of wine/beer, chocolate/Coca Cola or whatever.

Q^1	Q^2	Q^3
2 glasses wine	1 glass wine	2 glasses wine
1 can beer	2 cans beer	1 can beer
.	.	.
.	.	.
.	.	.
Bequest of species	Bequest of species	No bequest of species— it goes extinct

Make pairwise comparisons of these alternatives, recording the results below. If you prefer one alternative to the other, write, for example, Q^1PQ^2. If you are indifferent between the alternatives, write, for example, Q^1IQ^2. If you are unable to make a choice, (i.e., are unable to express either preference or indifference), write, for example, Q^1NQ^2.

A total of 38 students were given the sheet of paper. None expressed any difficulty in comprehending this question. One response only reported violation of the completeness axiom in respect to comparisons involving Q^3. Three responses reported violations of the transitivity axiom. Two responses involved complete and transitive, but unusual orderings: Q^1PQ^2, Q^3PQ^2, Q^1IQ^3; Q^1PQ^2, Q^3PQ^2, Q^1PQ^3. The remaining 32 responses, 84.2% of the total, fell into two groups. Group A involved 19 responses expressing a preference as between Q^1 and Q^2, with both of these preferred to Q^3. Group B involved 13 responses expressing indifference between Q^1 and Q^2, with both of these preferred to Q^3. The group B responses, 34.2% of the total, are interesting in that they are perhaps somewhat suggestive of a lexicographic ordering, which would have some intuitive plausibility in this sort of context. The group A responses,

50% of the total, are entirely consistent with the existence of a utility function.

If the lexicographic suggestion associated with group B is ignored, 84.2% of responses are consistent with the existence of a utility function.

The second question asked the students whether they thought that "decisions about species preservation should be made by comparing the costs involved with the aggregate of individuals' willingness-to-pay," and 79% answered "no" to this question. A "no" response is consistent with the variant Sagoff hypothesis. A third question simply asked for comment, and elicited a variety of responses. Blamey and Common (1992) report the main features of these and describe the scenario for the first experiment in detail.

Clearly, there are a number of reasons why the results of these two exercises do not support strong conclusions. However, we think that they are worth reporting in so far as they indicate possible directions for further research. The results of the first exercise show some support for the Sagoff hypothesis, while the results from the second show some support for the variant Sagoff hypothesis. The results from the first exercise can also be taken as suggesting that it could be possible to get some indication as to citizen-type preferences by interrogating individuals as citizens. The limited evidence considered in this section does not, at any rate, warrant dismissal of the Sagoff hypotheses, which, as noted in the previous section, are consistent with a number of other contributions to the literature. If it is accepted that some CVM respondents are acting as citizens, or are influenced by the view that they should be acting as citizens, this has implications for the interpretation, and possible uses, of CVM results.

THE INTERPRETATION OF CONTINGENT VALUATION RESULTS

If CVM results are to be used in cost-benefit analyses of projects as suggested earlier in this chapter, then it is necessary that they are taken to be results pertaining to WTP/WTA on the part of consumers. It is also necessary that they are taken to be consumers' appraisals in relation to the environmental impacts of the project, EC, which are to be compared with the net value of the project, B_d–C_d. What is required from an application of CVM is not, that is, consumers' appraisals of the net benefit of the project to them. CVM questions are not supposed to elicit responses as WTP/WTA in regard to the project. They are supposed to elicit responses relating to the environmental impacts of the project. Thus, the CVM scenario and questioning must isolate the environmental impacts from other aspects of the project, and elicit consumers' valuations of those impacts. Table 7.3 provides a possible matrix of CVM responses.

Table 7.3. 2x2 Matrix of Possible CVM Responses*

	Relating only to EC	Relating to EC and B_d–C_d
Consumer	A	B
Citizen	C	D

*Following Blamey (1991).

If the responses are to be properly used in cost-benefit analysis, they must be category A responses. The problem of picking up category B responses has been fairly widely noted in the literature (see below). It may be noted that type-B responses would presumably be in the nature of the outcome of a personal, consumer-type cost-benefit analysis. The possibility that responses are of category C has been discussed in previous sections. It is quite conceivable that many responses are, in fact, category D responses. Individuals responding as citizens may well incorporate into their replies citizen assessments of implications for jobs, for example. It appears reasonable, in the current state of knowledge about how individuals respond to CVM-type surveys, to speculate that D responses are actually more likely than B responses, generally, where it is existence benefits that are at issue. Except where the project inputs and outputs captured in B_d and C_d impact directly, as with employment prospects, say, on a responding individual, it is more plausible that they would influence a citizen than a consumer.

Clearly, if respondents to a CVM application are not solely of type A, this has implications for any attempt to use the results in the cost-benefit analysis framework.

There are several consequences for the interpretation of CV studies if individuals respond as citizens rather than consumers. Firstly, citizen behavior may account for a large proportion of non-responses if individuals refuse to be "pulled" into a consumer role by the CV scenario. Some individuals may reject the whole notion of trading off dollars for the environment. Biases will result if their true type A responses are higher (or lower) than the sample average. Secondly, a percentage of actual responses to the CV question may be a product, wholly or partly, of citizen considerations. Such responses can be seen to fall into two sub-categories—those where the dollar figure supplied to respondents is actually considered by respondents, and those where it is not. The latter case may be referred to as "committed-yes responses," the occurrence of which can pose considerable problems for CV. An individual who has formulated prior beliefs on a particular environmental issue may make a "yes" or "no" response in this light without regard for the magnitude of the payment figure. The former case may involve individuals formulating citizen strength of preferences in favor of preservation or development, and trading this strength of preference off with the dollar payment. These "cross-role" considerations may result in severe biases in CV results, since studies in behavioral psychology show that individuals can exhibit a high degree of "stickiness" in respect to their trading off of moral commitments (Etzioni 1988). Individuals may thus respond as citizens unless the costs to them of doing so are perceived to be "unacceptably high."

Two recent Australian CVM exercises will now be discussed in the light of the above discussion. Imber et al. (1991) report the results of a CV, conducted as part of a Resource Assessment Commission (RAC) inquiry, which lead to the assessment that Australians would be willing to pay (at least) $647 million per annum to have the Kakadu Conservation Zone incorporated into the Kakadu National Park, and thus made unavailable for mining. Imber et al. refer to the "commodity" to which this aggregate WTP attaches as "preservation benefits." In our terminology, these would be mainly, but not entirely, existence benefits. This result generated considerable interest and some controversy, especially since the net present value, B_d-C_d, of the proposed mining operation that lead to the inquiry was assessed at some $80 million for a ten year life of the mine. In fact, it appears that the CVM results played little part in leading to the inquiry advice to the government that the mining development should not go ahead.

Of the many issues raised in connection with this CVM exercise, only those relevant to the hypothesis that a percentage of respondents failed to give purely type A responses will be covered here.[10]

---

10. For three critiques of Imber et al. (1991), as well as responses thereto by Carson, see RAC (1991).

The CVM involved using separate samples drawn from the population of the Northern Territory (NT), the state in which Kakadu is located, and of the Australian population as a whole. Individual WTP was lower for the former sample. This has been taken to indicate that individuals in that sample were incorporating into their responses valuations relating to non-environmental aspects of the mining project. Northern Territorians, it is argued, stated lower WTPs because their responses were "contaminated" by awareness of the losses, in terms of jobs, tax revenues, etc., to their state if the project did not go ahead. Carson (RAC 1991, 8) argues that proper statistical analysis suggests that "there is not a 'general' NT depressing effect on the willingness-to-pay estimates beyond that explained by differences in the covariates." It is interesting to observe that these covariates actually include citizen-type variables, such as responses to questions pertaining to (1) the importance of jobs in determining best resource use, (2) willingness to proceed with development when the adverse effects are considered possible, but unlikely, and (3) the importance of financial benefits to Australia from developments of natural resources. Carson's observations regarding the differences in WTP for the NT and Australian samples thus appear to be consistent with the former diverging more from the required type A responses.

A second criticism of the RAC study relevant to the above discussions is that of ABARE (1991; see also Quiggin 1991), who present a statistical analysis of the data generated by this CVM application, based on "an alternative interpretation of the survey data in which respondents base their answers primarily on prior beliefs" (ABARE, 20). This interpretation is that some individuals were actually responding as voters, rather than consumers. The Kakadu CVM used the discrete choice method of WTP elicitation in which individuals are asked "yes/no" on a specified sum. According to the response to the first such choice offered, individuals were given a second "yes/no" choice in respect to a higher or lower sum. The ABARE/Quiggin analysis investigated their voting proposition by considering whether responses were insensitive to income, and by testing the restriction that individuals responding as voters answered "yes/yes" or "no/no" regardless of the sums involved. The first involved simply drawing on the findings of the RAC study, namely that income does not have a statistically significant effect on estimated willingness-to-pay for either Australian population or NT samples. Carson (RAC 1991) shows that this result no longer occurs when other attitudinal and demographic variables are included in a multivariate regression model. The citizen-type variables identified above in relation to the NT discussion are again largely behind this result, however. Indeed, the fact that variables such as income become significant when citizen-type explanatory variables are included within the model, tends to suggest that a combined consumer/citizen model may be the most appropriate for explaining CV responses. Appendix 6 of the RAC report also reveals that responses to the following question have a significant relationship with willingness-to-pay probabilities, "Do you think Australia needs to concentrate more on protecting the environment, or more on developing the economy, or would you say we currently have a reasonable balance?" This question clearly involves responses as citizens, not as consumers.

A second aspect of the ABARE/Quiggin analysis pertains to the assumption that some individuals respond as citizens who are committed to a position, one way or the other, on the project and that the commitment is unaffected by the size of monetary sums mentioned in connection with the project. The results presented in ABARE (1991) are interpreted as being consistent with 53% of individuals responding as voters, of whom 39% support preservation (i.e., are committed to not allowing mining). Carson (RAC 1991) disputes this interpretation of the statistical results reported in Appendix B of ABARE (1991). However, Carson does not appear to dispute the more general proposition that some individuals responded as citizens/voters rather than consumers. His objection is to the interpretation that voters were unresponsive to the postulated income loss:

> ABARE seems to be arguing that Australians are incapable of understanding and answering questions of the form: "would you vote for this policy if the cost to you was $x, yes or no," whether in an actual referendum or on a survey (3).

It was previously noted that Mitchell and Carson (1989) expressed the view that for goods with which respondents have little familiarity, the appropriate model for CVM is referendum voting rather than the market model. This view suggests that CVM results are not appropriate for use in cost-benefit analysis. This is the central point of the ABARE/Quiggin critique of the Kakadu CVM exercise. If CVM surveys are to be considered as surrogates for referenda, rather than for markets, this does have implications for their design. Such a position also raises questions about the cost-benefit analysis approach to social decision making on projects with environmental impacts. If CVM is not regarded as capable of generating consumer valuations, and given that no alternative has been proposed as being so capable, then it would appear that the cost-benefit approach is non-operational at the level of principal.

A recent Australian study conducted by one of the authors did depart from the strict cost-benefit analysis framework. It concerned preservation values in regard to forests on Fraser Island, which is in the state of Queensland.[11] Survey respondents were provided with arguments for and against the continuation of logging, provided by participants in the public debate on the question. They were then asked whether they favored a ban on logging or its continuation. Only those who favored preservation, a ban on logging, were asked about WTP for preservation.

The rationale for this approach was as follows. The issue was controversial and had received a great deal of publicity in the period prior to the survey. It was considered that the majority of respondents would have taken a position on the logging issue on the basis of some appreciation of the implications for jobs in the area and similar matters, as well as an appreciation of preservation benefits. It was considered unlikely, that is, that many would respond in the A mode from the table above, as cost-benefit analysis requires. It was anticipated that many would respond in B or D mode.

The WTP estimates arising were interpreted as willingness-to-pay to prevent logging, not as willingness-to-pay to preserve the forest areas in question, on the part of those who had taken the view that logging should be prevented. The results were taken to provide an estimate of the strength of preference of those who favored preservation. The report on the survey explicitly acknowledged the departure from the standard cost-benefit analysis framework, and recommended that its results be interpreted as conservative estimates of the type A results required by that framework. Blamey (1991) gives the main results arising and discusses a number of matters bearing upon their likely reliability when so interpreted. Several possible sources of upward bias are identified, and the maximum conceivable total effect is assessed at overstatement by a factor of 10. If the calculated aggregate WTP is divided by 10, it then exceeds the assessed commercial net benefits $(B_d–C_d)$ of logging by a factor of approximately 10.

---

11. Blamey (1991) provides a summary account of the study and its results.

This study appears to be the only one that explicitly addresses the problem of B/D type CVM responses in its design. It did not attempt to distinguish between B and D type responses. As noted above, it appears that type D responses would be more likely to occur than type B responses. Clearly, there is scope for empirical research here.

A problem that has been raised in regard to the use of CVM responses in cost-benefit analysis of projects with environmental impacts is the disparity between the size of inferred WTP and inferred WTA. As set out by Knetsch (1990), the problem is that WTA is generally found to be much larger than WTP with respect to the same environmental "commodity." The divergence should not, it is generally understood, be as large as is commonly estimated. The issue has been discussed in the literature within the framework of the CV respondent as consumer, i.e., within the context of consumer demand analysis and utility theory. For respondents to existence value questions in citizen mode, the "every citizen has a price" phenomenon may well be operative and do much to explain the observed disparities. If individuals regard an environmental asset as the property of the citizenry of which they are members, then moral considerations may asymmetrically affect their responses to WTP/WTA questions seeking to elicit a consumer response. Requested to pay as a consumer, the citizen will likely find the question inappropriate, but not wildly inappropriate. Thus, one might strongly believe that the relief of poverty is properly a matter for collective social action, yet not refuse a request for a donation to a private charity. On the other hand, a request to accept a payment to oneself in return for giving up what is regarded as a truly collective asset would jar greatly—one is being asked to accept a bribe to act immorally. Consider the question: how much would you need to be paid to accept the complete abolition of all welfare payments to the poor? There is no doubt some non-infinite but large answer to this question for most people, i.e., some price at which prospective consumer gain is sufficient to compensate for abandonment of citizen responsibilities. Further, presumably few would accept the proposition that the answers to such a question by individuals should be relevant, by way of comparing the aggregate of such answers with the savings in government expenditure, to a decision on whether or not government should make welfare payments. If individuals regard questions relating to the existence of environmental assets as falling within the domain of citizen rather than consumer choice, then one might expect that CVM responses on WTA would be higher than on WTP.

Harris and Brown (1992) consider the WTA/WTP discrepancy question in the context of a discussion of the context in which valuation responses are given. They focus particularly on the matter of implicit property rights, but also discuss questions of "motives like personal responsibility and altruism" (73). They report the results of a mail questionnaire sent to residents of Idaho, in which the following question was asked:

> Suppose that land development might result in a major reduction of nongame wildlife and endangered species. Suppose also that this loss would not occur if enough dollars were spent to prevent it. Which one of the following best describes your response to this situation?

Four alternative responses were offered. Five percent of respondents went for the alternative, "The loss of Idaho's nongame wildlife and endangered species does not concern me." Ten percent went for: "Only those people to whom Idaho's nongame wildlife and endangered species are important should pay to prevent the loss." Fifty-three percent went for, "The state of Idaho should pay to prevent this loss with tax dollars from all Idaho taxpayers." These results appear to be consistent with the hypothesis that the majority of individuals, 53%, responded that this was a matter for citizens. The 10% response could be interpreted to express the view that it is a consumers' matter. The remaining respondents, 32%, opted for, "Only those people responsible for this loss should pay to prevent it." Harris and Brown (1992) interpret these responses as reflecting the view that "society in general is the loser from the proposed development and society's members should be compensated by the gainers" (85). With this interpretation, it appears that these responses can also be classified as citizen responses. Then, the citizen response proportion is 85%, and includes citizens' WTP and citizens' WTA. Harris and Brown do not report any results relating to dollar amounts for WTP or WTA.

CONCLUSIONS: FUTURE RESEARCH DIRECTIONS

This chapter has identified the dominant form of sustainability-relevant pseudo market valuation as the use of the CVM to estimate the non-use values of environmental assets for incorporation in cost-benefit analysis. While this involves the assumption that individuals have utility functions defined over arguments, which comprise both ordinary commodities and "environmental commodities," this assumption does not appear to have been subjected to any empirical research. On the other hand, there exist many contributions to the literature that contend that individuals cannot be adequately understood within the single utility function framework. A number of these contributions relate this specifically to the question of social decision making on "projects" with environmental impacts. In this context, the chapter especially noted Sagoff's distinction between the individual as consumer and as citizen, and his contention that it is the second of these selves that is relevant to such social decision making. The very limited amount of evidence bearing directly upon this distinction and contention has been considered. The last section examined some surveys, which while they did not directly address these issues, generated some relevant evidence.

We cannot claim that any firm positive conclusions are warranted. The material reviewed in this chapter does add weight to the view that the extant approach to pseudo market valuations and their use is likely based on weak foundations. It has been established that there is a case for new directions of research in regard to environmental valuation and its use in social decision making. We now briefly indicate what we think those directions are.

First, there is a need to investigate directly whether the utility functions required for the standard approach can reasonably be assumed to exist.

Second, the Sagoff hypotheses require further examination. Do individuals respond to CVM non-use value questions as citizens rather than consumers? Do they think that they should? If the answer to either of these questions is "yes," how does that affect their responses to questions posed on the assumption that their only response mode is as consumer, and what are the implications arising for the interpretation of aggregate WTP/WTA estimates based on their responses?

Third, if individuals relate to aspects of the natural environment as citizens rather than consumers, do they have citizen preference orderings that can be used to inform social decision making in relation to sustainability-relevant policy questions? If such preference orderings exist, can means be devised to interrogate citizens that will reveal useful information on those orderings?

In this chapter we have given some indications of how one might start to think about trying to answer some of these questions. There is much in the existing CVM-related literature that is also relevant, of course. Many of the problems that attend attempts to interrogate individuals as consumers will also attend attempts to interrogate them as citizens. The problem of informational conditioning is as relevant to a citizen as to a consumer, for example. The point is not that, if research confirms it as appropriate, a switch from seeking sustainability-relevant valuations from individuals as consumers to individuals as citizens will solve all problems. It is that it would then put those problems in a more appropriate context.

REFERENCES

ABARE. 1991. Valuing Conservation in the Kakadu Conservation Zone. Submission to the Resource Assessment Commission. Canberra: Australian Government Publishing Service.

Andreoni, J. 1990. Impure altruism and donations to public goods: a theory of warm glow giving. *The Economic Journal* 100: 464–77.

Bennett, J. W. 1984. Using direct questioning to value the existence benefits of preserved natural areas. *Australian Journal of Agricultural Economics* 28: 136–52.

Bishop, R. C. 1978. Endangered species and uncertainty: the economics of a safe minimum standard. *American Journal of Agricultural Economics* 60: 10–18.

Bishop, R. C., T. A. Heberlein, and N. J. Kealy. 1983. Contingent valuation of environmental assets: comparisons with a simulated market. *Natural Resources Journal* 23: 618–33.

Blamey, R. K. 1991. Contingent Valuation and Fraser Island. Paper presented at Twentieth Conference of Economists, Economic Society of Australia, October, Hobart.

Blamey, R. K., and M. Common. 1992. Sustainability and the Limits to Pseudo Market Valuation. Paper presented at the International Society for Ecological Economics Conference on "Investing in Natural Capital: A Prerequisite for Sustainability," August, Stockholm.

Boulding, K. E. 1969. Economics as a moral science. *American Economic Review* 59: 1–12.

Collard, D. 1978. Altruism and Economy: A Study of Non-Selfish Economics. Salisbury: Martin Robertson.

Common, M., and D. W. McKenney. In press. 1994. Investigating the reliability of a hedonic travel cost model: a Monte Carlo approach. *Canadian Journal of Forest Research.*

Common, M., and T. Norton. 1993. Biodiversity, Natural Resource Accounting and Ecological Monitoring. Centre for Resource and Environmental Studies Working Paper 1993/1. Canberra: Australian National University

Common, M., and C. Perrings. 1992. Towards an ecological economics of sustainability. *Ecological Economics* 6: 7–34.

Costanza, R., S. C. Farber, and J. Maxwell. 1989. Valuation and management of wetland ecosystems. *Ecological Economics* 1: 335–61.

Crocker, T., and J. Shogren. 1991. Preference learning and contingent valuation methods. In Environmental Policy and the Economy, eds. F. Dietz, F. van der Ploeg and J. van der Straaten. Amsterdam: North-Holland.

Cummings, R. G., D. S. Brookshire, and W. D. Schultze. 1986. Valuing Environmental Goods: A State of the Art Assessment of the Contingent Valuation Method. Totowa: Rowman and Allanheld.

Dawkins, R. 1978. The Selfish Gene. Granada: St. Albans.

Deaton, A., and J. Muellbauer. 1980. Economics and Consumer Behaviour. Cambridge: Cambridge Univ. Press.

Downs, A. 1957. An Economic Theory of Democracy. New York: Harper and Row.

Ellis, G. M., and A. C. Fisher. 1987. Valuing the environment as input. *Journal of Environmental Economics and Management* 25: 149–56.

Etzioni, A. 1988. The Moral Dimension: Toward a New Economics. New York: The Free Press.

Friedman, M. 1953. Essays in Positive Economics. Chicago: Univ. of Chicago Press.

Goodin, R. E. 1991. A green theory of value. In The Humanities and the Australian Environment, ed. D. Mulvaney. Canberra: Australian Academy of the Humanities.

Gregory, R., E. Niemi, and R. Mendelsohn. 1989. A model for evaluating the impact of forest management regulations. *Journal of Environmental Management* 29: 129–44.

Hanley, N. D. 1989. Valuing rural recreation benefits: an empirical comparison of two approaches. *Journal of Agricultural Economics* 6: 361–74.

Harris, C. C., and G. Brown. 1992. Gain, loss and personal responsibility: the role of motivation in resource valuation decision-making. *Ecological Economics* 5: 73–92.

Harsanyi, J. C. 1955. Cardinal welfare, individualistic ethics, and interpersonal comparisons of utility. *Journal of Political Economy* 61: 309--21.

Howarth, R. B. 1991. Intertemporal equilibria and exhaustible resources: an overlapping generations approach. *Ecological Economics* 4: 237–53.

Imber, D., G. Stevenson, and L. Wilks. 1991. A Contingent Valuation Survey of the Kakadu Conservation Zone. RAC Research Paper Number 3. Resource Assessment Commission, Canberra.

Kahneman, D., and J. L. Knetsch. 1992a. Valuing public goods: the purchase of moral satisfaction. *Journal of Environmental Economics and Management* 22: 57–70.

———. 1992b. Contingent valuation and the value of public goods: reply. *Journal of Environmental Economics and Management* 22: 90–94.

Knetsch, J. L. 1990. Environmental policy implications of disparities between willingness to pay and compensation demanded measures of values. *Journal of Environmental Economics and Management* 18: 227–37.

Lutz, M. A., and K. Lux. 1988. *Humanistic Economics: The New Challenge*. New York: Bootstrap Press.

Margolis, H. 1982. Selfishness, Altruism and Rationality: A Theory of Social Choice. Cambridge: Cambridge Univ. Press.

Maslow, A. H. 1954. Motivation and Personality. New York: Harper and Row.

———. 1968. Toward a Psychology of Being. New York: Van Nostrand Rheinhald.

Mitchell, R. C., and R. Carson. 1989. Using Surveys to Value Public Goods: The Contingent Valuation Method. Washington, DC: Resources for the Future.

Norton, B. G. 1986. On the inherent danger of undervaluing species. In The Preservation of Species, ed. B. G. Norton. Princeton: Princeton Univ. Press.

Page, T. 1991. Sustainability and the problem of valuation. In Ecological Economics: The Science and Management of Sustainability, ed. R. Costanza. New York: Columbia Univ. Press.

Penz, C. P. 1986. Consumer Sovereignty and Human Interests. Cambridge: Cambridge Univ. Press.

Quiggin, J. 1991. Referendums and Pseudo-Referendums in Contingent Valuation. Mimeo. Department of Economics, Research School of Social Sciences, Australian National University, Canberra.

R.A.C. 1991. Commentaries on the Resource Assessment Commission's Contingent Valuation Survey of the Kakadu Conservation Zone. Canberra: Resource Assessment Commission.

Randall, A. 1986. Human preferences, economics and the preservation of species. In The Preservation of Species, ed. B. G. Norton. Princeton: Princeton Univ. Press.

Repetto, R., W. Magrath, M. Wells, C. Beer, and F. Rossini. 1989. Wasting Assets: Natural Resources in the National Income Accounts. Washington, DC: World Resources Institute.

Sagoff, M. 1988. The Economy of the Earth. Cambridge: Cambridge Univ. Press.

Samples, K. C., J. A. Dixon, and M. M. Gowen. 1986. Information disclosure and species valuation. *Land Economics* 62: 306–12.

Sen, A. K. 1977. Rational fools: a critique of the behavioural foundations of economic theory. *Philosophy and Public Affairs* 16: 317–44.

Smith, V. K. 1991. Can we measure the economic value of environmental amenities? *Southern Economic Journal* (April): 865–78.

———. 1992. Arbitrary values, good causes and premature verdicts. *Journal of Environmental Economics and Management* 22: 71–89.

Willis, K., and G. D. Garrod. 1992. On-site recreation surveys and selection effects: valuing open access recreation on inland waterways. In Tourism and the Environment, eds. H. Briassoulis and J. van der Straaten. Dordrecht: Kluwer.

World Commission on Environment and Development. 1987. *Our Common Future.* Oxford: Oxford Univ. Press.

PART III

IMPLEMENTATION AND POLICY

8 HISTORICAL AND FUTURE MODELS OF ECONOMIC DEVELOPMENT AND NATURAL ENVIRONMENT

Jeroen C. J. M. van den Bergh
Department of Spatial Economics
Faculty of Economics
Free University
De Boelelaan 1105
1081 HV, Amsterdam
The Netherlands

Jan van der Straaten
European Centre for Nature Conservation
Tilburg University
P.O.Box 1352
5004 BJ, Tilburg
The Netherlands

INTRODUCTION

This chapter will examine several issues related to the environmental sustainability of long-term development, both on the level of concept and implementation. Attention is devoted to the use of systematic and formal approaches for dealing with the topic of integrating economic analysis—"economics"—with knowledge of natural, environmental processes—"ecology." "Sustainable development" is often used as an analytical benchmark, ideological perspective, or long-term policy objective in the context of economic development and natural environment. Regardless of the precise interpretation of this concept, it is important for both theoretical and operational study that attention is paid to the likelihood of occurrence, as well as to the economic and environmental characteristics of unsustainable development. This means that frameworks used to elucidate the potential development interactions with the natural environment must be capable of recognizing and characterizing unsustainable patterns within economic-environmental systems, rather than adhering to only those development plans that are sustainable. These plans can merely give limited understanding for policy making because they represent pictures of a system reflecting static, unstable, unlikely, or very sensitive time patterns.

The search for a broader range of potential development paths, sustainable and unsustainable, may render information that is helpful to both scientific knowledge and policy preparation. It means first of all that an integrated perspective towards economic-environmental analysis is adopted. In the context of long-term analysis, a recently more supported conviction is that we must learn from "la longue durée" and adopt a more or less historical analysis (Wilkinson 1973; Common 1988; Ponting 1991; Pezzey 1993; Simmons 1989). This may even go beyond the level and time-span of phenomena that have occurred over the past few decades. In the context of long-term development and natural environment, we look therefore at some frameworks of relationships between economy,[1] institutions, and environment at different important phases in the history of mankind. The chapter concludes by noting particular inconsistencies in the steps to be taken when the implementation of sustainable development is attempted. They include valuation and analysis, evaluation and social decision making, and instruments and institutions.

SUSTAINABLE DEVELOPMENT: DEFINITIONS AND CONDITIONS

The title of this section is critical to resolving the confusion that is likely to result from the existing literature on sustainable development. A definition of sustainable development may take a teleological point of departure by focusing on such indicators as income, production, and welfare (per capita), and by requiring indicators to move along non-declining

---

1. The term "economy" is used here in a narrow sense. Especially from an environmental point of view, one might argue that "economy" includes the "environment" in terms of production factor, source of amenities, etc. However, for the sake of clarity, we prefer a distinction analogous to a system's approach, which identifies elements such as environment, economy, and development. The implication is that readers may sometimes interpret "economy" as "society," but not as an economic-environmental system.

paths over time.[2] One can then derive conditions on control variables such as investment, resource extraction, and waste emission (e.g., Van den Bergh and Nijkamp 1991a).

Contrary to this approach, one can opt for a deontological type of definition of sustainable development, starting with conditions such as those based on the concept of a capital stock. The interpretation of sustainability is then based on maintenance of (the size of) a stock.[3] What this means is not immediately evident since one may refer to the physical size or the economic value.[4] A more disaggregative approach perceives the natural environment as a composition of many stocks of capital. One division is into renewable and non-renewable stocks. Another is into regenerative and assimilative capacities. Furthermore, one may also add an acceptability constraint for restricting compensation and substitution strategies with a harmful effect on biodiversity and environmental integrity.

In addition to these two approaches, one may distinguish between strong and weak versions of sustainable development. Therefore, one has to recognize the relationship between man-made or economic and natural capital (both aggregates), as well as their changes over time. Strong sustainability may mean that whatever indicator is used, whether it based on quantity and/or quality factors, it must be non-decreasing over time. Consistent with this, weak sustainability should be interpreted as reflecting temporary decreases.

There is a second interpretation of strong and weak sustainability based on substitution and complementarity of economic and natural stocks of capital. Strong sustainability requires that both are non-decreasing in the sense of some relevant indicator. The weak version takes their sum, or some other aggregate measure, and requires that this should not decrease over time. Based on the latter notion is the idea of compensa-

---

2. See Pezzey (1989), who makes a distinction between different types of sustainability, and furthermore separates sustainability from survivability and efficiency (optimality).

3. This approach is clear in the literature on sustainable use of renewable natural resources in resource management (Clark 1976).

4. Based on capital theory, one may regard the value of a stock as the value of the goods and services (or work) it generates in the future. This is related to future prices, discount rates, and technological conditions. Technological progress may increase the effective resource stock size by allowing for the same amount of work derived from one unit of the resource at a later time compared to the present.

tion[5] in which a loss in natural capital must be compensated for by an addition in man-made or a combination of man-made and semi-natural capital.

It may be clear that in formulating a definition of sustainable development, one is faced with the difficulty of choosing a point of departure. Many authors have commented on this "definitional hiatus." It seems pointless to continue to engage in this discussion. There seems to be no apparent boundary between those developments that are sustainable and unsustainable. For this reason a more fruitful direction of research can be taken, namely one which concentrates on determining a set of qualifications of unsustainable development, for instance: (1) unstable behavior (e.g., negative trends, unstable cycles) in variables like income, welfare, and production; (2) highly variable patterns or negative trends in variables with high risks of collapse, such as renewable natural resource stocks; (3) positive trends in population, and agricultural or industrial pressure on land; and (4) positive trends in pollution stocks. Likewise, one can formulate very strict conditions that are sure to realize sustainable development. In between, one finds a zone where the difference between sustainability and unsustainability is dominated by uncertainty and lack of information. For putting strict definitions and conditions in a right perspective, one should finally also consider the open, regional character of many regulated spatial systems (e.g., nations). Ignoring this will inevitably lead to a purely theoretical approach.

INTEGRATION OF ENVIRONMENTAL CONSIDERATIONS IN ECONOMIC ANALYSIS

Here, it will be argued that for a useful, integrated method of analysis for sustainable development questions, an extensive interpretation of "integration" is required. The integration of economics and environment is much discussed, but can only become explicit after a distinction is made between mutual relationships that exist between economy, environment, and development. The integration concept is usually kept vague, and it can refer to combining concepts (e.g., in a verbal or qualitative sense), data (e.g., for statistical analysis), theories (e.g., micro-economic and resource-ecological), or models (e.g., regional economic and

---

5. For a fundamental discussion see Klaassen and Botterweg (1976), and for a
    neoclassical interpretation see Hartwick (1977).

ecosystem models). For the purpose of studying sustainable development, one should not be satisfied with static images of interactions between environment and economy. What may be a final goal in terms of
models can be signified as a two-way environment-economy interaction
scheme. One can regard this as a misuse or overuse of terms, but it is just
to distinguish it from one-way impacts, for which often, and
inappropriately so, the terminology "interactions" is used as well. This
can immediately be linked to the misuse of the term "integration" in the
context of economics and environment, or between the disciplines of
economics and ecology.[6] Sometimes the natural environment is included
in economic studies by taking constant environmental limits as given. In
such cases the use of the phrasing "one-way impact" is in order. Many
existing approaches in linking environmental considerations to economic
analysis take such an approach. They will be discussed below in a
classification of possible lines of work towards integration. Anyway, for
the study of long-term development, one cannot eliminate impacts in one
direction without losing some interpretive ability. It is very likely that the
magnitude of such a loss is increasing with the time-horizon of the study
that is being conducted.

A tentative grouping of types of integration of economic analysis and
models with understanding of environmental-ecological processes and
systems is the following one:

- calculating admissible economic activity levels in view of environmental safety limits;

- taking into account costs of adjustment actions to meet environmental
  standards;

- including economic-monetary valuation of environmental goods and
  services or environmental effects, losses, and damages; and

- describing physical-material interactions between economic and environmental systems.

The first approach describes either physical economic relationships
between inputs and outputs, different activities and sectors, or relates
physical interactions with the environment in terms of resource extraction and waste emission to output levels in one way or another measured

---

6. For more discussion on this in the context of integrated modelling see Van den Bergh
   and Nijkamp (1991b); for a formal approach see Van den Bergh (1993).

in monetary units (for an overview, see Briassoulis 1986). An example is the input-output model with emission coefficients developed by Leontief (1970). Physical environmental limits may be imposed on resource extraction, waste emission, and land use. The disadvantage of this approach is that the environment is regarded as fixed, providing merely static constraints for economic activities. This approach is not very suitable for development studies, because such constraints cannot be satisfied over longer periods of time, and too many changes occur in the natural environment that may affect the necessary safety constraints. Though for many practical reasons and lack of sufficient knowledge fixed environmental limits may be reasonable, we need different approaches for development studies that are more theoretical and explorative in nature.

The second approach considers the cost of performing activities like waste abatement, treatment (e.g., Jantzen and Velthuijsen 1991), the use of resource efficient techniques, and recycling materials. Economic efficiency is an objective on a micro level (maximizing profits or minimizing costs) or on a macro level (maximizing social welfare, national production or income, or economic growth exceeding some minimum rate). If one is specifically interested in answers to questions of sustainable development, then dynamic considerations of costs, substitution, capacity, and income effects seem more obvious than mere static ones. One is typically searching for levels of interactions with the natural environment that are optimal from an economic efficiency point of view. The approach therefore derives from cost-benefit analysis. Alternatively, it can be combined with the first approach by appending the physical environmental constraints (representing standards), which give rise to constrained optimization. A third, intermediate option is to include the levying of taxes or donation of subsidies in the model as financial checks on the level interactions with the natural environment. Again, as in the first approach, the assumed fixed character of the natural environment is the main deficiency of this method for long-term studies of development.

The third approach is based on estimating the monetary value of services provided by the natural environment or changes therein (e.g., through damages). It can serve as an input to evaluation, notably on the basis of CBA. Various valuation techniques may be used, based on, for instance, travel cost, contingent valuation, and hedonic pricing. Usually the orientation is towards one specific part of the natural environment, a small isolated ecosystem, or a specific problem (disappearance of a natural area). This approach does not take a general, multi-activity view on economic-environmental relationships. One may consider this approach as comparative static, because it can only deal with discrete states, such as existence or non-existence of a natural system. Transition periods involving dynamic processes from one state to another are not dealt with. Finally, this approach may be regarded as indirect and based on implicit and hidden assumptions, since many causal relationships and complex interdependency patterns are bypassed. The main advantage of it is which monetary outcomes are generated which fit easily into economic methods of evaluation. More will be said about this approach in a later section.

The last approach can be regarded as little inquired into, for the obvious reason of being interdisciplinary in nature. Integration in this approach takes place by descriptions on four levels (cf. Van den Bergh 1991): (1) material flows between economy and natural environment based on materials balance conditions; (2) effects of human systems (economy and population) on environmental quality through immaterial or less-tangible categories of impacts, such as land use, noise, and soil exploitation; (3) effects of environmental conditions on economic production, consumption, and health, including for instance, negative pollution effects; and, (4) production functions with a mix of economic and natural factors of production, such as can be found in renewable and non-renewable resource extraction, in recreation, and in agriculture. Such an approach requires a lot of input from various disciplines and is therefore rather time-consuming. The main advantage of this approach is that external effects can be dealt with explicitly, in addition to economic effects occurring through price processes. Consequently, the external effects are "internalized" in the method of analysis. Therefore, this type of modeling can be insightful for long-term issues of environment and economic development.

MODELS OF HISTORY

Before implementing models of the latter type, we consider different conceptual representations of long-term economic-environmental relationships, although in a very general schematic way. This includes two main aspects: (1) interactions in various periods of historical time are sketched; and (2) processes relevant to long-term change are indicated.

Figures 8.1 to 8.3 show economic-environment relationships in different periods of time. Each figure can be compared with the others since similar elements are represented by similar boxes or terms. The total set of figures can thus be regarded as a development of one economic-environmental system over a very long period of time. The addition of a term or box denotes then the change of the system from one given structure to another. The hunting-gathering era, in which mankind was completely dependent on hunting, fishing, and gathering for its food supply, is chosen as a starting point. Recognizing that it is difficult to pinpoint exact times in this context, this period extends from about 2 million years ago, (i.e., when prototype men Homo habilis and Homo erectus evolved), or perhaps 90,000 B.C. (when Homo sapiens appears) to about 10,000 B.C. (the slow introduction of cereals and domesticates in a few regions around the world). An evolutionary trait with considerable ecological effect falls in this period, namely the control over fire, estimated to occur around 500,000 B.C. (Simmons 1989).

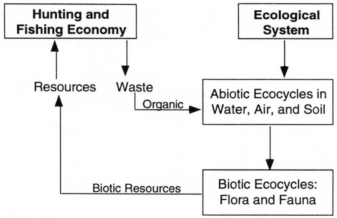

Figure 8.1. Hunting culture.

The traditional economy in Figure 8.1 is composed of two production sectors—hunting and fishing—which supply food for final consumption. The effects of these activities on the natural environment occur through use of biotic resources and organic pollution of air and water. Such effects are local and small in scale. This traditional economy is quite stable as a result of the absence of technological progress and population increase. Two types of culture are possible, namely a tribal one where people are living in harmony with their local natural environment, and a nomadic one where people are continually migrating as a reaction to a disequilibrium between an economy and its natural environment (cf. Wilkinson 1973).

The second scheme represents an agricultural society. Here, fuel wood is introduced in the economy, and land is used to grow crops or herd animals. People can concentrate so that both population density and population levels can increase. Such increases create a need for improving the production per acre, leading to technological development and change in the organizational structure of society. The latter is accompanied by changes in distribution of incomes and ownership to re-sources and means of production. Over-exploitation of resources and land may thus occur. The environmental effects are mostly local and still small in scale, except for land degradation. However, some interdependent relationships arise from regional interactions. For instance, problems and development of cities depend indirectly on the food potential op-portunities offered by agriculture. The change from the situation depicted in Figure 8.1 to that of Figure 8.2 can be understood as a transformation of a hunting culture to a farming society.

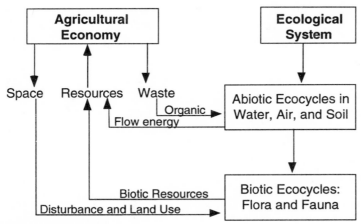

Figure 8.2. Agricultural society.

With the introduction of mineral resources in economic processes, a more complex economy can evolve. This will include several types of production processes (manufacturing, conversion, and generation of services), as well as different types of time delays, through investment and residuals recovery processes. Recovery is here meant to also include such diverse activities as recycling of materials, reuse of products, abatement, and waste treatment. Numerous activities making up the complex economy give rise to a large demand for energy, so that more wood is being used for energy production. Accordingly, the complex economy based on minerals gives rise to new major influences on the economy in terms of space use, resource use, and non-organic residuals emission. Mineral inputs cause new chemical compositions or concentrations of otherwise (potentially) dangerous substances to appear. More interactions between economic activities (including intersectoral deliveries, international trade, exploitation of colonies, migration, etc.) accompanies interdependencies of environmental effects, as a result of spatial dispersion of economies (including transport). Furthermore, the larger scale of many individual and regional activity levels gives rise to transboundary and global environmental problems. A very strong development of organizational structures (with respect to policymaking, education, R & D) causes a high rate of technological progress. This, in turn, can have major consequences for culture, economy, and, importantly, regional demographic processes. The well-known example is, of course, very high population growth as a result of advanced medical care, in combination with uncoordinated birth control. Taken together, distributional consequences and disparities manifest themselves more strongly on an international than regional or national level.

Figure 8.3 shows a modern economy that includes the use of both minerals and fossil fuel resources for energy conversion and certain material production activities. A high energy consumption goes along with high activity levels in all sectors and accordingly much use of minerals, space, water, and high levels of noise, organic and non-organic emissions, and disturbance of vegetation and fauna. The Industrial Revolution is an important phase in the transition from the situation shown in Figure 8.2 to the one in Figure 8.3.

In the complex system of Figure 8.3, it is clear that each box or element stands for a multitude of items. The fossil fuels include coal, gas, and petroleum. The energy conversion process can be based on fossil fuels, fuelwood, and nuclear power and hydro power generation. The minerals can be classified in terms of various characteristics, e.g., (non)metallic, (non)scarcity, and potential of specific pollution problems at a later stage. The agricultural, fishery, and forestry products consist of animal food, plant food, textiles, paper, and timber. The final consumption incorporates fuels, food, durable goods, and other non-durable goods. Finally, the residuals can also be classified by way of various criteria, e.g., (non)degradability, reactiveness (inertness), natural biological recyclability, small (large) quantity, and (in)toxicity.

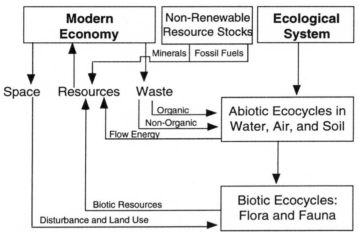

Figure 8.3. Economic-environmental relationships based on fossil fuel and mineral use.

Finally, Figure 8.4 shows the internal structure of the economic system that represents the modern economy block of Figure 8.3 where only the physical relationships are listed. The Appendix contains an example of a set of relationships between variables based on these two figures. In addition, Figure 8.5 shows its underlying decision system, composed of actors, namely government, consumers and sectors, and collective and market decision processes.

In conclusion, we can safely say that development still occurs on various levels—economic, organizational, technological, educational, demographic, interregional, and international—with immense impacts on local, regional, national, and global environmental systems. This can, to a large extent, be compared—and traced back—to historical processes that changed the interface between economies and natural environments. It seems that the tendency of modern economic processes to give rise to processes of resource depletion, environmental destruction, and pollution

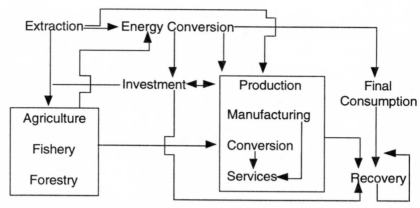

Figure 8.4. A modern economy based on fossil fuel and mineral use.

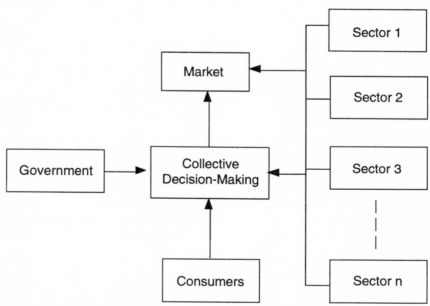

Figure 8.5. The decision framework of the modern economy.

is still not exhausted. Modern economies are even inclined to reach environmental and organizational limits time and time again, and therefore are forced to adjust and develop in new directions.[7] It is uncertain whether this development process of adjustment is converging to become an economic-environmental state that is both acceptable, from the point of view of equity and efficiency, and ecologically sustainable.

SYSTEMS, EXTERNALITIES, AND VALUATION

Figures 8.1 to 8.3 show that significant changes in the use of natural resources have taken place over the course of time. The Industrial Revolution created the possibilities to generate products on a large scale for a world market. This process dramatically increased both the level of production and the amount of pollutants. In earlier times pollution problems, occurring in an agricultural society, had a more local character. Adam Smith had already recognized that industrial production would increase the geographical scale of pollution, so that in fact it would become an international problem. Inevitably, an incompatible situation arose, since the regional organization of society was unable to deal with cross-boundary, multi-regional environmental issues. The existence of this problem was hardly addressed seriously before 1950.[8] It is a main cause of, on the one hand, a lack of instruments and institutional arrangements up to the present day, which are required for dealing with pollution problems like acid rain, the greenhouse effect, depletion of the ozone layer, and pollution of the common seas. On the other hand, there is a serious political barrier for implementation of a number of promising ideas and instruments. The causes of this seem to be: (1) a reluctance to stimulate drastic and permanent changes with several uncertain effects; (2) the sluggishness of the international process of cooperation and harmonization of policies; and (3) the pressure of existing economic interests that prevent the formation of political majorities to decide for effective environmental strategies.

The transformation towards an industrial society was accompanied by a change in the use of resources, an example of which is the use on a large scale of non-renewable resources such as iron and coal. New types

---

7. This seems to be most clearly explained by Wilkinson's "ecological view" on economic development (Wilkinson 1973).
8. Of course, it went along with a general delay of environmental awareness.

of waste, which were in some way or another emitted into the environment, resulted from the use of them. This created pollution problems never thought of before. The increased use of resources is not the sole source of pollution problems. Some of the waste residuals have certain characteristics that cause damage to living organisms, ecosystems, and ecocycles. The residuals of renewable resources are organic, so that they are mainly limited by the cleansing capacity of ecocycles. However, such capacity is zero for non-renewable resource residuals such as heavy metals, synthetic organic compositions, SO_2, and NO_x. Consequently, these substances are accumulating in environmental systems and living organisms. Such problems remained unrecognized for a long time by society at large, including economists.[9] Of course, sometimes pollution in industrial towns and residential areas was discussed, but mainly as a resolvable side effect of modern economies. Mostly optimism—for good and bad reasons—dominated the economists' view on consequences and even the pace of resource depletion and environmental pollution, as related to economic activity, development, and growth.

It is not so surprising, after all, that neoclassical theory, having its roots in the period of the Industrial Revolution, hardly devoted any attention to these issues. Not until Pigou (1932) introduced the concept of a negative external effect was a neoclassical framework available that allowed for an analysis of problems of resource use and emission of waste residuals. But as shown in Blaug (1978), this framework was hardly used before 1960. Only at the end of the sixties were economists inclined to apply the framework to various environmental problems. It soon became clear, however, that it had a very limited use.

The framework of externalities can only be used to deal with questions on a rather theoretical level, related mainly to economic efficiency, environmental effectiveness (controllability), and distributional consequences associated with the use of specific types of instruments for reaching a social welfare optimum. One can never really use the framework for supporting the phase of actually introducing instruments in environmental policy. Indeed, one can merely obtain insights about the theoretical advantages c.q. deficiencies of one versus another instrument.

---

9. The admirable contribution to the field of economic history by Martinez Alier (1987) shows, however, that already in the 19th century and the first part of the 20th century, a lively debate took place about the relevance of energy for the valuation of goods and services.

First, it seems that the theory of externalities is incapable of analyzing—beyond a quite abstract frame such as transaction cost theory—the consequences of specific and diverse characteristics of social institutional solutions to environmental problems. These include conflicting objectives, compromising processes, dominating pressure groups (more generally, distribution of lobby power), influencing of policy by vested interests, bargaining, and establishing multi-level goals, multi-objective decision making, voting systems, etc. (see Dietz and Van der Straaten 1992; Opschoor and Van der Straaten 1993).

Second, it is difficult to assign (close to) objective values to environmental services and elements. This holds as well for vague services (e.g., life-support, an intact ozone layer, clean oceans, preserved biodiversity, and stable climate and ecocycles) as for more well-defined natural resources and components of ecosystems (fish populations, forests, ores, fossil fuel resources, etc.). Of course, one can find many reasons why objective valuation of these services and systems is impossible, for example, related to missing markets, multiple uses, ethical stance, uncertainty, future generations, and free rider behavior. But especially because one cannot isolate any element of a natural environmental system from the system without destroying some link with it, it is difficult to assign a value to it or to a particular service that is generated by it.[10] The issue can be made clear by comparing the internal environmental relationships to economic interactions on markets, as represented by a general equilibrium framework. In order to find a correct price of a certain good or service, one has to solve the entire set of interdependent prices (and quantities). In other words, one can only solve for one price if one knows all the others, (i.e., they all have to be solved at the same time). There is a similar type of requirement for finding the value of an environmental service, namely that its value can only be assessed if one knows all the environmental components connected to it. But this is not sufficient. The exact nature of a mutual relationship between two components, (e.g., via a production or damage function), must be clear in advance, since it determines the "value" or "cost" that is transferred from one to another component.

---

10. The value of the element (stock) can be derived from its services over time (flows) when a capital theoretical framework is chosen as the base of valuation. But, of course, this does not solve any of the fundamental problems of valuation discussed in the text.

Instead of pursuing such a type of "systems" approach, one may of course adopt a less ambitious approximate and partial valuation. This can be done by considering a single environmental service or element separately, which is the common practice in environmental economic studies of valuation. But in such a case, one still lacks important information that is required to obtain a measure of the reliability of the estimation. A second comparison with a typical economic "value system" further supports and clarifies the point. It is difficult to find the value that is added to total social value (i.e., welfare) by some process (activity) generating some product (output), when one lacks values of all the labor, capital, intermediate products and services, and material inputs that are needed in the process (i.e., costs). Thus, one has to take the view of a system of interrelated values that can only be solved as a whole. While prices generate the adequate signals to estimate the values of products in market systems, with external physical effects one can only find analogous signals through a simulation of reality, notably via a systems analysis. This illustrates the importance of a system of interrelated values for valuation of environmental elements and services. In order to reach that phase, the underlying physical-biological system it is based on must be clarified. In conclusion, one cannot escape study of the relationships in the environmental system when solving the value estimation problem satisfactorily.

Altogether, it seems that if partial valuation of an environmental element or service is approximately correct, this means that the assumption of partiality is in order. This implies that the element or service is rather independent from the environmental system as a whole. One may conclude this particular element or service is of little concern in a wider environmental perspective of sustainable development and behavior of environmental systems. Furthermore, one can conclude that in the case of relevant or important environmental elements or services (i.e., strongly interrelated with the rest of the natural environment), it is hardly acceptable to estimate their values by way of partial methods. Consequently, the relevance and impossibility of partial valuation seem to be strongly related to each other.

One can safely say that there are enormous complications involved in value estimation as a result of both conceptual and informational deficiencies. The neoclassical approach too easily avoids considering them. That is no problem in itself, if it is accepted that this approach serves an important theoretical purpose of clarifying and generalizing. But other methods should be acquired for approaching policymakers who have a serious interest in the economic and environmental effects of using specific environmental policy instruments. One can argue that no satisfying alternative economic method exists to the neoclassical approach. However, in order to address more seriously the interrelationships between elements in environmental systems, for instance, one may turn to integrated (systems) modeling.

In any approach one adopts, it is necessary to consolidate the well-known concept of sustainable development for policymaking. This may mean a somewhat loose interpretation, but one, in any case, based on a long-term point of view. It involves a demarcation of environmental policy and sustainable development policy. The latter should be regarded as a composite of economic investment and environmental policy. The reason for this interpretation is that no automatic solutions exist to the observed conflict between economic activities and development on the one hand, and the preservation of environmental qualities and quantities on the other hand. If automatic solutions were possible, the introduction of the concept of sustainable development would be needless. It is very likely that sustainable development will only be realized when it is pursued as a purpose in itself, (i.e. when it is an explicit policy objective). An alternative view may be based on the belief that (1) sufficient "natural" mechanisms are present between economy and environment to generate sustainable development, or (2) the use of instruments for environmental policy generally will provoke sustainable development. The first belief does not take into account the very extreme character of "natural" economic reactions on unbalanced economic-environmental relationships in order to adjust for an "ecological equilibrium" (in the sense of Wilkinson 1973). The second belief forgets that many environmental policies and instruments are partial, local, and short term in both their purpose and effect. Especially the short-term effectiveness—more precisely, the long-term deterioration of effectiveness—of environmental policy requires some illustration. It may result from changes in economic processes that in turn change characteristics of materials use, waste emissions, and natural resource use. Furthermore, (not unrelated to the first point), economic agents may try to evade the restrictiveness of environmental policy instruments.

An important conclusion is that sustainable development policy will have to embrace both environmental and (many) economic policies, (i.e., it is not equivalent to environmental policy). However, the mere intro-duction of a concept like sustainable development will not bring forward sustainability, as is discussed in the next section.

PITFALLS IN EVALUATION AND SOCIAL DECISION MAKING

Traditional economic theory takes for granted that economic values can be assigned to environmental systems, elements, or services. The very impossibility of this was argued in the previous section. The next step is usually that environmental problems can be solved—meaning actually that the social optimum is realized—by using the estimated environmen-tal values to obtain corrections on market prices or to introduce prices (costs) for use of non-market goods and services provided by nature (Baumol and Oates 1988). The clearest example of this is provided by the set of charges on products, processes, etc. that aim to approximate the (optimal) Pigouvian taxes. However, the problems of valuation men-tioned imply that this approximation may be very imperfect. Dietz and Van der Straaten (1992) argue that one should include environmental standards in the economic theory itself, meaning that one should go be-yond the approach of taking environmental limits into account after eco-nomic analysis has been performed. In fact, one is then outside the eco-nomic sphere, which would be an approach that some economists could support—namely to leave the trade-off between economic and environ-mental goals outside economics (i.e., for politics). However, the previous section showed why the trade-off is hard to perform in a single, monetary value dimension. This section demonstrates that the complicated compar-ison of different dimensions, in which economic and environmental con-sequences are measured, can foster dominance of certain pressure group interests in political and social decision making. The real alternative can, for instance, include the assessment of uncertainty or lack of knowledge about natural systems and processes, and their importance for economic processes and health. This can then lead to establishing safety standards that can not be traded off against economic objectives. This does not mean that the economic market principle—today often employed to pro-mote the introduction of economic instruments for environmental pol-icy—should not be used, (e.g., implementing a standard on an aggregate level by way of a tradable permit) (Opschoor and Van der Straaten 1993). An example of incorporating environmental standards in economic theory is to avert growth theory towards inclusion of environmental factors (e.g., land, pollution, and resource indices, and absolute scarcity measures) that influence processes of development, technology, population, and growth.

The political institutional difficulty of introducing environmental standards can be illustrated by an example of an attempt in the Netherlands to introduce energy taxes for curbing the use of fossil energy (in order to stop the greenhouse effect; the standard here is a lower level of CO_2 emissions). In the beginning of 1992, the Minister of Environmental Affairs in the Netherlands proposed that an energy tax be introduced as quickly as possible. Even before an official advisory commission of experts on this topic could publish a report, the Minister of Economic Affairs made clear that the energy tax was not amenable to serious discussion. The main objection was that the competitive position of Dutch industries would be harmed by such a tax, and that the introduction of such an instrument required international cooperation. This view was of course that of the leading Dutch companies, who did not welcome an increase in the price of energy in the Netherlands, in spite of the fact that energy prices in the Netherlands—of natural gas as well as electricity—are the lowest in Europe. They did not argue, using competitiveness and cooperation arguments, that such prices should be equalized for the whole of Europe. Clearly companies were motivated by direct protection of profits against intrusion of environmental costs, rather than by the necessity of international cooperation.[11]

The general cause of this passivity is obvious. As one cannot calculate all costs resulting from the greenhouse effect ("values" in the previous section), the introduction of a CO_2 emissions' standard is delayed on the basis of economic sacrifices' arguments. These are based purely on traditional indicators such as employment and income. The discussion is therefore hardly an honest comparison of all gains and losses. The problem finally comes down to the separation between economic theory (and policy), and considerations of values and functions of natural resources. The previous section made clear that an honest comparison of gains and losses must consider information on estimated effects of economic activi-

---

11. Similarly, the European Community did not reach an agreement regarding an energy tax. Consequently, the UNCED "Earth Summit" conference in Rio de Janeiro, June 1992, lacked a possibly influential proposal by the European Community on this issue.

ties on environmental change, and estimated effects of environmental change on economic costs. This way all possible and relevant information can be integrated while also incorporating indicators of economic performance. The difference with traditional analysis and evaluation is that one has to look into more distant future effects of present-day economic activities.

INSTRUMENTS AND INSTITUTIONS: MISBELIEFS

Two types of instruments are used in environmental policymaking. When introducing environmental policies in the beginning of the 1970s, most countries in Western Europe put their trust in the instrument of legislation. Several laws against air pollution, water pollution, toxic substances, and so on, were the result of societal debate about environmental pollution in the 1960s. Since then the interest in the use of economic instruments has been rising (Opschoor and Vos 1989). Usually economic instruments are considered to be more effective (less control required) and more efficient than other instruments (Baumol and Oates 1988; Peeters 1991; Verbruggen 1991).

Many authors, stressing the importance of the use of economic instruments, refer to the "Tragedy of the Commons" (Hardin 1968), which suggests that some environmental resources can be used free of charge and are publicly available.[12] Over-exploitation belongs then to the more likely use patterns. It is usually suggested that the introduction of an economic instrument or property right can solve the problem of a tendency towards over-exploitation. However, this is not the whole story. Regulation of open-access resources can also result by transforming them into a common property. It is important, of course, that the rules of the common property are clear and obeyed or enforced (Clark 1991). Hardin's focus on a common property resource makes it impossible to regard common property as a policy for dealing with open-access resources, which actually describes environmental resources much more adequately in most circumstances. Furthermore, one might argue that the use of the term "common property" by Hardin is incorrect since it would

---

12. In fact, resources described in such a way satisfy open-access characteristics. Hardin in his article talks about common property resources ("commons"). This is, depending on one's interpretation, either a different class of resources, or a more narrow class. In the text it is made clear that open access is at the heart of the problem, while common property may even be at the heart of the solution.

really imply that common rules are accepted and obeyed by individual users (belonging to the community). In that case, an environmental problem of the type sketched by Hardin is very unlikely to arise.

Returning to the discussion on legislation vs. economic instruments in the context of environmental policy, it is important to recognize the analogy between the open-access resource on a small, local scale and the open-access character of the natural environment in general, as well as the analogy between the common property rules and environmental legislation. One should be aware that during the last two decades in Western Europe, there has been a practice of very weak maintenance of environmental legislation. Furthermore, after a certain period of bad maintenance of environmental legislation, the practice of behavior dominates the prevailing legal and formal arguments at present. As soon as polluting industries are confronted with major actions of authorities to protect the environment, they do not behave in accordance with these formal and legal arguments. This makes it difficult to conclude that economic instruments are a preferred solution over legislation (i.e., common property rules). It is possible that consistent control and (moral and political) support of legislation will be much more effective than it has been in the past.

In addition, Bromley (1992) is of the opinion that there are no common resources, but only resources under either a state property regime, an individual property regime, or a common property regime. In all these situations, the access to use or exploit these resources, has been regulated in some way. Bromley demonstrates that in cases where over-exploitation occurs, there has previously been a breakdown of institutional arrangements. So the over-exploitation is not the result of the common property character, but rather of the creation of a situation of open-access by destroying institutional arrangements in favor of certain economic groups. Therefore, one can not argue, according to Bromley, that only privatization of resources solves the problem of over-exploitation.

In conclusion, one cannot say formally that there is any doubt about the formulation of the property rights of unpriced natural resources. However, as was stated previously, most governments have maintained environmental legislation in such a way, that polluting industries can behave as if they have the right to pollute the environment. This means that there has been a breakdown of the institutional arrangements regarding the use of unpriced natural resources. The fact that society is now con-

fronted with a very weak maintenance of environmental legislation provides insufficient argument for stressing their weaknesses to solve environmental problems.

CONCLUSIONS

The following conclusions emerge from the contemplative discussion in
this chapter:

- Frameworks used to elucidate the potential development interactions
  with the natural environment must be capable of recognizing and characterizing unsustainable patterns within economic-environmental systems, rather than sticking to only those development plans that are sustainable; the latter can give only limited insight, for instance, because
  they represent pictures of time paths within the system that may be
  static, unstable, unlikely, or very sensitive to little changes in external
  influences. Seeking a broader range of potential development paths,
  (sustainable and unsustainable), may render more insightful information, for both scientific and policy purposes.

- The discussion of Figures 8.1 to 8.3 makes it clear that changes of economic structures have been very significant factors in the occurrence of
  unsustainability in the economic process. Development still takes place
  on various levels—economic, organizational, technological, educational, demographic, interregional, and international—with immense
  impacts on local, regional, national, and global environmental systems,
  as well as within the economy-environment interface. It seems that the
  tendency of modern economic processes to give rise to processes of resource depletion, environmental destruction, and pollution is still not
  exhausted. One can even see that modern economies are inclined to
  reach environmental and organizational limits time and time again, and
  therefore are forced to adjust and develop in new directions (note
  Wilkinson's "ecological view" on economic development, Wilkinson
  1973). It is uncertain whether this adjustment process of development is
  converging to a sustainable and acceptable situation.

- The implementation of traditional economic solutions to environmental
  policy is heavily based on valuation of environmental goods, services,
  and elements (ecosystems, species, etc.). There are fundamental problems associated with partial valuation, and it should be recognized that
  there is a need for alternative approaches. These may include the use of
  methods stressing interrelationships between elements in environmental
  systems. Ultimately, this comes closer to meeting demands for analysis

related to critical environmental problems, in the context of the broader notion of sustainable development.

- Because of a neglect of the institutional framework related to environmental legislation, one cannot infer that economic instruments are to be preferred to environmental legislation.

- It is of great importance that in representations of economic-environmental interactions, more attention is given to institutional factors that are relevant to environmental policies, such as multi-level goals, multi-objective elements of and compromising processes in social decision making.

- There is still a significant lack of integration of ecological insights into economic theory, leaving too much space for economic activities (and related pressure groups) to use traditional economic arguments for not implementing required policies for sustainable development.

- Environmental legislation should not be discarded as ineffective by mere reference to past experience. Institutional arrangements and economic instruments should be combined to realize an effective and efficient policy toolbox.

APPENDIX: A FORMAL ILLUSTRATION OF THE MODERN ECONOMY-ENVIRONMENT SYSTEM

Here a complete example set is given as an illustration of the relationships among physical variables in the modern economy, which are depicted in a general sense in Figures 8.3 and 8.4. The variable names are chosen to speak for themselves. A single function f(), is used for simplicity and denotes various specific (i.e., different) relationships.

The Environment and Nature

soil quality	=	f(agriculture, air quality, water quality, organic residuals, nonorganic residuals)
air quality	=	f(nonorganic residuals, vegetation)
water quality	=	f(vegetation, agriculture, forestry)
vegetation	=	f(soil quality, air quality, water quality, organic residuals, nonorganic residuals, space_use, heat, radioactivity, forestry)
fauna	=	f(vegetation, noise, nonorganic residuals, space_use, radioactivity, forestry)
fish	=	f(sea quality, fishery)

sea quality	=	f(organic residuals, nonorganic residuals)

Economic Activities

extraction	=	f(production)
energy_conversion	=	f(forestry, extraction)
investment	=	f(production, agriculture, forestry, energy conversion) -g (final_cons)
agriculture	=	f(soil quality, water quality, air quality, investment)
fishery	=	f(fish, investment)
forestry	=	f(vegetation, soil quality, air quality, water quality, investment)
production	=	f(final_cons)

Economic-Environmental Interactions

change_stock_fossils	=	–extraction
change_stock_mineral	=	–extraction
space_use	=	f(production, agriculture, forestry, fin_cons)
heat	=	f(energy_conversion)
noise	=	f(production, energy_conversion)
radioactivity	=	f(energy_conversion)
organic residuals	=	f(agriculture, fishery, forestry)
nonorganic residuals	=	f(extraction, investment)

In this simple example, final consumption is exogenous and activates the model; population may be based on population, which in turn may be dependent on health to close the circle.

ACKNOWLEDGMENTS

We are grateful to Herman Vollebergh of Erasmus University, Rotterdam, for useful comments.

REFERENCES

Baumol, W. J., and E. E. Oates. 1988. The Theory of Environmental Policy. 2nd ed. Cambridge: Cambridge Univ. Press.

Bergh, J. C. J. M. van den. 1991. Dynamic Models for Sustainable Development. Ph.D. dissertation. Amsterdam: Thesis Publishers/Tinbergen Institute.

————. 1993. A framework for modeling economy-environment-development relationships based on dynamic carrying capacity and sustainable development feedback. *Environmental and Resource Economics* 3: 395–412.

Bergh, J. C. J. M. van den, and P. Nijkamp. 1991a. Aggregate dynamic economic-ecological models for sustainable development. *Environment and Planning A* 23: 1409–28.

————. 1991b. Operationalizing sustainable development: dynamic ecological economic models. *Ecological Economics* 4: 11–33.

Briassoulis, H. 1986. Integrated economic-environmental-policy modeling at the regional and multiregional level: methodological characteristics and issues. *Growth and Change* 17: 22–34.

Blaug M. 1978. Economic Theory in Retrospect. Cambridge: Cambridge Univ. Press.

Bromley, D. W. 1992. The commons, common property, and environmental policy. *Environmental and Resource Economics* 2: 1–18.

Clark, C. W. 1976. Mathematical Bioeconomics: The Optimal Management of Renewable Resources. New York: Wiley-Interscience.

————. 1991. Economic biases against sustainable development. In Ecological Economics: The Science and Management of Sustainability, ed. R. Costanza. New York: Columbia Univ. Press.

Common, M. 1988. Poverty and progress revisited. In Economics, Growth and Sustainable Environments, eds. D. Collard, D. W. Pearce, and D. Ulph. New York: St. Martin's Press.

Dietz, F. J., and J. van der Straaten. 1992. Rethinking environmental economics: missing links between economic theory and environmental policy. *Journal of Economic Issues* 26: 27–51.

Hardin, G. 1968. The tragedy of the commons. *Science* 162: 1243–48.

Hartwick, J. M. 1977. Intergenerational equity and the investing of rents from exhaustible resources. *American Economic Review* 67: 972–74.

Jantzen, J., and J. W. Velthuijsen. 1991. An Integrated Environment-Economy Simulation Model for the Netherlands. Paper presented at the 2nd conference of the European Association of Environmental Economists, June 1991, Stockholm.

Klaassen, L. H., and T. H. Botterweg. 1976. Project evaluation and intangible effects—a shadow project approach. In Environmental Economics, Vol. 1: Theories, ed. P. Nijkamp. Leiden: Martinus Nijhoff.

Leontief, W. W. 1970. Environmental repercussions and the economic structure: an input-output approach. *Review of Economic Studies* 52: 262–71.

Martinez-Alier, J., and K. Schluepmann. 1987. Ecological Economics. Oxford: Basil Blackwell.

Opschoor, J. B., and J. van der Straaten. 1993. Sustainable development: an institutional approach. *Ecological Economics* 7(3): 203–22.

Opschoor, J. B., and J. B. Vos. 1989. Economic Instruments for Environmental Protection. Paris: OECD.

Peeters, M. G. W. M. 1991. Legal aspects of marketable pollution permits. In Environmental Policy and the Economy, eds. F. J. Dietz, F. van der Ploeg and J. van der Straaten. Amsterdam: North-Holland.

Pezzey, J. 1989. Economic Analysis of Sustainable Growth and Sustainable Development. Environmental Department Working paper no.15. Washington, DC: The World Bank.

————. 1993. Sustainability: an interdisciplinary guide. *Environmental Values* 1: 321–62.

Pigou, A. C. 1932. The Economics of Welfare. 4th ed. London: Macmillan,

Ponting, C. 1991. A Green History of the World. London: Sinclair-Stevenson.

Simmons, I. G. 1989. Changing the Face of the Earth. Culture, Environment, History. Oxford: Basil Blackwell.

Verbruggen, H. 1991. Political economy aspects of environmental policy instruments. In Environmental Policy and the Economy, eds. F. J. Dietz, F. van der Ploeg and J. van der Straaten. Amsterdam: North-Holland.

Wilkinson, R. 1973. Poverty and Progress—An Ecological Model of Economic Development. London: Methuen & Co.

9 DISTRIBUTIONAL CONFLICTS AND INTERNATIONAL ENVIRONMENTAL POLICY ON CARBON DIOXIDE EMISSIONS AND AGRICULTURAL BIODIVERSITY[1]

Juan Martinez-Alier
Department d'Economia i d'Historia Economica
Universitat Autònoma
Bellaterra (Barcelona)
Spain 08193

INTRODUCTION

Environmental movements have tried to keep environmental resources and services outside the market, but now there are attempts to establish property rights on and to give monetary values to environmental resources and services, such as agricultural genetic resources and the CO_2 absorption capability provided by the oceans and new vegetation. This chapter considers European "green" proposals to impose an "eco-tax" and proposals from India to create a world market for CO_2 emission permits. The issue raised by the growing Third World agroecology movement of payment of "farmers' rights" for in situ agricultural biodiversity is discussed. The chapter includes a short discussion of the free trade agreement (NAFTA) between Mexico and the United States in so far as it

---

1. Previous versions of this chapter were presented at the 2nd meeting of the International Society for Ecological Economics, Stockholm, August 3–6, 1992; the 27th Congress of the International Geographical Union, Washington DC, August 10–15, 1992; a conference organized by the Latin American Centre, University of Oxford, on "Latin America and Europe, 1992," September 9–11, 1992; and the meeting of the Transnational Institute, Amsterdam, November 20–21, 1992. A longer version has been published in *Environmental Values*, May 1993.

involves so-called "ecological dumping," (i.e., trading at values that do not include environmental costs). In the last sections, the chapter asks how prices in ecologically extended markets would be formed, how much such prices will depend on distribution, and how much (or how little) such payments would change distribution of income. Environmental movements of the poor are faced with the dilemma of keeping environmental resources and services out of the market, or instead, of asking for property rights to be placed on them. The main conclusion is that, even leaving intergenerational effects aside, inequality in income distribution within the present generation implies that property rights and monetary values are a weak substitute for social responses.

The main political and intellectual input for the UNCED in Rio in June 1992 was the concept of "sustainable development" as used by the Brundtland Commission, which was meant to separate environmental policy from distributional conflicts by arguing that increases in income are beneficial for the environment. This is so in some cases, but higher incomes have meant higher emissions of greenhouse gases and higher rates of genetic erosion. The UNCED conference failed to reach effective agreements on climatic change and on the conservation of biodiversity. This was the starting point for this chapter, which grew out of research interests in the relations between distributional conflicts and environmental policy, and in the environmentalism of the poor.[2] The main objectives in Rio were to reverse the trend towards increased emissions of CO_2 and other greenhouse gases, and to stop the increase in genetic erosion. Such historical changes would affect the geography of emissions and the geography of biodiversity, and would have different distributional impacts for different countries and their citizens. In Rio a convention was signed on global warming that lacked firm commitments. The U.S. government and therefore, under its authority, the major seed and biotechnology firms failed to sign the biodiversity agreement. The present U.S. administration has now signed the biodiversity agreement, but this agreement makes no provision for payments for the genetic materials preserved *ex-situ*, nor does it contain safeguards for the conservation of *in situ* agricultural biodiversity through concrete measures of support for agroecology. Thus, the official UNCED at Rio failed on the issue of the greenhouse effect,

---

2   Research funded by D.G.XII of EC, Brussels, through the Institut fuer Oekologische Wirtschaftsforschung, Berlin, and from the MacArthur Foundation, Chicago, through the Social Sciences Research Council, New York.

and also on agricultural biodiversity. The lack of success is due to distributional conflicts that became a hindrance for environmental policies geared to an ecological economy.

The regulation of external environmental effects has strong intra- and intergenerational distributional impacts since it implies the expropriation of environmental property rights that used to belong (in practice) to the polluting agents. Conversely, inequalities in income distribution have an influence on the values placed both on environmental resources (e.g., genetic resources, which up to now were considered the "patrimony of humankind" even at this dawn of the biotechnological age), and on environmental functions (e.g., CO_2 absorption by oceans and new vegetation). Thus in Rio, the rich[3] saw the CO_2 absorption capability provided by the oceans and new vegetation as basically a free access good available on a first come, first serve basis. Some well-informed and intelligent voices from the poor (Agarwal and Narain 1991) argued for ownership rights to this CO_2 sink function to be instituted and shared equally by all of humankind in such a way that poor people, making little use of it because of their low CO_2 emissions, could sell their unused part to the rich. Naturally, additional questions arise. Would such quotas be available if the poor become richer? What would be their price? Which authorities would collect the receipts, and to what ends would they be applied?

Genetic resources for agriculture have been developed in many parts of the world over the last few thousand years through traditional methods of plant breeding, mostly outside the market. The ownership rights to and the values placed on such environmental resources are now a subject of political contention. Similarly, the ownership rights to and the values placed upon the environmental sink function for CO_2 emissions have become hotly contested. Behind such disputes there are distributional conflicts. Different outcomes will imply different environmental policies. Of course, such policies will also be influenced by today's views on uncertain, future changes in technology, and the assessment of technological change is itself also subject to political disputes.

---

3. The North (which is an inappropiate name because there are rich countries in the South), or the First World (but then what should the Third World be called now? Perhaps it should be upgraded to the Second World?).

SOCIAL AND MARKET RESPONSES TO EXTERNALITIES

The main focus of this chapter is on the valuation of environmental resources and services, particularly with regard to CO_2 emissions and agricultural biodiversity. The role of environmental movements in the North and in the South, and their practical influence on environmental policies will also be covered. Environmental movements sometimes use conventional scientific language like that found in the anti-nuclear movement in Europe or the United States since the 1970s, if not before. Sometimes they use local languages (as in Chipko) distinct from the language of conventional science. Some environmental movements deal only with local issues and take pride in this, while some (such as Greenpeace) deal with global environmental problems.

Elsewhere I have expressed the view[4] that environmental movements are social responses against actual or threatened externalities. They grow out of the conflicts between the economy and people's livelihood. They perform a function at which the market fails (i.e., the complaints and actions of environmental movements raise the costs that firms or governments have to pay for their use of resources or for polluting the environment). The word "externalities" refers here to environmental impacts whose values are not captured by market prices—they remain external to the market. "Externalities" is the appropriate word only in a generalized market system. That some effects are external to the market may be noticed only after the market extends *almost* everywhere. Then we wonder about the consequences of such market valuation failures for the allocation of environmental resources and functions, and we also ask how income distribution will change once such environmental resources and functions are "properly" valued. In other words, the abuse of humans and the abuse of nature are older than the generalized market system, and the interesting question is whether such *Raubwirtschaft* works now mainly through the market system, and whether it would continue to work, even through an ecologically extended market that gave chrematistic significance and valuation to externalities.

There have been many local movements against externalities. For instance, comparative studies could be made of complaints against sulfur dioxide, from Rio Tinto in 1888 to La Oroya in Peru eighty years ago, to Puracé in the Cauca Valley of Colombia and Ilo in Southern Peru in re-

---

4.   Taken from Leff (1986) and O'Connor (1988), possibly anticipated by other writers.

cent times (Patiño 1991; Diaz Palacios 1988). If environmental movements are social responses to externalities, are there movements against the increased greenhouse effect at world or regional levels? Yes, although not exactly mass movements, (i.e., the proposals by the Greens in the European Parliament, and before this, in several northern European states, for a carbon-and-energy tax, and also some proposals from India by Agarwal and Narain on equal rights to the Earth's "cleaning facilities" for CO_2). Ecological movements are characteristically small-scale, and this has been preached as a virtue: "Think globally, act locally." But global warming requires global action, and it is difficult to articulate a response based on local-action groups. There has been no specific Latin American answer to global warming, either at official or NGO levels.

We might also ask whether there are eco-social movements against genetic erosion, in favor of agricultural biodiversity. Beyond the work of ethnobotanists and the agronomic institutions (belonging or not to the Consultative Group of the Institutes of Agronomic Research, CGIAR), there is now a growing agroecological movement (i.e., CLADES, a Latin America consortium for agroecology), including perhaps some peasant organizations in low-income countries, which preach conservation and further co-evolution of agricultural biodiversity *in situ*. They ask for the payment of Farmers' Rights (*not* patents, *not* Intellectual Property Rights) as an incentive and reward for the preservation of agricultural biodiversity, which will compensate traditional farmers for the fact that the introduction of commercial varieties and modern farming practices increases money revenues. The questions of what will be the price of such Farmers' Rights and who will collect the receipts naturally arise.

Before economic values are given to environmental resources or services, a necessary condition is the social perception that they exist. This is the present stage regarding the CO_2 sink function and genetic resources. The values attributed to such resources and services will depend on the different possible outcomes of conflicts over income distribution. And the reverse also applies—if certain environmental resources (agricultural genetic resources) or services (the CO_2 sink function) are considered economically valueless, this will imply a different income distribution than if such resources and services had well-defined ownership rights and were transacted in ecologically extended markets.

The market is a wonderful, non-bureaucratic institution where deals are made between individuals, but it is difficult to reach a rational consensus on the economic values of concrete externalities that the market fails to value. Usually, economic values are arrived at by market bargaining, but reliance on contemporary individual preferences evades the issue of giving present values to future, uncertain contingencies. There is a double uncertainty: (1) about facts (e.g., how much CO_2 is absorbed by the oceans), and (2) about the adequacy of our representations of environmental reality (whether formally scientific or not). We enter the realms of "post-normal science" and "political epistemology" (Funtowicz and Ravetz 1991) where, because of the nature of the issues, the experts are necessarily subject to an "extended peer review," and where "communication wars" try to influence public opinion.

The following sections present the argument that environmental resources (genetic resources) and services (the CO_2 sink function) should become marketable commodities, acquiring suitable chrematistic values, so that ecologically extended markets become instruments of environmental policies. The inability of future generations to come to today's actual or surrogate markets, although a crucial fact, will not be considered. This discussion will stress that market valuations depend partly on the distribution of income at present, and that therefore, environmental policies based on markets will not be the same if the distribution of income changes. The chrematistic valuation of environmental resources and services "owned" by the poor in ecologically extended markets will change income distribution, and it is therefore opposed by the rich. But *if the poor sell cheap*, then there is no reason to expect that such valuation will be an effective instrument of environmental policy. Thus we cannot simply rely on ecologically extended markets. Environmental policies are needed that are based on social movement, beyond the operation of an ecologically extended market where such environment as belongs to the poor, will be sold cheap.

A EUROPEAN ECO-TAX?

The reconvened Brundtland Commission met in London a couple of months before the Rio de Janeiro conference, and courageously called for a specific timetable of concrete reductions of greenhouse gases. But Gro Harlem Brundtland herself was at the official Rio conference as one of the main actors in this great act of procrastination. The agreement in Rio is so feeble in content that it was signed quite legally by the Spanish government, despite the fact that this government publicly announced in

Madrid and in Rio that the Spanish emissions of CO_2 (which are above the world per person average and much above the world median) would *increase* substantially. The figure in the official Spanish report for UNCED was a 25% increase in CO_2 emissions from electricity generation in the next ten years. Inside the EC, Spain opposed the proposal by the Environmental Commissioner, Ripa di Meana, to impose a carbon-and-energy tax of about U.S. $10 per barrel of oil-equivalent energy, which would include nuclear energy but would exclude renewable energies (Luke 1992). The European Greens had *first* proposed an eco-tax of U.S. $20 per barrel of oil-equivalent energy (Green Agenda 1992). Because of distributional conflicts, the EC could not agree to take to Rio a unilateral decision on a carbon-and-energy tax; Ripa di Meana was so irritated that he refused to attend the Rio conference, and he then became the Italian Minister for the Environment. His idea was to present the United States and Japan with the fait accompli of a European decision, which would challenge them to follow suit.

A carbon-and-energy tax does *not* mean that we know how to correct the market value in order to have an ecologically correct present-day value that internalizes the relevant future and uncertain externalities. The internalization of externalities into the price system stumbles upon the following obstacles: (1) the preferences of future generations are not known at all; (2) there are many uncertainties regarding the functioning of ecosystems and changes in technologies; and (3) even the preferences of the present generation are only partly known (Dietz and Van der Straaten 1992). A tax is merely a technical instrument on a level with a system of legal standards and fines, or with a system of tradable emission permits, in order to reach a reduction in emissions. This reduction objective must be determined outside economics, through a scientific-political debate conducted in a terrain of factual and scientific uncertainties and stakeholder politics. So, the question is not the internalization of externalities into the price system, (which is an impossible task), and then business-as-usual setting priorities by the market. The question is rather to set ecological limits to the economy through an open, democratic scientific and political debate, and then to force the economy to remain under such limits by a mixture of policy measures, not excluding market-oriented measures.

In some cases, a cultural change in consumers' awareness, as in the case of tobacco consumption, is an alternative route to environmental objectives more effective than fiscal or other market-oriented measures. This is relevant to the demand for "organic" agricultural products, and also to the demand for alternatives to the private car, which are very much under discussion. Changes in tobacco consumption, or the conspicuous rejection of private cars in the West by ecological groups with names such as "Friends of the Bicycle," are not so trivial as they might appear to economists who blandly describe them as shifts in demand curves. Such changes in needs mean that, instead of conforming with society's rules, a growing minority of people change towards a self-determined structure of needs. It must be remembered that humans have genetic instructions regarding only the endosomatic consumption of energy and materials. Exosomatic consumption, which is extremely variable, depends on economic, social, and cultural differences.

FREE TRADE AND ENVIRONMENTAL COSTS—A CRITIQUE OF NAFTA AND THE GATT

Naturally, a carbon-and-energy tax on oil, gas, or coal, collected in importing countries on top of existing taxes, irritates the exporting countries. Demand for fossil fuels would go down (the reason for the tax is to curb CO_2 emissions), and export prices would not increase; rather, they would decrease due to diminished demand. For oil exporting countries, many of which (Mexico, Russia, Nigeria, Algeria, Indonesia, Iran, Iraq, Ecuador, Venezuela) are poorer than the United States, the EC, and Japan, the proper place to collect the tax would be at the point of extraction. This is why in Rio there was strong opposition to the greenhouse treaty by some governments of oil-exporting countries. Would the receipts from eco-taxes be used to lower other forms of fiscal pressure on the rich, or for development in the poorer countries? Could eco-taxes be collected by the United Nations? In the case of tropical timber, there have been proposals to impose an import levy that would be repatriated to tropical timber exporting countries via an environmental fund (Daly and Goodland 1992).

In the United States oil prices are relatively cheap, though the United States has become a great oil-importing country. A small energy tax was unsuccessfully proposed by the Clinton administration, and further discussions on this tax backed by environmental arguments are still on the political agenda. From a Mexican point of view, the situation is paradoxical. Mexico exports cheap oil to the United States. It is "cheap" in the sense that it includes no allowance for environmental costs at the extraction zones of Campeche and Tabasco, nor for the environmental costs of CO_2 (and NO_x) emissions, and moreover the price implicitly discounts heavily the value of future demand for oil in Mexico. Now, oil might be ecologically taxed in the United States rather than in Mexico! This will certainly produce distributional fights. As things stand now, Mexico will probably be prevented by NAFTA from taxing exports. It will export cheap oil to the United States, and in return, it will take goods such as maize, produced in part with cheap Mexican oil. This U.S. maize has very little genetic merit because it is hybrid, and in part relies on the flow of unpaid Mexican genetic resources. U.S. maize exports are and will be subsidized at least in the sense that their prices include no allowance for ecological costs. Such exports will undermine Mexican peasant maize production, which is more efficient in terms of use of energy from fossil fuels, and it is biologically more interesting. In other words, U.S. agriculture works with lax environmental norms compared to Mexican peasant agriculture.

What will be the environmental costs of the likely boom of several sectors of the Mexican economy under NAFTA? A misguided environmental lobby in the United States has placed exclusive attention on the potential effects of NAFTA in increasing production in the maquiladora industry across the border, and in other industries, including commercial fruit-and-vegetable growing, which work with less stringent environmental standards in Mexico than in the United States. This is an important issue. The exportation of domestic and industrial waste from the United States to Mexico is another important issue. But there are *also* the environmental costs of cheap oil exports from Mexico to be considered, as well as the threat to its agroecological farming system and food security. Such issues have gone almost unnoticed in the environmental debate about NAFTA.

The conclusion of the NAFTA negotiation in August 1992 with ratification still pending, was greeted with pleasure by U.S. maize planters and hog farmers, who foresaw an increase of exports to Mexico. The description of the situation by the press (*New York Times* 1992) still ignored the ecological critique against modern agriculture. Thus, it was correctly argued that Mexican barriers to maize imports have prevented U.S. farmers from dominating Mexican food markets and from perhaps ruining hundreds of thousands of peasant maize farmers in southern

Mexico. Under NAFTA, Mexico will immediately allow the duty free import of 2.5 million tons of corn a year. The tariff against imports above this very high quantity will be phased out over fifteen years. It was further argued that this free trade policy would benefit both countries, since U.S. maize growing is more efficient than Mexico's. However, we do not really know which system is more efficient until there is an agreement on how to correct the measure of agricultural productivity by a factor that takes into account the use of fossil fuels and the loss of biodiversity in modern agriculture. Agricultural exports from the U.S. (incidentally, also from Europe) profit not only from direct but also from indirect subsidies, since the costs of environmental degradation are not part of the prices of such agricultural exports. They are a case, if one wishes, of "ecological dumping." Probably, the best agricultural production system would combine the ecological advantages of traditional Mexican farming, which is excessively based on hard human labor, and U.S. farming, which does not count the negative externalities it produces. The ecological critique of conventional agricultural economics leaves much room for different political views to be expressed on this issue, because the ecological critique says that the prices are wrong. However, it is unable to say what the prices are that internalize the externalities.

A unifying theme for the opposition to NAFTA should be how market prices for Mexican oil exports and for U.S. maize exports do not include environmental costs. This does not mean that there is some magic method in order to ascertain the "full environmental costs" of economic activities with future and uncertain ecological consequences. There are no "ecologically correct" prices, in the sense that they convincingly internalize all the externalities—there are only "ecologically corrected" prices, which make a provision for environmental externalities. "Adequate" carbon and energy taxes on oil collected in Mexico, and "anti-depredatory agriculture" taxes collected in the United States, would then allow free trade flows based on ecologically corrected absolute or comparative advantages. This is, however, not on the political agenda in the United States because of the distributional impacts it would have. It could still become part of the political agenda in Mexico, where there are somewhat faded traditions of political agrarianism (going back to Zapata) and of oil nationalism (going back to the Cárdenas of the 1930s) that could link up with the new ecological awareness.

There is a growing debate about *trade and environment*, of which NAFTA offers only one particular case study. In general, GATT has wrongly argued that free trade is good for the environment, because trade promotes economic growth, and growth provides resources to "clean" up the environment. Although there are examples of a positive correlation between economic growth and a better environment (for instance, reduction of SO_2), the argument is clearly spurious in view of domestic and industrial waste, nuclear power, and CO_2 emissions. The increasing liberalization of trade, if it promotes growth, is, for this very reason, damaging to the environment. Leaving the growth argument aside, there are two main objections to increased trade from the environmental point of view:[5] (1) the ecological cost of transport—witness the reaction in Austria and Switzerland to the externalities of increased EC traffic; and (2) "ecological dumping," (i.e., the fact that trade often takes place at prices that do not make any allowance for ecological costs). Certainly, it is difficult to express ecological costs in monetary terms (how to value now the negative impact of plutonium in 24,000 years), but nevertheless, ecological costs exist. Today there is a rhetorical demand for "full cost pricing of environmental assets" and "internalization of external costs," which comes from some new quarters such as the Business Council for Sustainable Development, which represents multinational corporations. It might in the near future also come from GATT or the new Multilateral Trade Organization. First, the environmental issues must be solved, then free trade should be allowed to exert its beneficial influence.[6] However, the internalization of future and uncertain externalities into the price system is not a mere economic technicality, but an open political issue. If Mexican tuna exports should be penalized because the fishing methods employed involve the killing of dolphins, a case could also be made for penalizing Mexican oil exports, and U.S. agricultural exports, since they also imply a loss of environmental values. Here are some examples of trade at ecologically incorrect prices, beyond the NAFTA case:

- Agricultural exports from the United States and the EC are directly subsidized but also indirectly subsidized since their prices do not in-

---

5. Some critical writings on trade and environment are Arden-Clarke (1991), Daly and Cobb (1989), and Røpke (1992.)
6. This has been argued by S. Barrett and D. W. Pearce in working papers from CSERGE (1992).

clude costs of lost agricultural biodiversity, high energy input, pollution, and soil erosion.

- Electricity exports from France, liberalized inside the EC, do not include the present and future costs of nuclear industry.

- Gas exports to the EC from Russia and Algeria do not include in their prices the costs of CO_2 (also of NO_x) emissions, and future demand is heavily discounted in their price.

Historically, discussions on "unequal exchange" have focused on two issues: the underpaid labor of the poor (and therefore cheap exports from poor countries), and the worsening of the terms of trade for primary products. The notion of *ecologically unequal exchange,* which should be carefully defined, could now be added. From such *ecologically unequal exchange* has risen an *ecological debt* that is increasingly claimed by the poor.

EQUAL RIGHTS TO THE EARTH'S CO_2 "CLEANING" CAPABILITIES?

In Western Europe and in the United States, the eco-tax is the main instrument of environmental policy under discussion against the increased greenhouse effect. In India, a complementary proposal for an international market in tradable permits for CO_2 emissions was made in a deservedly famous pamphlet from the Centre for Science and Environment in Delhi, entitled *Global Warming: A Case of Environmental Colonialism*. The objective would be to lower worldwide CO_2 emissions so that they do not exceed absorption by the oceans and new vegetation. This sink function is at present insufficient to capture current emissions of CO_2. The distribution of CO_2 emissions per person is very unequal inside and across countries, both historically and at present. Against a policy of proportional reductions for every country proposed by the World Resources Institute of Washington, DC, Agarwal and Narain argued, for the first time in the long social history of the greenhouse effect, that the capacity of the oceans and of the new vegetation as a sink for CO_2 should be shared equally among all persons. Thus, human respiration does not nourish the increase in the greenhouse effect, although it produces CO_2, and burning a little charcoal for cooking makes a different contribution from driving a car regularly. Agarwal and Narain proposed that people with low emissions should not be subject to any reduction, while greater reductions would be demanded from those with high emissions.

Furthermore, countries or regions with emissions lower than their share of the Earth's "cleaning" capabilities (shares being determined according to population) could sell their unused quota to other countries or regions.[7]

Large countries like China or India do appear in the statistical tables of CO_2 emissions *per country* near the top, but the U.S.S.R. has disappeared from the table because it is now partitioned into its constituent nations. What matters then is emissions *per person*, although international agreements must apparently still be made between states. On a different tack, it could be argued that Agarwal and Narain's proposal does not impose a penalty on population growth, rather the reverse. This is true. In order to counteract this effect, CO_2 emission quotas could be pegged to today's population. Historically, the remarkable demographic fact of the last 500 years in a continental comparative perspective is the expansion of the European populations, in Europe and overseas, particularly in the Americas because of the demographic collapse of native Americans after 1492. If a shorter timespan is considered, then non-European populations are growing more quickly. Which base line to take for comparisons of population growth becomes, therefore, another topic of political contention.

Bringing history into the greenhouse dispute has other consequences. The increase of the greenhouse effect because of CO_2 emissions was already discussed one hundred years ago by Svante Arrhenius, and it was judged to be positive (Grinevald 1990). "Socially constructed ignorance" is not an excuse for the rich countries that have belched out so much CO_2 from fossil fuels; they should be held accountable. From the poor's point of view, there is an ecological debt from the rich to the poor.

Agarwal and Narain's position, which became widely known in the world (though it was absent from the official proposals in Rio), touched on some raw nerves. Nevertheless, the impact in terms of income distribution of their proposal remains unclear. If CO_2 emissions per person in the world were lowered to the Indian standard, then the CO_2 sink function provided by the Earth's oceans and new vegetation would have some spare capacity. If, less stringently, CO_2 emissions per person were brought down to the aggregate level that equals that sink function, then most members of the human race would be still under their allowance; they could either reserve it for later use by themselves, or, if equal rights

---

7. See in comparison Markandya (1991).

are instituted, they could trade such quotas. One may fear that, given the poverty of India and countries in a similar position, the supply price of such quotas would be cheap unless they could manage to establish an oligopoly. It could be assumed that reduction of CO_2 is costly for the rich, in terms of the cost of achieving increased efficiency of energy use and/or reduction of output, and therefore, the demand for such quotas would be high. However, if the poor compete among themselves to sell quotas and the supply price is low, then the rich, even if they are very keen on buying such quotas, could profit by making agreements among themselves, paying little, and enjoying a large consumer surplus. If quotas were auctioned off, perhaps the demand price would be high, but the low supply price would allow the difference to be appropriated by intermediaries belonging to the rich portion of humankind.

INTRODUCING AGRICULTURAL BIODIVERSITY

Regarding CO_2 emissions (one of the main causes of the increased greenhouse effect), the main lines of conflict are fairly well drawn. Distributional conflicts prevent solutions. Biodiversity was the other key issue at the Rio conference, and it raises questions for environmental policy that are more difficult to analyze than the increased greenhouse effect. Also, the distributional conflicts are barely understood even by the social actors themselves, since only recently has a widespread awarenesss of the value of agricultural biodiversity arisen in poor countries. Some of these countries comprise the original "centres of biodiversity" identified by Vavilov (e.g., maize in Mexico and Central America, potatoes in the Andes, cassava in Brazil Paraguay). Moreover, in such countries there are still poor farmers, experts in traditional plant breeding, practicing "clean technology" and low-input agriculture based on hundreds of "landraces" (which Pat Mooney has proposed to call "folkseeds" in Cooper et al. 1992; see also Querol 1992).

The threat to such agricultural biodiversity comes mainly from the market advantage to be gained by switching over to modern agriculture and the "high response varieties." Questions arise as to the value that agricultural biodiversity has now and will have in the future as an asset of "cultivated natural capital" that cannot be substituted for by the products of modern plant breeding or genetic engineering; whether such value that the market leaves aside ought to have a chrematistic translation; and who should collect such monetary revenues. Also, what should be transacted? The right to use such traditionally improved varieties without excluding other users, or the acquisition of their property? There is also the issue of the complementarity between agricultural biodiversity and the biodiversity of wild life, which is the main platform of bodies such as the WWF, and is emphasized far more than agricultural and agroforestal biodiversity in the IUCN's conservation strategy (McNeely et al. 1990).

Agricultural genetic resources as "cultivated natural capital" are not a substitute for, but a complement to the human-made capital equipment used in modern agriculture; in its turn, such "cultivated natural capital" needs the complement of "natural capital," (i.e., the wild and weedy relatives of the same species of cultivated plants[8]). The ethnobotanical diversity of the poor has been recently emphasized by different authors inside a wider framework of agroecology based on indigenous, peasant knowledge that continuously evolves (Richards 1984; Guha and Gadgil 1992; Toledo 1988/1991, 1989; Posey 1985; Descola 1988; Rocheleau 1991). Agricultural biodiversity cannot be understood unless we also understand the whole human ecological complex of each society that has managed to create, preserve, and further create such wealth of genetic resources. They are valuable, but such value is not easily translatable into monetary terms. The crucial question is whether genetic resources in general (those from the wilderness, those from traditionally improved varieties, those from modern varieties, and those genetically engineered) should be commercialized or should remain the "patrimony of humankind." Genetic resources produced by traditional plant breeding and collected in the fields, up to now, have not been paid for, while firms selling modern improved seeds insist on payment for them, and the products of genetic engineering will be, not only sold, but monopolized through a patent system.

---

8. Herman Daly's classification includes Natural Capital, Human-Made Capital, and also, as a special case, Cultivated Natural Capital. He has discussed the question (which was previously raised by Frederick Soddy of Oxford) of whether such categories of Capital are substitutes or complements. Ecological economists have insisted that natural resources should be called natural capital for two reasons. First, the change in name points to the lack of depreciation provisions for natural resources. Second, the change in name points to the problematic nature of the substitution of capital for natural resources as in orthodox production funtions. However, the change in name also might mean that resources not produced as commodities and that were not commodities should now be treated as capital, (i.e., commodities). Examples are traditional agricultural genetic resources and the Earth's CO_2 cleaning facilities.

A new socio-political movement, part of a worldwide slowly emerging trend of *ecological neo-narodnism*, will be able to use the ecological critique developed in the rich countries over the last forty years against modern agriculture. In Western Europe and the United States, agricultural historians and agricultural economists have paid almost no attention to the biological impoverishment of modern agriculture, swept under the carpets of "increases in productivity" of conventional economics or "development of productive forces" in mainstream Marxist historiography. Even before Rachel Carson in 1962, there had been a number of local episodes against the use of pesticides. For instance, techniques of integrated pest management were used in coastal Peru, in the cotton plantations of the Cañete Valley in the 1950s (conference paper in Farvar et al. 1972), even though at the same time, there was in coastal Peru a successful campaign to eradicate pre-Hispanic varieties of colored cotton as sources of pests for the commercial cotton plantations. This campaign is now regretted by Peruvian agronomists.

Some years after the alarm over the use of pesticides arose in different parts of the world, another approach was taken in order to understand and criticize modern agriculture. This was the study of the flow of energy in agriculture (Pimentel 1973; Leach 1975; Naredo and Campos 1980), which showed that modern agriculture made an increasingly inefficient use of outside energy inputs, while traditional agriculture had used no energy source from outside agriculture other than energy from the sun. The question was immediately asked by ecological economists whether the increased economic productivity of modern agriculture was merely an artifact of the low price of fossil fuels. Discussion of this issue continues to this day. It figured as a political argument in the SAM program for food security in Mexico in the early 1980s (Schejtman 1983; 1987).

While a traditional peasant farmer who has rights to land, will automatically also have access to energy from the sun and at least some water through rainfall, and will also command a "fourth resource," (i.e., the seed for his or her crops), modern farmers depend much more on an external energy subsidy from fossil fuels, which are more polluting. And modern farmers have lost control over the "fourth resource."[9] Here again

---

9. This is Henk Hobbelink's description. He is the founder of GRAIN (Genetic Resources Action International), an NGO based in Barcelona, which provides information on the importance of and the threats to agricultural biodiversity.

we could examine the evolution of ideas,[10] tracing back long ago to the first use of expressions such as "genetic erosion," not as an exercise in erudition but in order to show how ignorance of the ecological and social impacts of technological change was socially hidden under the ideology of progress.[11] Thus, peasant farmers have insisted in sowing traditional varieties not because of the recent efforts by ethnobotanists and the agronomic institutions, and certainly not because of monetary incentives, but because their logic has not been limited to the logic of the market. In Mexico, modern hybrid maize has *not* yet taken over. In the rich countries, the extension of the market meant great, ignored losses of genetic resources, rarely mentioned in textbooks of agricultural history. Perhaps in the poor countries an ecologically extended market, where genetic resources are properly valued, would combat genetic erosion.

The economics of technology took as a classic case the study of the rate of return on the research and development of hybrid maize in the United States fifty years ago (Griliches 1958). The ecological context was left out. No item measured the costs of the loss of biodiversity, which makes hybrid maize in the United States dependent on the imported genetic wealth of Mexican folkseeds and wild varieties; this was given away gratis, a beneficial externality to U.S. agriculture for which there was no market, and which therefore had no chrematistic value. The development of hybrid maize, and later of the HYV of wheat and rice, gave a large impulse to the process of genetic erosion, which is a corollary of the new farming system based on mechanization and a monoculture in every field.

There is now an increasing awareness that the history of modern agriculture is a history of biological impoverishment. Vellvé (1992) in focusing on the European experience, shows that modern agriculture has replaced diversity with uniformity, and security with vulnerability. What is being done in practice in order to safeguard genetic resources for the future, so as to escape the contradiction between apparent increases in agricultural productivity and the destruction of the genetic resource base? Vellvé concludes that genetic resources are increasingly vested in industrial, multinational hands, while the efforts of public institutions for

---

10. As was done for the history of the study of the flow of energy in agriculture in Martinez-Alier and Schluepmann (1991).

11. Mario Tapia in Peru has been writing a history of the Andean scholars who started the tradition of collecting peasant varieties in the 1920s and 1930s.

ex-situ storage in genebanks suffer many drawbacks. There is, however, a third actor, and not only in countries of the South, which are the main repositories of agricultural biodiversity, but also in Europe, where the crucial conservation work has been done by individuals and grass roots organizations, as an example of popular environmentalism—underfinanced, and unrecognized.

Since the so-called improved varieties of modern agriculture cannot do without a continuous flow of new genetic resources in order to cope with new pests and new environmental challenges, and since they provide a short-run economic advantage (in the chrematistic sense) over traditional agroecology, the growth of production for the market undermines its very conditions of production (i.e., agricultural biodiversity) and a new socio-ecological movement was born, which is now is growing, in order to resist this degradation.[12]

FARMERS' RIGHTS

Modern agriculture, which represents a radical ecological break, has used the biodiversity of the poor in order to produce new varieties, such as the HYV (or High Response Varieties) of the Centres of Agronomic Research in the CGIAR, (whose headquarters are not in FAO in Rome, for instance, nor in any other U.N. institution, but at the World Bank in Washington, DC).[13] The flow of genetic materials, and the incorporated knowledge, (which is inevitably lost to some extent when the seeds stored *ex-situ* are divorced from the farmers' knowledge) has not been paid for, another item in the *ecological debt* that the rich owe to the poor. Sometimes, a little has been paid for the traditionally improved varieties, a cheap peasant price for folkseeds bought in peasant markets, and then shipped to gene banks *ex-situ*. Nobody pays for medicinal plants discovered and nurtured by indigenous knowledge, which are then developed by pharmaceutical firms that charge prices and royalties for their medicines. In contrast with medicines, the modern improved seeds have not been patented. Protection against duplication by farmers was secured

---

12. This fits in with O'Connor's (1988) notion of the "second contradiction" under capitalism.
13. The reason is that the CGIAR is controlled by the so-called "donor countries." Donor countries are the countries that finance the CGIAR's centres, not the countries whose farmers donated the genetic resources now stored *ex-situ* in the Centres for Agronomic Research.

to some extent, not by a legal monopoly, but by selling hybrid varieties or varieties that degenerate quickly. It seems that the new legal framework required by the biotechnological industry will allow patenting "forms of life," including agricultural genetic resources. This is why GATT is now pushing for the international recognition of patents on "new" genetic materials (as it has always tried to do for medicines), while some CGIAR's centres are now proposing to take patents on the genetic resources they hold (Hobbelink 1992). Activists in the agroecological movement (GRAIN, CLADES) are against the patenting of "forms of life." On this issue they concur with many other green activists who fear that the development of biotechnology, with its promises and menaces, will be subject only to the logic of the market. Specifically, agroecologists are against the patenting of the genetic resources in the CGIAR's centres. They are in general against "Intellectual Property Rights," in the sense that they do not think this is the appropriate way to defend and reward agricultural biodiversity. They are somewhat divided over the issue of Farmers' Rights, which would be paid to farmers or farmers' organizations, or governments of poor countries, for the labor and knowledge in traditional plant breeding.

Payments for Farmers' Rights would not buy the exclusive use of such genetic resources, they are not the equivalent to buying Intellectual Property Rights; rather the analogy would be a fee or honorarium for professional services. From the economic point of view, the issue is to provide the required incentive to secure the conservation and further development of agricultural biodiversity, but some agroecological activists think that the payment of Farmers' Rights will interfere with the peasants' own non-market logic for maintaining and increasing biodiversity, without really implying a considerable transference of money from the rich to the poor in exchange for such non-exclusive rights to use the improved folkseeds. Perhaps it would be better from the point of view of conservation to keep *all* genetic resources as the "patrimony of humankind," at the same time introducing social and legal safeguards against dangerous or absurd applications of biotechnologies. An example of these is increasing plant resistance to pesticides, instead of resistance to pests. In addition, an economic compensation can be established *via product prices* (or income transferences) for the producers of low-input, "clean" agroecology so that they will be motivated to preserve and further develop their traditional biodiversity.

The technologies of modern agriculture outcompete the products of "organic" farming in the large markets. There are small, specialized markets for products of "organic" farming that command higher prices. A massive change in consumers' preferences could change the economic advantage that now favors the adoption of modern technologies; this might come about slowly through ecological awareness and consumer education. However, since many of the damages caused by modern agriculture will have impacts only in the long run, much depends on the weight that the present generation gives to the uncertain needs of future generations. It is likely that the conflict between economy and ecology will stay with us; therefore, the issue of Farmers' Rights as payments for specific environmental resources will also stay on the political agenda for some time. Who would be, in any case, the recipient of Farmers' Rights? Farmers' organizations? Individual farmers? Governments? What would be their price? Apart from the immediate use value of folkseeds, there is also their option value, even perhaps their existence value, although many would be readier to apply the notion of "existence value" to wild biodiversity than to a humble domesticated variety of potatoes. The reality is that *peasants and indigenous peoples are likely to set a low price to their hypothetical Farmers' Rights*, not because they themselves attribute a low social value to their labor and agronomic knowledge, and not because they give a low present value to the benefits from biodiversity for future generations, but *because they are poor*.

THE POOR SELL CHEAP

The expansion of market exchange implied not only the actual inclusion in the market of inputs and products that were outside it, but it also implied, on another plane (emphasized by Martin O'Connor, following Baudrillard), the *ideological appropriation* by capitalism of elements of nature hitherto external to the market system. Thus, the ecologically extended market implies giving *chrematistic significance* to environmental resources and functions that were outside the market. Agricultural genetic resources and the Earth's CO_2 sink function were outside the market, but they were of great ecological significance for the human economy (in the sense of *oikonomia*). Once humankind has been immersed in a generalized market system (and it also has grown in numbers, and for some groups in the exosomatic consumption of energy and materials), then the lack of market valuation of such resources and services that were the common patrimony of humankind has perhaps led to a wasteful use of them. Hence the idea that, in principle, placing chrematistic values on environmental resources and services would be conducive to a more ecological economy, and in these instances, it would also favor the poor. Therefore, further negotiations after Rio on the increased greenhouse effect and on biodiversity might eventually be conducted under the proposals outlined in this chapter, which imply a redistribution of income as part of such environmental policies. How large the redistribution of income would be is impossible to say, because we cannot know what the price of such environmental resources and services would be. We are aware, however, that the poor sell commodities cheap, and they also sell cheap environmental commodities. There have recently been some glaring examples of this.

The first example is the low indemnities for the victims of the Bhopal disaster (in a settlement approved by the Courts in India), indemnities that were lower (although the criminal case is still pending) than the indemnities already paid for by the Exxon Valdez oil spill. Here one sees the truth contained in the memorandum "Just between you and me" by Lawrence Summers, chief economist of the World Bank:

> The measurement of the costs of health-impairing pollution depends on the foregone earnings from increased morbidity and mortality. From this point of view a given amount of health-impairing pollution should be done in the country with the lowest cost, which will be the country with the lowest wages. I think the economic logic behind dumping a load of toxic waste in the lowest-wage country is impeccable and we should face up to that (The Economist 1992).

Union Carbide would have been bankrupt by the damages to be paid had the accident taken place in a North Atlantic country.

The second example is the Costa Rican deal with the Merck Company in 1992 through INBIO (Instituto Nacional de Biodiversidad) (Brugger and Lizano 1992). It is not a case of agricultural genetic resources, but rather of "wild" genetic resources. However, it is most relevant to this discussion. While the World Resources Institute (WRI 1992) typically praises the "recent agreement between a major drug company and Costa Rica (which) deserves to be widely copied," the deal is creating a major uproar in Latin America, because Costa Rica shares genetic resources with neighboring countries. The deal implies, of course, the recognition of rights on genetic resources ("wild" resources, in this case) but, on the

other hand, it gives no assurance that traditional knowledge and the conservation of biodiversity will be able to compete by themselves with
other land uses that give a higher rate of return in the market. The deal is
for a little more than one million U.S. dollars to be paid in two install-
ments for the access to the information in a large amount of samples collected by INBIO from the protected areas of Costa Rica. The deal also
includes the payment of a royalty by Merck on any commercially valuable products developed from those samples. Barring some extraordinary
piece of luck, it is a low price in the sense that "existence" value is not
paid for, and also in the sense that immediate utilitarian value is low, and
that perhaps nothing profitable will come out of the chemical screening
by Merck. Unless there were additional costly measures for conservation
(legal regulation, police vigilance) paid for by the Costa Rican authorities
or private foundations, plus the self-interest in conservation of parts of
the local populations, the small chrematistic incentive provided by Merck
would be too low in order to prevent deforestation and genetic erosion.
However, it is only normal that Costa Rica should sell cheap.

There is a parallel here with debates within the feminist movement
some years ago. The analogy is not far fetched, since the debates were
connected with the same root economic cause (i.e., the failure of the
market to measure services essential to the human economy in the sense
of *oikonomia*). Should the reality of unpaid domestic work given by
women because of their social subjection be denounced at the moral and
political planes, and changes be sought to the unequal distribution of
labor by moral persuasion and social changes, or would it be a good idea
to give *chrematistic significance* to such work by attributing to it a
domestic wage similar to the wage the market determines for remunerated domestic work by outside help? Peculiar labor markets make such
remunerated domestic work relatively cheap, but apart from this, many
feminists felt that a domestic wage would add insult to injury, since the
social value for the *oikonomia* (for the human economy) of caring for
children and for the family would not, and could not be properly reflected in a price established by market criteria.

In the case of environmental externalities, there is the further issue of
distant intergenerational effects. There is no guarantee at all that the ecologically extended market in which today's preferences are expressed
will give sufficient importance to future needs. The unborn cannot come
to the market, ecologically extended or not. The implicit discount rates

might be too high, not only because of selfishness but also because of ex-aggeratedly optimistic views regarding technical progress and economic growth. But, apart from the short time horizons they might share with the rich, there are other reasons why the poor sell cheap. First, the distribution of assets in the world is very unequal. Second, the world labor markets are terribly segmented by racial discrimination, gender inequality, unequal access to education, and by the poor's inability to move freely in the world, as we see in the many deaths at sea in Haiti and Morocco. In the third place, while free mobility is practically forbidden, on the other hand, open markets are forced upon people; nobody is allowed in practice to live outside the market. Even subsistence peasants cannot retreat from the market if they do not have enough land, and sufficient water, and their own seed. In such circumstances, poor people will have to sell cheap commodities, they will also sell cheap environmental resources, and they will accept pollution cheaply. Thus, in the history of the world economy, even when rights to health protection are instituted due to pressure from labor unions or international norms, free wage workers in poor countries who suffer a disproportionate share of environmental hazards (in mines, in plantations) accept such hazards cheaply, if not gladly.

If the poor sell cheap, the environmental resources and functions they would own, once suitable ownership rights were established, are likely to reach low values once they are brought to the market, and therefore, the ecologically extended market will not necessarily direct the economy towards sustainability.

THE ENVIRONMENTALISM OF THE POOR

So far I have suggested that the establishment of new property rights on environmental resources and services might work to the benefit of poor sections of the population, although perhaps their very poverty will lead to a low valuation of such resources and services in the ecologically extended markets. The fact that the poor put low chrematistic values on the environment, which can be expressed by the aphorism "the poor sell cheap" (it could also be called the "Lawrence Summers' principle"), does not mean, however, that the poor have no interest on the environment. Rather the contrary.

One prevalent interpretation of environmentalism sees it as a movement of relatively affluent populations that arises because of a shift from materialist to "post-materialist" values. Thus, in rich countries, forests and even the maintenance of agricultural landscapes are increasingly seen as "quality of life" issues, while in most of the world full use of forest products and of agricultural production is essential to the precarious livelihood of the population. In rich countries people can afford to care about clean air, while in most of the world air pollution is accepted as a sign of industrialization. Another interpretation of Western environmentalism contends, from the opposite angle, that the economies of rich countries are *not* "post-materialist" but, on the contrary, use and destroy natural resources and services at much greater rates per capita than the economies of poor countries. Thus, the movement against the civilian use of nuclear power was born in the 1960s and 1970s in countries that have high rates of consumption of electricity per capita. Movements against industrial toxic waste arose because of the high level of consumption of chemicals that characterizes rich countries, although here it should be noticed that the geography of waste dumping often discriminates against relatively poor communities inside rich countries. The movement in favor of recycling domestic waste came about because the amount of waste (over one kilogram per person per day), and its composition, made it difficult or dangerous to dispose of it in waste dumps or incinerators. Such environmental movements react against "the effluents of affluence." If the preservation of forests appears to be in the West a question of "quality of life" rather than livelihood, the reason is that the functions the forests fulfilled, namely as sources of woodfuels, of building materials, and of medicinal plants, are now performed in other ways that certainly are not less materialistic, such an cooking with electricity, building with cement, glass, and aluminum, or with imported tropical woods.[14] If agriculture is increasingly seen in the rich countries as a way of preserving green landscapes, enhancing the "quality of life," this is because agriculture and meat production make such as intensive use of external inputs that surpluses are produced, as is the case even in overpopulated, carnivorous Western Europe. Green policies of reforestation on agricultural land now set aside are proposed. Such high agricultural productivity does

---

14. Moreover, the forests are now seen again by the rich in terms of livelihood, because of the services they perform as sinks for carbon. This is why in Rio there were attempts to impose an agreement on International Principles for Forests, which would deprive not only local communities but even independent states of control over the forests, which would be vested instead in international ecological managers.

not arise from a "post-materialist" recipe but rather from the intensive use of external inputs that also results in large material flows of waste. The environmental movements of the rich born in reaction against high levels of resource use and waste, could be called the "Environmentalism of the Rich, the Ecology of Affluence."

Both the "post-materialist" and "materialist" interpretations of the "Environmentalism of the Rich" have some merits. The intent here, however, is rather to show that there is another type of environmentalism that arises from materialist concerns—"the Environmentalism of the Poor, the Ecology of Survival." The focus here is not on the search for "quality of life" once material needs are satiated. It is again on the social responses against resource depletion and the production of waste, which in rich countries may occur because of a generally high standard of living, but which may also occur because of increasing inequality in the allocation of resources (internal to each country, and internationally). Some sections of the population make such large use of environmental resources and services that they deprive the poorer sections of the population of their access to them. The reaction against this could be called the "Environmentalism of the Poor," or the "Ecology of Survival" (or Ecological Neo-Narodnism), in so far as it demands equitable and non-destructive use of natural resources and services for livelihood, and not for commercial gain. The conclusion will summarize the main issues of this chapter, which are the attribution of property rights on some environmental resources and services, and the values that such rights would achieve in the market, in the light of this notion of the "Environmentalism of the Poor."

CONCLUSION: AGAINST THE MERCHANDISING OF NATURE?

In the aftermath of the Rio conference, this chapter has addressed the issue of distributional obstacles to environmental policy. The Brundtland Report of 1987, which has dominated discussions over the past few years on the relations between inequality and environment, took an easy way out by adopting the convenient view that both poverty and environmental degradation might be alleviated by overall economic growth (called "sustainable development"). After all, Brundtland herself is a social-democratic leader, and the position of social-democracy has always been favorable to growth rather than redistribution, and this apparently worked well in Western Europe in the Keynesian era. Ecological considerations have only recently become part of the social-democratic perspective, mainly because of challenges by Green political parties. It is only natural that the first approach has been that ecological problems can be solved by growth. This comes as easily to Keynesian social-democrats as the belief that the market has solutions for environmental problems comes to neo-liberals. This chapter takes instead a more realistic view, showing that in general we cannot rely on economic growth as a solution both to environmental problems and to income inequality, because economic growth is unsustainable from an ecological point of view. However, there are some exceptions as in the case of fuels for domestic cooking, or atmospheric pollution with sulfur dioxide, or some aspects of public health. In such cases, economic growth is good for the environment. In many other cases, distributional obstacles to environmental policy should be removed by redistribution rather than growth. This point of view has been discussed with reference to two concrete issues: genetic erosion and the increased greenhouse effect.

The poor through their conservation and creation of agricultural genetic diversity, and through their disproportionately low use of the Earth's CO_2 sink function, have made contributions to sustainability. These contributions have not been rewarded through the market since no rights were established on such environmental resources and services. Rio missed the opportunity to establish such rights, as a step towards effective agreements on the greenhouse effect and on biodiversity. However, if such rights were instituted, the question remains of the prices at which they would be transacted. Inequality and poverty would possibly depress their supply prices. The attribution of *chrematistic significance* to environmental resources and services does not, therefore, provide a guarantee for their conservation, and might even be counterproductive. Rights and money values are a weak substitute for social responses. In fact, in the Environmentalism of the Poor, the most frequent type of action (as in the Chipko movement, or by Chico Mendes) *denies* the inclusion of environmental resources in the generalized market system, and tries to keep them in the non-market sphere of a "moral economy" (in E. P. Thompson's or J. Scott's sense). In the case of Chico Mendes' *reservas extractivas* (which were actually *productivas*), it has been argued sometimes (Aragón 1991) that the production in terms of rubber, Brazil nuts, and other resources, was able to compete in monetary terms with the agropastoral use of the land, (without counting the negative externalities of the latter) were it not for the direct money subsidies to cattle ranching. This might well be true, but Chico Mendes' movement arose as a non-violent social response by people who made a sustainable use of the forest against its privatization and commercial use; it did not appeal to market advantage. In this, it is quite similar to the Chipko movement (Guha 1991), or to other social movements against the expansion of the market and its threat to livelihood, (i.e., movements in India that try to prevent water needed for domestic use, or for the irrigation of food gardens, being used for commercial sugar cane plantations (Rao 1989). The livelihood of the poor, their material provisioning (i.e., *oikonomia*) is for them too crucial to be left to the results of market exchanges (*chrematistika*).

The emphasis on a "moral economy" is not environmental posturing but rather a spontaneous reaction against the threats coming from the generalized market system against the livelihood of the poor. Therefore, the main proposals considered in this chapter, on payments in money for Farmers' Rights on agricultural genetic resources, and payments in money for rights to the CO_2 sink function, coming as they do from NGOs identified with the poor, are somewhat surprising as instances of "Environmentalism of the Poor," because they wish to give chrematistic significance to resources and services that up to now were outside the market. The measures proposed are weak in two senses. First, (and this has not been the main point of this chapter), they do not secure at all the demands of future generations. In the second place, if the poor sell cheap, such payments would be low, and perhaps would not provide a strong environmental inducement. Nevertheless, even such weak measures would imply a flow of money from the rich to the poor (because of the actual geographical and social distribution of CO_2 emissions and of agricultural biodiversity), and they would also put on the table the issue of the *Ecological Debt* that the rich owe to the poor due to past emissions of CO_2, non-payment for collection of genetic resources, and destruction of biodiversity. For these reasons, such weak measures were not agreed to at Rio. It is still doubtful whether they will provide a basis for further negotiations on the greenhouse effect and on biodiversity.

REFERENCES

Agarwal, A., and S. Narain. 1991. Global Warming: A Case of Environmental Colonialism. Delhi: Centre for Science and Environment,

Aragón, L., ed. 1991. A Desordem Ecológica na Amazônia. Belém: UNAMAZ.

Arden-Clarke, C. 1991. The General Agreement on Tariffs and Trade, Environmental Protection and Sustainable Development. Gland: World Wildlife Fund for Nature.

Brugger, E. A., and E. Lizano, eds. 1992. Eco-Eficiencia. La Visión Empresarial Para el Desarrollo Sostenible en América Latina, 289-293. Bogotá: Oveja Negra, Business Council for Sustainable Development.

Cooper, D., R. Vellvé, and H. Hobbelink, eds. 1992. Growing Diversity. Genetic Resources and Local Food Security. London: Intermediate Technology Publications.

Diaz Palacios, J. 1988. El Perú y su Medio Ambiente: Southern Peru Copper Corporation, Una Compleja Agresión Ambiental en el sur del País. Lima: IDMA/CONCYTEC.

Daly, H. E., and J. B. Cobb. 1989. For the Common Good. Boston: Beacon Press.

Daly, H. E., and R. Goodland. 1992. An Ecological-Economic Assessment of Deregulation of International Commerce under GATT. Discussion draft, Environment Department, September. Washington, DC: The World Bank.

Descola, Ph. 1988. La Selva. Culta. Simbolismo y Praxis en la Ecología de los Achuar. Quito: Abya Yala.

Dietz, F. J., and J. van der Straaten. 1992. Sustainable development and the necessary integration of ecological insights into economic theory. In Sustainability and Environmental Policy, eds. F. J. Dietz, U. E. Simonis and J. van der Straaten. Berlin: Sigma.

The Economist. Let them eat pollution. February 8, 1992.

Farvar, M. Taghi, and J. P. Milton, eds. 1972. The Careless Technology. Ecology and International Development. Garden City, NY: The Natural History Press.

Funtowicz, S., and J. Ravetz. 1991. Three types of risk assessment and the emergence of post-normal science. In Theories of Risk, eds. D. Golding and S. Krimsky. New York, NY: Greenwood Press. Also in Ecological Economics: the Science and Management of Sustainability, ed. R. Costanza. New York: Columbia Univ. Press.

Green Agenda. A publication of the Greens in the European Parliament for the UNCED conference, May 1992.

Griliches, Z. 1958. Research cost and social returns: hybrid corn and related innovations. *Journal of Political Economy* 66: 419–31.

Grinevald, J. 1990. L'effet de Serre de la Biosphère. *Stratégies Énergétiques, Biosphère et Société* 1: 9–36.

Guha, R. 1991. The Unquiet Woods. Ecology and Peasant Resistance in the Himalayas. Delhi: Oxford Univ. Press.

Guha, R., and Gadgil, M. 1992. This Fissured Land: An Ecological History of India. Delhi: Oxford Univ. Press.

Hobbelink, H. 1992. La Diversidad Biológica y la Biotecnología agrícola. *Ecología Polític* a 4: 57–72.

Leach, G. 1975. Energy and Food Production. Guildford, Surrey: IPC Science and Technology Press.

Leff, E. 1986. Ecología y Capital. Mexico: UNAM.

Luke, A. 1992. Spain: too poor to be green? *New Scientist* (July 25).

Markandya, A. 1991. Global warming: the economics of tradable permits. In Blueprint 2. Greening the World Economy, ed. D. W. Pearce. London: Earthscan.

Martinez-Alier, J. with K. Schluepmann. 1991. Ecological Economics: Environment, Energy and Society. 2nd ed. Oxford: Blackwell.

McNeely, J. A., K. R. Miller, W. V. Reid, R. A. Mittermeier, and T. B. Werner. 1990. Conserving the World's Biological Diversity. Gland; Washington, DC: IUCN, WRI, CI, WWF-US, World Bank.

Naredo, J. M., and P. Campos. 1980. Los Balances Energéticos de la Agricultura Española. *Agricultura y Sociedad* 15.

New York Times, August 15, 1992, 34.

O'Connor, J. 1988. Introduction *Capitalism, Nature, Socialism* 1(1): 11–38.

Patiño, A. 1991. Ecología y Compromiso Social. Itinerario de Una Lucha. Bogota: Cerec.

Pimentel, D., et al. 1973. Food production and the energy crisis. *Science* 182: 443–49.

Posey, D. 1985. Indigenous management of tropical forest ecosystems: the case of the Kayapo Indians of the Brazilian Amazon. *Agroforestry Systems* 3(2): 139–58.

Querol, D. 1992. Genetic Resources: Our Forgotten Treasure. Penang: Third World Network.

Rao, B. 1989. Women and water in rural Maharashta. *Capitalism, Nature, Socialism* 1 (2).

Richards, P. 1984. Indigenous Agricultural Revolutions: Ecology and Food Production in West Africa. London: Hutchinson.

Rocheleau, D. 1991. Gender, ecology and the science of survival: stories and lessons from Kenya. *Agriculture and Human Values* (Winter–Spring): 156–65.

Røpke, I. 1992. Trade, development and sustainability. a critical assessment of the free trade dogma. *Ecological Economics* 9: 13–22..

Schejtman, A. 1983. Análisis Integral del Problema Alimentario y Nutricional en América Latina. *Estudios Rurales Latinoamericanos* 6(2–3): 141–80.

———. 1987. Campesinado y Seguridad Alimentaria. *Estudios Rurales Latinoamericanos* 10(3): 275–311.

Toledo, V. M. 1988. La Sociedad Rural, los Campesinos y la Cuestión Ecológica. In Las Sociedades Rurales Hoy, ed. Jorge Zepeda. Conacyt: El Colegio de Michoacan. Also in *Ecología Política*, Vol. 1, 1991, 11–18.

———. 1989. The ecological rationality of peasant production. In Agroecology and Small Farm Development, eds. M. Altieri and S. Hecht. Boca Raton: CRC Press.

Vellvé, R. 1992. Saving the Seed. Genetic Diversity and European Agriculture. London: Earthscan.

WRI. 1992. World Resources 1992-93. Oxford: Oxford Univ. Press.

10 ECOLOGY, ECONOMIC INCENTIVES, AND PUBLIC POLICY IN THE DESIGN OF A TRANSDISCIPLINARY POLLUTION CONTROL INSTRUMENT

John H. Cumberland
Maryland International Institute for Ecological
  Economics
University of Maryland
P.O. Box 38
Solomons, MD 20688

INTRODUCTION

An important aspect of investing in natural capital is instituting policy instruments designed for effective protection against pollution. Therefore, a major challenge facing ecological economics is not only to create a transdisciplinary science that will improve capabilities for describing and analyzing complex systems, but which will also help design policy instruments that are more effective than those now in use. The acceleration of environmental pollution since the Industrial Revolution, despite intense remedial efforts for more than two decades, remains a major threat to the sustainable development of the earth (Daly and Cobb 1989). Buchanan (1988) and other contributors to the literature on public choice have acknowledged the inadequacies of current regulatory processes for environmental management. The failure of society to come to grips with environmental pollution cannot be attributed simply to the failure among various branches of natural and behavioral sciences to address the problem. Indeed, surveys of the literature yield a rich harvest of imaginative pollution control policy instruments, ranging from the most hardline command and control regulatory regimes to the most imaginative and theoretical incentive schemes. It is not surprising to find, each arguing from the concepts of their own disciplines—ecologists leaning toward the total prohibition of emissions that they regard as life-threatening, while economists accept with equanimity, and even with enthusiasm, the sale of what conservationists pejoratively term licenses to pollute. Given the conflicting approaches by specialists from different fields, environmental administrators cannot be blamed for crafting policy instruments serving their own separate agendas.

Since thermodynamic imperatives guarantee that continued population and economic growth will increase pollution pressures (Georgescu-Roegen 1971), one of the most valuable contributions ecological economics could make is to develop criteria for improved environmental policy instruments needed for sustainable development. The objective of this chapter is to carry forward the design of policy instruments "...which are scientifically valid, economically efficient, and distributionally equitable between regions, interest groups, and generations" (Cumberland 1991, 355).

THE INCENTIVE-BASED ECONOMIC EFFICIENCY MODEL

While specialized disciplines such as economics and ecology are essential to the advancement of theory and knowledge, they seldom individually provide the best basis for policy design. An example that illustrates both the strengths and weaknesses of a single-purpose pollution control instrument is the proposed use of pollution taxes, marketable pollution permits, and comparable incentive-based (I-B) environmental policies. Economic theory demonstrates that in a large number of cases and under a wide range of circumstances, these I-B instruments can provide the most efficient, least-cost method of pollution control, primarily because they provide economic incentives for the most efficient pollution abaters to perform most of the abatement. Most I-B policies also have the additional advantage of raising revenues needed for environmental and other public purposes. This well-known model is summarized in Figure 10.1.

If the marginal damage and treatment cost functions can be derived, their intersection yields two important estimates:

1.   on the horizontal axis, optimal environmental quality, as measured by efficient emission levels, and

2. on the vertical axis, the shadow price of pollution (optimal tax per unit of emission) needed to provide emitters with the financial incentives for limiting their emissions to the socially desirable level.

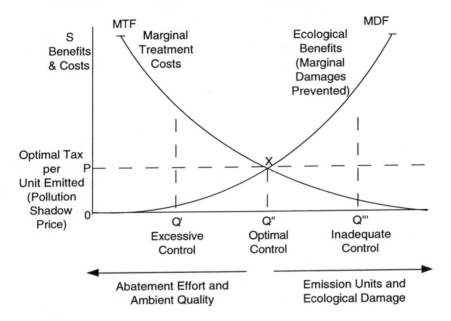

MDF = Marginal Damage Function
MTF = Marginal Treatment Cost function
Ambient quality in parts per million.
Emissions in units per time period.
Based upon a transformation function relating ambient quality to emission rates.

Figure 10.1. Economically efficient pollution control and environmental quality.

In terms of economic logic, this instrument also has the attractive quality of achieving optimal environmental quality at lowest social cost in the static case, and of harnessing and rewarding competition to achieve improved, cost-reducing pollution control technology in the dynamic case. Economic literature extensively supports this approach as an alternative to the current regulatory or command and control approach. Regulation, in this view, is unnecessarily costly and inefficient (Baumol and Oates 1988).

SOME OBJECTIONS TO THE EFFICIENCY APPROACH

Despite its powerful appeal to economists, public policy debates have revealed numerous objections to the concept of fees or taxes on pollution, including the following (see, among others, Dietz and Van der Straaten 1992):

- pollution taxes are merely a "license to pollute";

- pollution taxes simply become "a cost of doing business" and are passed on to the consumer;

- pollution taxes may impinge inequitably upon some firms, potentially giving large firms the advantage of driving out small firms;

- the effects of pollution taxes are less certain than are the effects of emission control regulatory powers vested in administrative agencies;

- data requirements and uncertainty make it difficult to estimate the damage and abatement cost functions needed to set efficient pollution charges and to achieve optimal environmental quality;

- in the absence of well-defined damage functions and of the transdisciplinary research needed to set appropriate tax levels, those pollution taxes that have been applied tend to have been too low to reduce pollution and are used primarily to raise revenue;

- it is inequitable to impose regulatory limits on emissions and then to add pollution taxes on legally-permitted emissions;

- some pollutants are too toxic to risk being emitted for any level of taxes, (e.g., plutonium);

- in many western countries, such as the United States, the familiar regulatory approach has become so embedded in legal custom and business practice that powerful interest groups resist pollution taxes to the extent that their introduction would be politically infeasible; and

- damage functions based upon emissions are difficult to estimate, and may not encompass the full range of ecological interrelationships involved in global phenomena, such as the greenhouse effect, ozone depletion, acid rain, and nuclear damage.

Some of these points are more substantive than others, but each of them merits discussion. Concerning licenses to pollute, present regulatory practices already license pollution, but polluters are given the right to use the limited assimilative capacity of the environment without charge, as though it were a free good. To the extent that emission charges, fees, or taxes become a cost of doing business and are passed along to the consumer, they serve economic efficiency, since they tend to reallocate spending away from pollution-intensive activities.[1] The equity aspects of taxing pollution depend upon one's view of the locus of property rights as between emitters vs. the public (Pearce and Turner 1990). The equity aspects of impacts upon small and existing firms vs. large firms also merit attention here. The point that most pollution taxes to date have been set too low to change behavior is less an objection in principle than an argument for improved calibration of this policy instrument. A comprehensive review of the literature on I-B instruments has been provided by Oates and Cropper (1992).

However, since economic efficiency remains as one goal, if not the only goal of environmental policy, these points and other more serious objections to single purpose I-B policies can assist in the search for a new generation of environmental policy instruments. Innovations are needed that would be more relevant to sustainable development and more responsive to a broad spectrum of physical science and social purposes than are the pure forms of pollution taxes and narrowly-focused I-B approaches. The design of acceptable pollution charges can benefit from more transdisciplinary research than has been achieved to date, and from a broader public policy perspective than has guided environmental policy design to date.

Recent work has suggested that a public choice approach could offer the guidelines needed for effective and acceptable environmental management policies (Cumberland 1990). The criteria to be sought are:

- consistency with the realities of physical science,

- economic efficiency,

- distributional equity and justice,

- interest group acceptability, and

- political feasibility.

---

1. Anderson et al. (1990), in a detailed analysis of the incidence of emission fees, conclude that, at least in the short run, emission fees will be borne not necessarily by consumers, but "...will be largely borne by producers, or shifted backwards to their suppliers, workers, or stockholders." (56). Long-run incidence depends upon the elasticities of supply and demand functions, industry structure, and other factors.

It is the thesis of this chapter that because current policy instruments fail to meet the full range of these criteria, such instruments are inadequate for meeting current environmental threats and that chances for significant improvement of these instruments will be enhanced if they are designed to meet all five of the above criteria.

BEYOND ECONOMIC EFFICIENCY: AN ECOLOGICAL ECONOMICS APPROACH

The proposed transdisciplinary framework, which supplements economic insights through a team approach by explicitly including concepts from ecology and the physical sciences, as well as concerns for equity, distribution, and political feasibility, is illustrated in Figure 10.2.

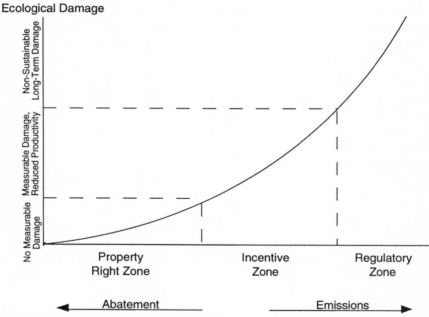

Figure 10.2. An ecological economic approach to pollution control.

This model is proposed as an alternative to the purely economic model, which is predicated upon marginal damage and treatment cost functions whose intersection yields a single uniquely efficient level of pollution tax, treatment, and environmental quality. In contrast, the proposed approach recognizes three separate ranges of environmental quality or levels of ecological health, each with its appropriate policy measure. The model allows for a zone of low levels of emissions, within which assimilation reduces pollutant concentration and within which damage is too low to measure, or too low to reduce the productivity of the system. Until emissions and concentrations of pollutants reached a level at which damage could be detected, emitters would be permitted to release waste within legal limits without charge as under the present practice in the United States. This is termed the *property right zone*. For equity reasons, emitters are not taxed for emission levels below which (1) no damage occurs, (2) no accumulation results, and (3) ecological productivity is not impaired. In this zone, the marginal cost of monitoring and administration would probably exceed marginal ecological damage, and thus, not justify intervention.

The next level of policy concern is that at which ecological criteria indicate that pollution emissions and concentrations have measurably damaged the environment and threatened the productivity of the system. Within this zone a pollution charge, calibrated like the optimal tax in Figure 10.1 and set at a level sufficient to prevent transgression into the cumulative damage zone, is imposed upon each additional unit of pollution emitted. This is termed the *incentive zone*, because the pollution tax is used as an economically efficient measure for confronting emitters with financial incentives to reduce pollution to optimal levels, as in Figure 10.1. Despite an understandable reluctance by regulators to place exclusive reliance on financial incentives, establishing an incentive zone could serve the important goal of achieving the highest level of environmental safety per unit of social cost. The establishment of an incentive zone also creates a discrete threshold which provides emitters with incentives to limit their emissions to non-damaging, assimilable levels.[2] The central importance of the incentive zone here and of I-B policies in general is that they apply the powerful forces of competition to the reduction of pollution through economic rewards to those who act in the public interest. Thus, they shift entrepreneurial talents away from regulatory evasion towards benign technical improvement. Within these first two management zones, the proposed instrument is similar to a Pigouvian tax.

However, even the willingness to pay pollution taxes should not permit the privilege of purchasing rights to unconstrained emissions beyond

---

2   The author is grateful to an anonymous referee for this point.

ecologically acceptable limits. A third level of policy concern is therefore reached when pollution emissions and concentrations threaten to rise to the point that ecological criteria indicate irreversible, non-sustainable damage to the system. This is termed the *regulatory zone,* because at this threshold, the option of pollute-and-pay would be superseded by regulatory prohibition of any further increases in emissions. While an optimal pollution tax would have been designed to preclude taxed emissions from reaching an unsustainable level, back-up regulatory authority would serve as a safeguard against miscalculation and uncertainty.

There is an efficiency disadvantage in the proposed approach. Strict efficiency requires that each unit of emission be taxed at the same rate.[3] However, in this proposal those emitting within a no-damage zone could continue to emit at initial levels even after new emissions pushed the total into the taxable incentive range. This equity-efficiency tradeoff in the incentive zone is introduced in order to provide a measure of protection to existing firms against the possible impact of future entrants having greater market power. Also, the absolute cutoff of further emissions, once the regulatory zone had been reached, would preclude the entry of new, more efficient firms. Both the equity and efficiency goals, however, could be served by a variant of this tripartite approach, using tradable permits instead of charges.

Provided that markets could be established for them, permits would be issued without charge in the property right range of no measurable damage. After the threshold of measurable damage was crossed, additional permits would be offered for sale on the open market, but their number would be limited to a level set by ecological criteria to prevent irreversible damage in the regulatory zone. Thus, additional emission permits would not be available at any price once the regulatory range had been reached. Economic efficiency would automatically result from the equilibrium price of existing permits set by bidders in the market. Existing firms would not receive absolute guarantees against the competition of more efficient firms for emission permits, but equity would be served by their rights to sell their emission permits. Thus, limitations on sales of marketable permits to ecologically safe levels combines the best features of both regulation and economic incentives (Zylicz 1992). The option of selling emission permits in competitive markets would auto-

---

3.   The author is grateful to Wallace E. Oates for this point.

matically allow new and technologically efficient producers to emerge and to phase out more pollution intensive producers who, however, could receive compensation through sale of their emission permits. Resale and periodic renewal of permits would also automatically adjust markets for inflation, unlike Pigouvian emission charges, which would require administrative action for efficient response to price level changes.

Thus, provided that markets could be established for them, tradable permits under this system of tripartite water quality zones based upon ecological health standards would offer advantages over the use of Pigouvian charges.

IMPLEMENTATION AND OPERATIONAL CONSIDERATIONS

Clearly, numerous issues, including site-specific and related factors, would have to be faced in implementing these proposals. In deriving the damage and treatment cost functions, difficult decisions would have to be made concerning multiple pollutants, multiple species affected, and multiple spatial jurisdictions, depending upon the availability of data and knowledge. For example, Tietenberg has discussed techniques for dealing with multiple sources and multiple receptors of pollution damage (1988). Fine tuning would require different tax levels appropriate spatially and temporally for different pollutants, again depending upon the state of data and knowledge. Monitoring and enforcement would be essential. However, these imperatives are just as compelling for all existing environmental management systems.

One feature of this proposal would be precluded in places where pollutants were already causing measurable damage, which is already the case in much of the world.[4] In such instances, the property right zone would be forfeited and pollution taxes would become relevant on all emissions.[5] Rates on these taxes could then be increased to keep damages

---

4. The author is grateful to an anonymous referee for this point.
5 . In this case, the principle of Pareto fairness, or of not leaving any parties worse off by introducing a new economic incentive policy, could be achieved by granting subsidies for cutting back emissions to within the incentive zone. Subsidies are less efficient than fees for reducing pollution, and are less appealing on ethical grounds, but could be considered as a cost of introducing property rights and incentives as alternatives to regulation in situations where damaging but reversible pollution is already occurring. Under this proposal, direct regulation would still be appropriate to reduce pollution in areas where unsustainable damage levels had been reached.

within the incentive zone and prevent spill over into the non-sustainable damage zone. Where non-sustainable damage levels have already been reached, drastic regulatory and punitive (negative incentive) action is necessary. Examples include fines and damage judgments incurred from oil spills and the damage assessments against hazardous waste disposal under the U.S. Supervened program (Kopp and Smith 1993).

It should be noted that a variant of this approach has already been applied in the Netherlands (Anderson et al. 1991). Farmers are permitted to discharge the manure equivalent of 125 kgs of phosphate per hectare per year without charge. However, beyond that level, they are then charged the equivalent of 0.1 ECU ($0.11) per kg from 125 to 200 kgs per hectare. Above 200 kgs, the charge increases progressively to 0.2 ECU ($0.22) per kg per hectare per year, with a typical charge per farm of about 730 ECU ($810) annually. This innovative policy instrument, though similar in many respects to the tripartite approach suggested in this chapter, utilizes, in place of a regulatory level of capped, maximum discharges, a level of increased emission charges at twice that in the incentive zone. The two approaches can be made to converge formally by raising the emission charge in the zone of unacceptable damages to a prohibitively high level. Like the proposals here, the practice in the Netherlands diverges from the strict efficiency rule of taxing each unit of emission at the same price in order to provide some equity consideration to existing emitters.

Although the refinement and implementation of the policy proposed here would require a large-scale, transdisciplinary research program, some of the information needed has begun to emerge. For example, the U.S. Environmental Protection Agency (1991) has published for the Chesapeake Bay a list of 14 "toxics of concern," with supporting data that could assist in identifying the regulatory zones and ranges of ecological health envisaged in this approach. The Chesapeake Research Consortium has begun to provide estimates of safe contaminant levels for specific pollutants for individual marine species (Funderburk et al. 1991).

ASSESSMENT

This proposed pollution control instrument offers numerous improvements over the conventional command and control approach now typically in use. Its ethical basis permits individuals and firms to use environmental resources without charge as long as no damages result or the cost of monitoring exceeds probable damage. Polluters, however, would have to pay for environmental damage to ecological systems, and management agencies would have a clear mandate to impose regulatory limits on emissions exceeding scientifically defined damage thresholds.

Another advantage of this approach would be the introduction of economic incentives to reduce emissions in areas where environmental damage is occurring. Emitters would benefit financially by reducing their taxed emissions and by acting in the public interest. New incentives would have been created for redirecting the costly efforts now devoted to resisting regulation into more constructive research and development programs for improved pollution control technology.

Not the least significant benefit of this proposed multi-part approach is that it would raise public revenues from emission charges or from the sale of emission permits which could then be used for environmental and other public purposes.

Among the criteria noted above for the design of environmental policy instruments are (1) interest group acceptability and (2) political feasibility. This current proposal includes an initial range of emissions permitted without charge in the no damage zone. This is termed the property right zone, because current emitters would gain marketable property rights to emit current levels of these non-damaging emissions, provided they were in compliance with all current regulations and standards. The purpose of the property right zone is to provide equitable, Pareto fairness to existing emitters who are not generating measurable damage, to permit them to remain in production without charges, to create economic incentives for them to accept a more efficient management policy, and to permit them to benefit from any improvements they can make in pollution abatement technology. This feature, therefore, though failing the strict efficiency rule, has been added in order to meet equity and political feasibility objectives. Beyond the no-measurable-damage zone, if existing or new emitters proposed to make additional emissions that would raise the total into the taxable incentive range, the initial emitters holding property rights would have the options of continuing to emit at low levels without charge, or of selling all or part of their rights, giving them tangible incentives to compete in finding more efficient methods of reducing emissions. These same considerations should reduce the resistance to acceptance of this proposal by current emitters, who could be rewarded for acting in the public interest, by developing and adopting innovative abatement technology and cleaner processes.

In order to avoid creating perverse incentives for existing or new emitters to increase emissions preemptively within the no measurable damage range, the level of costless emissions should be frozen retroactively for each emitter at some cutoff date. Under these initial conditions, the most efficient and equitable method for allocating any further emissions, even in the no-damage range, property rights zone, would be for the management agency to sell them, or better, to auction them off to the highest bidder.

Another advantage of the proposed policy is that it could help bridge the resource management gap between emphasis upon emissions vs. emphasis upon ambient concentration of pollutants. By identifying levels of ecological health, this policy emphasizes the variable which most directly affects health, (i.e., ambient concentrations). Emission charges would not be triggered until ambient concentrations approached the damaging range, and concentrations would thereafter be controlled by taxing emissions or by selling permits. Precise prior knowledge of the transformation function between emissions and concentrations would thus be valuable, but not essential to the implementation of this policy instrument.

Many of those currently responsible for environmental protection are troubled by the prospect of shifting reliance from the familiar regulatory mode to an unfamiliar incentive system. It is for this reason that this proposal retains the regulatory zone as a safety and insurance range within which regulatory agencies would have the authority to prevent encroachment either by wealthy polluters or by over-zealous pollution taxers. Allocation of some of revenues raised from pollution taxes in the incentive zone to regulatory agencies might mitigate their resistance to such innovations.

This proposal is not actually a drastic departure from current practices and proposals so much as an evolution of current policies. Its primary intent is to introduce a new incentive option, which could significantly help environmental managers meet the formidable challenges ahead. The development of this, or of virtually any other improved environmental policy instrument, will depend upon more extensive collaborative and applied research.

Increasingly, environmental and ecological problems are spilling over national borders and becoming not only transboundary phenomena, but more seriously, threats to the global commons. Recognition of these increasingly serious global dimensions of the problem will require international solutions. One proposal has been to empower international agencies, such as OECD or the U.N., to impose emission charges on transboundary pollutants, with the proceeds being used for monitoring, enforcement, and research (Cumberland 1974).

CONCLUSIONS

Despite decades of effort at solutions, industrialized societies have failed to find policies adequate for controlling the expanding pollution generated by the growth of population and production. Proposals for alternative policies based upon economic incentives offer potentially significant gains, but have not received widespread acceptance among policymakers or the general public. This chapter proposes a pollution control policy instrument which, rather than being based exclusively upon present command and control measures or upon economic efficiency alone, would retain the essential features of both and would add strong, relevant transdisciplinary scientific input, distributional equity, interest group acceptability, and political acceptability. The heart of the proposal extends the economic concept of efficient levels of pollution and environmental quality, but also includes three science-based ranges of environmental concern, each with its appropriate management implementation. This tripartite policy would include (1) an initial range of no measurable ecological damage, in which transferable property rights to emissions would be recognized; (2) a range of measurable but not irreversible damage, in which economic incentives would be used to control damage efficiently; and (3) a regulatory range, in which absolute emission limits would be used to prevent damage from reducing the productivity of the system and to enhance sustainability.

ACKNOWLEDGMENTS

The author is grateful for valuable comments from Dennis M. King, Wallace E. Oates, and two anonymous referees, but is solely responsible for remaining shortcomings. Sandra Koskoff provided much appreciated editorial and word processing assistance.

REFERENCES

Anderson, R. C., L. A. Hofmann, and M. Rusin. 1991. The Use of Economic Incentive Mechanisms in Environmental Management, 55–63. Research paper #051. Washington, DC: American Petroleum Institute.

Baumol, W. J., and W. E. Oates. 1988. The Theory of Environmental Policy. 2nd. ed. Cambridge: Cambridge Univ. Press.

Buchanan, J. M. 1987. The constitution of economic policy. *American Economic Review* 177(3): 243–50.

Costanza, R., B. G. Norton, and B. D. Haskell. 1992. Ecosystem Health: New Goals for Environmental Management. Washington, DC: Island Press.

Costanza, R., and J. H. Cumberland. 1991. The Ecological Economics of Pollution Control in the Chesapeake Bay Region. Paper presented at Chesapeake Research Consortium Conference, December 4, 1990, Baltimore, MD. Summary published in conference proceedings: New Perspectives in the Chesapeake System, 19–27.

Cumberland, J. H. 1974. Establishment of international environmental standards—some economic and related aspects. In Problems in Transfrontier Pollution, ed. E. Gerelli. Paris: OECD.

———. 1990. Public choice and the improvement of policy instruments for environmental management. *Ecological Economics* 2: 149–62.

———. 1992. Intergenerational transfers and ecological sustainability. In Ecological Economics: The Science and Management of Sustainability, ed. R. Costanza. New York: Columbia Univ. Press.

Daly, H. E., and J. B. Cobb. 1989. For the Common Good. Boston: Beacon Press.

Dietz, F. J., and J. van der Straaten. 1992. Rethinking environmental economics: missing links between economic theory and economic environmental policy. *Journal of Economic Issues* 26(1): 27–51.

Funderburk, S. L., J. A. Mihursky, S. L. Jordan, and D. Riley. 1991. Habitat Requirements for Chesapeake Bay Living Resources. Solomons, MD: Chesapeake Research Consortium.

Georgescu-Roegen, N. 1971. The Entropy Law and the Economic Process. Cambridge: Harvard Univ. Press.

Kopp, R. J., and V. K., eds. 1993. The Economics of Natural Resource Damage Assessment. Washington, DC: Resources for the Future.

Oates, W. E., and M. L. Cropper. 1992. Environmental economics: a survey. *Journal of Economic Literature* 30: 675–740.

Pearce, D. W., and R. K. Turner. 1990. Economics of Natural Resources and the Environment. Baltimore: Johns Hopkins Univ. Press.

U.S. Environmental Protection Agency. 1991. Chesapeake Bay, Toxics of Concern List. Information Sheets, Chesapeake Bay Program, May, Annapolis, MD.

Tietenberg, T. 1988. Environmental and Natural Resource Economics. 2nd ed. Glenville, IL: Scott Forsman

Zylicz, T. 1992. Implementing Environmental Policies in Central and Eastern Europe. Paper presented at the second meeting of the International Society for Ecological Economics, August 3–6 1992, Stockholm.

INDEX